Politics of the Pantry

Dear Elaine,

Hope you enjoy
my ladies.

much love,
Emily

Politics of the Pantry

Housewives, Food, and Consumer Protest in Twentieth-Century America

EMILY E. LB. TWAROG

OXFORD
UNIVERSITY PRESS

OXFORD
UNIVERSITY PRESS

Oxford University Press is a department of the University of Oxford. It furthers
the University's objective of excellence in research, scholarship, and education
by publishing worldwide. Oxford is a registered trade mark of Oxford University
Press in the UK and certain other countries.

Published in the United States of America by Oxford University Press
198 Madison Avenue, New York, NY 10016, United States of America.

Library of Congress Cataloging-in-Publication Data
Names: LaBarbera-Twarog, Emily E., 1971– author.
Title: Politics of the pantry : housewives, food, and consumer protest in
twentieth-century America / Emily E. LB. Twarog.
Description: New York City : Oxford University Press, [2017] |
Includes bibliographical references and index.
Identifiers: LCCN 2017016871 (print) | LCCN 2017030024 (ebook) |
ISBN 9780190685607 (Updf) | ISBN 9780190685614 (Epub) |
ISBN 9780190685591 (hardcover : alk. paper)
Subjects: LCSH: Women—United States—History—20th century. |
Housewives—United States—History—20th century. | Consumers—Political activity—
United States—History—20th century. | Boycotts—United States—History—20th century.
Classification: LCC HQ1420 (ebook) | LCC HQ1420 .L33 2017 (print) |
DDC 305.40973/0904—dc23
LC record available at https://lccn.loc.gov/2017016871

1 3 5 7 9 8 6 4 2

Printed by Sheridan Books, Inc., United States of America

For my sons,
Nathan and Gabriel

Contents

Acknowledgments

THIS BOOK IS a product of collective action. And, as with all collective action, it required an enormous amount of support—emotional, financial, logistical, archival, and spiritual. Thank you to everyone who assisted me over the years to make this happen.

This book would not be a book without the interest and enthusiasm of Oxford University Press (OUP). From her first query about my book project, Susan Ferber has been dreamy to work with. Thank you so much for shepherding me through this crazy process. The external readers offered incredibly useful comments and feedback that helped me to clarify some critical concepts, and the OUP production staff was wonderfully attentive and responsive. I felt well-cared for all the way through this daunting process. Thank you.

It all started in graduate school at the University of Illinois at Chicago (UIC) when I wrote my first seminar paper on the 1935 meat boycotts in Hamtramck. My mentor Susan Levine embraced my passion for meat boycotts from the start along with a dedicated dissertation committee—Eileen Boris, John D'Emilio, Leon Fink, and Kevin Schultz.

Over the past decade, I have been given an enormous amount of financial support. Thank you to the Gender and Women's Studies Department at the University of Illinois at Chicago for giving me my first teaching assistantship and offering a wonderfully supportive space to transition back into graduate school after my stint as a community organizer. The UIC History Department provided significant support throughout graduate school by awarding me a History Doctoral Award, the Polish Resistance (AK) Scholarship, the Marion Miller Dissertation Fellowship, and several teaching assistantships. I spent many weeks traveling to archives across the country to piece together this narrative. All of this research would have been impossible without the financial support provided by the UIC Provost's Award for Research, the Travel to Collections Grant from the Sophia Smith Archives, and the Lubin-Winant Research Fellowship from the Franklin and Eleanor Roosevelt Institute while

I was a graduate student. The School of Labor and Employment Relations at the University of Illinois at Urbana-Champaign provided an excellent environment for me to complete this book through financial support as well as giving me time away from teaching for research and writing. Substantial grant money from the University of Illinois at Urbana-Champaign Campus Research Board, the School for Labor and Employment Relations Junior Faculty Research Grant, a Research Support Grant from the Schlesinger Library at the Radcliffe Institute for Advanced Study Harvard University, and the Sam Fishman Travel Research Grant from the Walter P. Reuther Library, Archives of Labor and Urban Affairs, Wayne State University gave me the opportunity to spend week after week conducting archival research away from my home in Chicago.

Throughout my research I met amazing archivists who preserve history. An enormous debt of gratitude must be paid to William LeFevre at the Wayne State University's Walter P. Reuther Library for helping me to learn the craft of archival research and remaining a constant resource even up to these final days. Thanks as well to the many archivists who helped me find the hidden history of housewives at the Burton Historical Collection at the Detroit Public Library; Georgia State University's Southern Labor Archives; the National Archives and Research Administration in College Park, Maryland; the George Meany Archives, then in Silver Spring, Maryland (now at their new home on the campus of the University of Maryland College Park); Smith College's Sophia Smith Archive; the Library of Congress; the Franklin D. Roosevelt Presidential Library in Hyde Park, New York; the Schlesinger Library at the Radcliffe Institute for Advanced Study, Harvard University; the Department of Special Collections and University Archives, San Diego State University; the State Historical Society of Missouri; and the Richard L. D. and Marjorie J. Morse Department of Special Collections, Kansas State University Library.

The history of housewives is often not found in the archives. There are a number of people who helped me to discover these lives. First and foremost, thank you to Don Binkowski for all your work to record and preserve the activism of the "generalissmo" of the 1935 meat boycott, Mary Zuk. Thank you as well to the children of Eleanor Fowler—John, Jane, and Ann—for sharing your memories; US Congresswoman Jan Schakowsky and Chairman Ruth Goldway for both taking time out of your busy schedules to talk with me; and Topper Carew, Mickey DeLorenzo, Lynne Heidt, Roger Hickey, Jackie Kendall, David Swankin, and Bonnie Wilson for allowing me to interview you.

There are so many individuals to thank for their intellectual enthusiasm and support: Eric Arnesen, Steven K. Ashby, Monica Bielski Boris, Robert Bruno, Eileen Boris, Heath Carter, Vicki Crawford, Alison Dickson, Tracey Deutsch, Hasia Diner, Jay Driskell, Daniel Gilbert, Stephanie Farmer, Leon Fink, Stephanie Fortado, Lawrence Glickman, Julie Greene, Julie Guard, Jeffrey Helgeson, Alice Kessler-Harris, Susan Levine, Caroline Luce, Jennifer Luff, Jamie McGrath Morris, Robyn Muncy, Kathryn Oberdeck, Jessica Weiss, Monica White, and Ann Folino White.

There are three people to whom I am deeply indebted. Emily Pope-Obeda, Eva Vaillancourt, and Michal Wilczewski all provided significant research assistance. Thank you so much for your hard work and dedication to this project. Your work was instrumental in getting me to the finish line.

Writing is a solitary process and the academy can be a very isolating space. I am grateful to have developed support systems to help pick me up when I am down and to cheer me on when I am on a roll. Over the past several years, I have had the pleasure of working with two support groups. Through the National Center for Faculty Diversity and Development, I was paired with three wonderful people who held me accountable every step of the way. Thank you Vanessa Cozza, Preetha Mani, and Alfonso Pedraza Martinez. And to the Hens—Katie Batza, Lara Kelland, and Anne Parsons—this book would not have been possible without you all. Outside of the Ivory Tower, I am privileged to be part of an amazing extended family who have bolstered me every step of the way. Thank you for the last minute bus stop pick-ups, childcare swaps, potlucks, and Coke Zeros on the stoop.

My immediate family deserves much of the credit for this book. My in-laws, Rita and Doug Miller, provided practical support of all kinds—especially in the form of childcare. Despite the distance, your willingness to fly to Chicago and take care of the kids was huge. Thank you for welcoming me into your family with open arms. When I was a kid, my mom—Rita Alfonso LaBarbera—wore a blue T-shirt that read on the front, "Women Belong in the House," and on the back: " . . . and the Senate!" My mother instilled in me my fierce feminism. Thank you for all of the encouragement throughout my life and moving to Skokie just in time to watch the kids, do the laundry, and wash the dishes as I finished the book. In the final days of revising, I opened my trusty Roget's *Thesaurus* and out fell my favorite picture of my late father. His smile lit the way during the final weeks of finishing this book.

My biggest champions are my two wonderfully loving and caring sons to whom this book is dedicated. At the end of the day, being your mother is truly a gift and the best part of my life. I adore you and love you more than all the sweet cherries in the world.

My husband—Dan Miller—has a heart that is more generous than I thought possible. I could never have pulled this off without your love and support. Your love and ridiculous sense of humor keep me going every day. Thank you for absolutely everything. I love you.

Abbreviations

AAA	Agricultural Adjustment Act
AFL	American Federation of Labor
AFL-CIO	American Federation of Labor-Congress of Industrial Organizations
ACTU	Amalgamated Clothing and Textile Union
CACHCL	Central Action Committee against the High Cost of Living (Detroit)
CCC	Civilian Conservation Corps
CCH	Consumers Clearinghouse
CFMA	Commodities Futures Modernization Act of 2000
CIO	Congress of Industrial Organizations
COPE	Committee on Political Education
COIN	Consumers Opposed to Inflation in the Necessities
CWA	Congress of Women's Auxiliaries
DBCFSN	Detroit Black Community Food Security Network
HALPM	Housewives of Azusa for Lower Priced Meat
HELP	Housewives Elect Lower Prices
LWS	League of Women Shoppers
LWV	League of Women Voters
NAM	National Manufacturers' Association
NCL	National Consumers' League
NCU	National Consumers' Union (national)
NCU	National Consumers' United (Chicago)
NOW	National Organization of Women
NWP	National Woman's Party
OPA	Office of Price Administration
SACA	Special Assistant for Consumer Affairs
SFCA	San Francisco Consumer Action
UAW	United Automobile, Aerospace and Agricultural Implement Workers of America
UE	United Electrical, Radio and Machine Workers of America
UFW	United Farm Workers of America

USDA   United States Department of Agriculture
VCCC   Virginia Citizens Consumer Council
WAC   Westchester (County) Action Council
WAD   Women's Activities Department (COPE)
YWCA   Young Women's Christian Association

Politics of the Pantry

Introduction

STRUGGLING TO DEAL with the high cost of food, housewives found themselves emptying the grocers' shelves of elbow macaroni as they searched for inexpensive alternatives to meat to feed their families. One Brooklyn housewife declared, "Doing something about meat prices is true women's liberation. The average housewife isn't getting a job as a banking executive—and she can't understand the life of someone like Gloria Steinem." In 1973, there was one thing that Americans could agree on: the cost of living was "the main problem facing Americans today," according to a Gallup poll. At the kitchen tables of working-class families across the country, people were forced to eat well below their usual standard for meals. One mother protested the high cost of meat by eating a can of dog food outside a Pennsylvania grocery store, while restaurants offered diners meatless menus. The message was the same across the country: Food simply cost too much, and housewives and politicians alike were through with listening to the "let's keep politics out of the pantry" message parroted by the food industry.[1]

The Politics of the Pantry is a study of how women used institutions built on patriarchy and consumer capitalism to cultivate a political identity and voice. Using a labor history lens, it places the home rather than the workplace at the center of the community, revealing new connections between labor, gender, and citizenship. Three periods of consumer upheaval anchor the narrative: the Depression-era meat boycott of 1935, the consumer coalitions of the New Deal and the rise of the Cold War, and the wave of consumer protests in the 1960s and 1970s. The book is framed around the lives of several key labor and consumer activists and their organizations in both urban and suburban areas—Detroit, Chicago, Long Island, and Los Angeles. The geographic diversity of these three periods allows for a national story about the influence of domestic politics between the New Deal and the election of

Ronald Reagan and the emergence of the conservative right. Some of these women have appeared in other historical work in limited ways; the remaining women are new to the literature of consumer activism. This book tells the story of these women as they enter the public sphere to protest the increasingly challenging task of feeding their families and balancing the household ledger.

In this book, the American housewife is both part of a political constituency group and an imagined ideal. Politicians, social norms driven by racism and sexism, and the advertising industry manufactured the ideal housewife in the image of a white middle-class woman devoted to her husband and her children. The housewives featured here used this imagined ideal to create a relationship between the domestic sphere and the formation of political identities. The book explores what is historically unique about the "mechanisms of democratic participation" that enabled American housewives to use it to claim their political citizenship.[2] In doing so, it shifts the focus away from the workplace as a site of protest and dissension and looks to the homefront as a starting point for protest in the public sphere.[3]

Politics of the Pantry makes three central claims. First, domestic politics is a distinctive form of activism that is not simply the feminine version of labor activism. Rather, domestic politics as a political strategy highlights the inextricable links between labor, community, home, and the market in the twentieth century. Second, the housewife—the actual and the representative—rose and fell as a political constituency group in the eyes of the state. Finally, second wave feminists missed a critical opportunity to build alliances with working-class and middle-class housewives in the 1970s. The lack of unity between the women's movement and community-based consumer activists comprised largely of housewives helped pave the way for the rise of a conservative women's movement made famous by anti-feminist icon Phyllis Schlafly and the conservative watch group the Eagle Forum.[4]

The American Housewife and Domestic Politics

Existing largely on the periphery, housewives are rarely studied as political actors. While historians have made critical links between consumption and citizenship, this work rarely focuses on working-class and middle-class housewives and the connections made by them with labor, gender, and citizenship.[5] To be clear, this book does not examine the craft of being a housewife. Instead, the focus is on the social and cultural construction of the housewife and how this identity evolved over time. Many working-class housewives did in fact labor as wage-earning workers prior to marriage and their transition to full-time homemaker. In some cases, women returned to the wage-earning workforce periodically, but their personal and political identity centered on their life and work as a housewife. This is also not a study of motherhood.[6] As theater studies scholar Ann Folino White so eloquently points out, " 'housewife' was, and continues to be, culturally constructed as a role, while 'mother' was, and continues to be, perceived as a state of being."[7] Furthermore, by the Great Depression, housewifery had evolved into an occupation in large part because of the professionalization of home economics as a field of study and research.[8] Despite the non-waged status of housework, those in the public sphere often turned to housewives as "experts" on topics such as family budgeting, food costs and availability, and nutrition.

For women engaged in consumer activism in the twentieth century, many intentionally invoked their housewife identity in multiple ways.[9] In the 1930s, housewives in Los Angeles, New York, and Detroit launched a meat boycott to protest President Franklin Delano Roosevelt's Agricultural Adjustment Act—a policy intended to help ease the financial burden of American farms during the Great Depression but which instead created a ripple effect that transferred that burden to consumers. The meat boycott was not an innovation borne of desperate times. It was a tradition that, in the United States, dates back to the founding of the republic but is most familiarly known from the 1902 Kosher Meat boycotts of New York City's Lower East Side when Jewish immigrant women rebelled against the monopoly of kosher butchers by boycotting and later founding a short-lived kosher meat trust.[10] The 1935 meat boycott, specifically in Detroit, marks a shift in political activism. Working-class women—both white and African American—took up the trope of the "housewife" to advance a political identity beyond the boundaries of their neighborhood. They shifted the protests beyond their local communities to ignite a national conversation.[11] Later in the twentieth century, housewives protesting outside supermarkets would turn their identity on and off as needed depending on their audience. One activist housewife recalled being in a street theater action outside a supermarket to protest the lack of labeling transparency. "The police had been called. By the time the police came—we didn't want to get arrested, so we weren't going to stick around. We just explained to them, 'Oh, officer, you see here, this is what's happening.' We could totally play the innocent housewife. Right?"[12] The ability to shift between consumer expert and innocent housewife was a common trait among most of the housewives.

Domestic politics evolved to influence policy and act as a conduit for working-class and middle-class housewives to increase their political participation. Writing on the labor upheavals of the 1930s, journalist Mary Heaton Vorse "recognize[d] that the new unionism of the 1930s '[did] not stop at the formal lodge meeting. It [saw] the union as a way of life which [involved] the entire community.'"[13] As historian Elizabeth Faue notes, this vision of the labor movement placed the family at the center. This was not just an "extension of domesticity to the political realm," but the "emergence of class politics in the urban sphere of social production."[14] Thus, domestic politics is not simply the feminine version of labor activism, nor is it "auxiliary or complementary to the masculine solidarity of labor." It is a distinctive form of activism that recognizes the inextricable links between labor, community, home, and the market in the twentieth century.[15] Further, it relies on the collective action of women who both challenge and embrace the social and economic order. As historian Temma Kaplan puts it, "A sense of community that emerges from shared routines binds women to one another within their class and within their neighborhoods."[16] Understanding this female "consciousness" has informed this book's argument that the domestic politics of working-class and middle-class housewives simultaneously embraced their socially ascribed roles as mothers and wives while demanding equality for the community as a whole. As "buyers of the nation," the American identity was within reach of housewives. Yet their lack of connection to institutional power both before and after the passage of the Nineteenth Amendment created a barrier to accessing this citizenship.[17] Throughout the book the term "domestic politics" is used to distinguish a recognizable model of activism that originates in the home and uses the language of the home to effect political change. It forged a bridge between the private and public sphere that critiques the imbalances between wage labor and consumption in a decidedly patriarchal environment, and it fuels the argument that public policy and political institutions must see unpaid labor as a valuable commodity.[18] This book demonstrates how housewives used domestic politics to build relationships and connections with social, economic, and political institutions.

The experiences of white working-class and middle-class women dominate the campaigns narrated here. To be clear, there is a substantial history of consumer activism among women of color, most notably during the civil rights and welfare rights movements.[19] However, the socially and culturally ascribed identity of the American housewife did and continues to describe a woman who is explicitly heterosexual, white, and financially secure. For women of color—especially African American women—efforts to achieve housewife status were often thwarted by economic and social restrictions despite campaigns to gain respectability.[20]

While housewives have often been interpreted as a conservative group that allowed the traditional family model to go unchallenged, *Politics of the Pantry* questions this characterization. Working-class housewives defended the rights of wage-earning women, challenged the notion and construction of equality from an economic standpoint, and demanded full access to a "good" life for white and African American workers. Tracing their steps from the home to the factory into the broader community and eventually national politics reveals a hidden history of women who used their identity as housewives and the strategy of domestic politics in the public sphere to exercise political citizenship beyond the voting booth.

The book opens in the 1930s with Mary Zuk, a working-class housewife from Hamtramck, Michigan who spearheaded a national boycott against the high cost of meat in 1935. Zuk's experience as a consumer activist gained her a place as the leader of a delegation to Washington, DC, to meet with Secretary of Agriculture Henry Wallace, and later, an elected seat on the Hamtramck City Council. Zuk used her identity as a working-class housewife to campaign and organize for economic equality and justice from the point of consumption rather than production. Prior to Zuk, working-class housewives faded into obscurity once the immediate consumer boycott activity ended, as was the case with the Jewish housewives during the 1902 kosher meat boycott in New York's Lower East Side. Zuk's capacity to transform from a community activist to a local political and union leader during the Popular Front period and the rise of the United Auto Worker union was a turning point for women and the role of domestic politics in the local and national debate about the cost of living.[21] The year 1935 was a key moment in the history of women's activism as working-class housewives engaged in politics beyond their neighborhoods and built lasting relationships with institutions and organizations.

By the late 1930s, workers across the industrial North joined unions en masse. For many, this organizing was a result of direct action such as the 1936–37 sit-ins in Michigan's automobile industry.[22] Working-class housewives joined the ranks of women's union auxiliaries, but the strike kitchens furnished the women with more than sandwiches and coffee. They fed the hunger of working-class housewives for economic equality as they sought ways to use their "domestic expertise" in their communities. Chapter 2 explores how women's labor union auxiliaries affiliated with the Congress of Industrial Organizations (CIO) created a space that helped housewives craft leadership skills that funneled this expertise into the public sphere. During cost-of-living campaigns and legislative battles, auxiliary members built a movement of housewives that spoke with a unified voice as they sought economic and political equality for working-class families beyond the bargaining table. In her study of "social disunity" in the World War II shipyards, sociologist Katherine Archibald characterized the pre-war period as a moment in time during which citizens had "the tools to defeat these evils . . . at hand: an activist liberal state, a revivified trade union movement, an ethic of pluralism and diversity, and the American ideals of equality and democracy."[23] This is the context in which the women's labor union auxiliaries developed and nurtured the political life of working-class housewives who were able to take these "tools" and make a claim for more complete political citizenship. This moment in time was unlike any other for working-class housewives in that they had institutional access to organized labor as well as agencies within the New Deal government in a way that was not available to participants in earlier neighborhood upheavals.

The wartime benefits of the 1940s were short-lived as women lost federally funded childcare and high-paid industrial jobs, and many bowed to the social pressure of media campaigns that focused on the revival of domesticity featuring a male breadwinner and female homemaker.[24] During the 1950s, the social and political gains of working-class housewives were devoured by the fear and insecurity of organized labor in the midst of the second Red Scare. Auxiliaries lost their influence as unions hemorrhaged membership and the newly merged American Federation of Labor-Congress of Industrial Organizations (AFL-CIO) reorganized the radical elements out of the auxiliaries. The hopes of the American housewife were raised when President Johnson appointed Esther Peterson as the first Special Assistant to the President for Consumer Affairs. Focusing on her efforts to create a space for housewives to voice their concerns, Peterson often found roadblocks within an administration that exhibited little real concern for the American consumer. Nonetheless, Peterson cultivated a national reputation as the voice of the American consumer in the White House by working within communities as well as collaborating with business leaders and the advertising industry. Chapter 3 tells the story of what happened when the White House and Main Street met during the Cold War.

With unionization at an all-time high during the 1950s and 1960s, working-class sons were, as historian Joseph McCartin put it, "staking claim to the middle-class lifestyle."[25] Through unionization, working-class jobs often enabled men to earn enough to allow their wives to stay home rather than work. And, with the boom in post-war suburbanization, workers who grew up in tight-knit communities in urban neighborhoods of Brooklyn or the Bronx flocked to places like Nassau County on Long Island in search of the American Dream. Chapter 4 explores two consumer rebellions by working-class and middle-class housewives that sparked protests across the country and contributed to debates about key pieces of consumer legislation in the 1960s. In 1969, suburban housewives in Chicago ramped up a campaign demanding more transparency in labeling. Their efforts gained national media attention and soon forced midwestern supermarket chains to change their labeling practices. Only three years after the Denver housewives ignited a national boycott against meat, housewives on Long Island launched a boycott demanding an explanation from the federal government about why food prices were so high.

Chapter 5 focuses on grassroots consumer organizing in the 1970s. In 1972, feminist activist and writer Robin Morgan opened her speech to the American Home Economics Association by saying, "As a radical feminist, I am here addressing the enemy."[26] Meanwhile, Esther Peterson was frustrated by the emphasis many in the women's movement placed on legislation such as the Equal Rights Amendment. "That's the kind of phony stuff that just got me," recalled Peterson. "Those women were for long-distance things but not for real gutsy immediate things. . . . [T]he long-range goal was not to have the Equal Rights Amendment until we had in place a little bit more equality for the low-income working women. . . . I think they really believed, they really believed that if you get the [ERA], that automatically we'd have equality. And that's stupid."[27] Morgan and Peterson were working in a period during which the political identity of the housewife was up for grabs. On the one hand, consumer activists continued to organize and developed a significant national voice. In 1973, housewives in California launched a national meat boycott that led to the formation of a national organization. Yet the women's and labor movements missed opportunities to collaborate on the engagement of housewives, opening the wedge needed for conservatives like Phyllis Schlafly to reclaim the housewife as a player in the growing conservative movement.[28]

In 1970, Pauli Murray, a pioneering African American lawyer, civil rights activist, and feminist, called on her friend and fellow feminist, Esther Peterson, to embrace what she called "imaginative feminism." Murray believed that women needed to "find new ways to make democracy truly participatory, to break new ground, to reject violence, war, etc., etc., and to introduce imaginative feminism (public housekeeping) into the political arena."[29] But the women's movement dismissed domestic politics because of its foundation in the traditional family model so vilified in Betty Friedan's *The Feminine*

Mystique. While Friedan and the leadership of the newly founded National Organization for Women were fiercely committed to gender equality, they fell into the trap that held back an earlier organization, Alice Paul's National Woman's Party. Women are not one-dimensional. There is not a "one-size-fits-all" solution to gender inequality. Murray and Peterson understood the complexities of gender inequality. In order to achieve Murray's "truly participatory" democracy, the women's movement of the 1970s needed to look beyond their comfort zone and natural allies. This is the story of one set of lost allies.

I

The 1935 Meat Boycott and the Evolution of Domestic Politics

THE ROOM OVERFLOWED with people, jubilant and inspired by the results of the recent election. Hamtramck residents filled every seat and stood around the room, radiating joy and relief. Finally, there was a "glimmer of something better in [their] gray life, especially for working women," reported the *Voice of the People* newspaper.[1] At the first gathering of the new Hamtramck's People's League—an organization formed to run a slate in the 1936 Common Council election—the crowd was ready to tackle the community's toughest issues, including citizenship, political corruption, and the high cost of living. This electoral success was even more significant because it included the first woman elected to the Common Council.[2] Mary Zuk—a petite woman with dark hair and eyes the color of coal—had gained notoriety the previous year when she became the public face of the 1935 meat boycott that attracted national media attention.[3] Now, she would push for change as part of a slate of progressive Hamtramck residents who ran for office to protest the "irresponsible, selfish politicians, who lead the city government on their behalf, to steal the city's money and taxes."[4] In less than one year, Zuk was transformed from an anonymous housewife in an eastside Detroit suburb to a national spokeswoman and elected political leader. This transformation would have ramifications long after her time in the spotlight.

In the summer of 1935, housewives from all over Detroit called for a boycott of meat to protest the high cost of living. This was not the first cost-of-living protest in the United States. In 1902, Jewish immigrant women from New York City's Lower East Side boycotted the high cost of kosher meat. Amid the Great Depression, New York City's housewives again protested the

FIG. I.I Mary Zuk Speaking to Housewives at a Meat Boycott Meeting in Hamtramck, Michigan, 1935.

Courtesy of Archives of Labor and Urban Affairs, Walter P. Reuther Library, Wayne State University, Detroit, Michigan.

high cost of living, taking their concerns to the mayor while he attended an upscale dinner at the Waldorf Astoria.[5] The 1935 meat boycott would mark a turning point for both consumer movements and the women's movement. While earlier boycotts were largely spontaneous, the 1935 boycott involved considerable forethought and planning by housewives. This boycott challenged the familiar pattern of waves within the women's movement, with a notorious downward spiral after the passage of the Nineteenth Amendment in 1919.[6] Housewives learned to use their gender identities to harness community strength, along with a commitment to what one scholar calls "a moral purpose."[7] Their family obligations did not "dampen militancy or weaken their identity as workers." Instead, "family ties may in fact be crucial in generating working-class solidarities."[8] Building on the maternal politics of the Progressive Era and the community organizing that marked an early response to the 1929 crash, the Great Depression's "meatless summer of 1935" provides an example of domestic politics.[9]

Domestic Politics

Both middle- and working-class housewives used their roles as consumers to expand the boundaries of the public sphere. With faith in a "collective obligation toward one another," politicized housewives held the state responsible for the well-being of its citizens.[10] An earlier era of women had fought hard to win public policies that protect women as mothers, and food protests broadened the scope of women's responsibilities to include both the family and the economy.[11] By articulating their concerns about providing meals on limited incomes, housewives politicized the obligation to feed one's family. This politicization included organizing food protests that demanded the attention of both the public and the state. Emphasizing the high cost of living turned the household budget into a public issue. It also created citizen housewives who were becoming amateur experts on the relationship between the cost of living and their family's income.

Food and consumer protests expose a type of grassroots activism rooted in how working- and middle-class women used their roles as housewives to advocate a moral economy in the marketplace. Domestic politics places class before gender equality. The fusion of domestic politics with consumer activism created a space in the public sphere that aspired to liberate the entire working-class community. These citizen housewives followed a tradition in which consumers took on the government with unprecedented militancy and was critical to readjusting the relationship between the state and its citizenry.[12] To be clear, domestic politics does not seek to alienate gender equity. Rather, the crafting of a political voice and the theater of the activism around pricing, quality, and transparency creates an environment in which gender empowerment and advocacy can flourish.[13]

Before the "meatless summer of 1935," the working class had first unleashed their rage in the early 1930s.[14] Throughout the decade, work stoppages increased, peaking in 1937. Between 1932 and 1935, work stoppages more than doubled, growing from a mere 324,000 workers in 1932 to 1,200,000 in 1935.[15] The meat boycott was an extension of these strikes. As workers made demands on the shop floor, their wives were calling for "the right to live" in the streets.[16] Like the 1902 housewives of the kosher meat boycott, many of the 1935 housewives called their boycott a "strike," demonstrating the influence of the language and culture of the shop floor. The use of labor-style tactics—such as picketing, passing out leaflets, and holding house meetings—to organize meat boycotts continued into the 1970s.[17]

Meat as a Class Marker

"Hamtramck families will go without the traditional Polish sausage and sparerib dinners Sunday as a result of a meat strike," reported the conservative *Detroit Free Press*.[18] The boycotts were about far more than Sunday dinner. To attain and maintain an American standard of living, housewives embraced their identity to defend the family economy, and the ability to feed their families meat was the symbol of that objective. The increased cost of meat was a financial burden for families. For Hamtramck's Polish working-class families, meat consumption represented financial security not available in the old country. In America, eating meat daily had become a right, not a luxury. Like other Eastern European immigrants, Hamtramck's Polish working class challenged anyone standing in the way of maintaining an American standard of living.[19]

Hunger represented a collective misery for Eastern and Southern European immigrants as well as for African Americans migrants. With food carts loaded with fruits and vegetables, butchers' windows full of fresh meat, and the scent of fresh bread wafting from the neighborhood bakery, the American city promised to end hunger for many.[20] While foods preferences varied among different groups of migrants, meat became the barometer of success in every community. Of all the food available to families, meat most represented class difference.[21] As one boycotter put it, "In the old home I never [had] enough meat. . . . Now fat meat was mine for the asking."[22] Meat boycotts represent part of the working-class struggle in American history that has been left out of most labor history narratives.[23]

For many immigrants in the early twentieth century, the United States was imagined as "a land of plenty" or, in the words of the early Jewish immigrant protestors, the *goldene medinah*.[24] This imagined plenty drove immigrants hungering for security in American cities and mining towns at the turn of the twentieth century. African Americans migrated from the American South, fleeing poverty and racism and hoping that northern cities would provide them with a better livelihood.[25] The promise of economic stability, represented by the potential for a living wage that could provide shelter, a full table, and the possibility of even more offered a glimmer of hope and long deferred justice. For many working-class families, however, providing their families with the basics—shelter, food, and jobs—proved more challenging than expected.

The twentieth-century marketplace flush with goods and customers created a distinctly female space of consumption. The rise of consumer culture led working- and middle-class women to become the family managers.[26] As such, women embraced their identity as "buyers of the nation" and negotiated within the marketplace, serving a "powerful mediating role."[27] As one historian put it, women consumers demanded "a crucial measure of fairness."[28] Policymakers and corporate leaders began discussions of a living wage. Historian Thomas Stapleford's study of the Consumer Price Index shows that there was bi-partisan support for "tying higher wages to economic prosperity and the growth of mass markets."[29] In fact, the chairman of General Electric's board of directors, Owen D. Young, insisted that workers needed "not merely a living wage, but a higher 'cultural wage' appropriate to American aspirations (and American production)."[30] The crash of the stock market, however, sent the consumer market into a tailspin and the working class into increasingly dire straits.

Meat was the symbolic good that both working- and middle-class women used to protect access to the American standard of living. The boycotts were mediated by the price of beef and were the housewives' response to perceived imbalances between consumers and producers.[31] Men relied on meat—specifically beef—for nutritional support to work. Thus, lack of meat on the family table compromised the capabilities of the family breadwinner, which meant less money in the family budget. The breadwinner's meat consumption was inextricably tied to his success as a full economic citizen.

In the late 1800s, the American Federation of Labor (AFL) became focused on workers' access to the marketplace. Calling on industry leaders to pay a living wage, the AFL and progressive public intellectuals like Henry Demarest Lloyd used the US Constitution to link the argument for a living wage to citizenship. In an 1893 AFL pamphlet, Lloyd declared that workers "have burned the new words of the living wage into the bill of rights . . . born equal, with inalienable rights to life, liberty, and pursuit of happiness."[32] The American labor movement also saw meat as a symbol of manhood and whiteness. In 1901, Samuel Gompers penned the pamphlet "Some Reasons for Chinese Exclusion—Meat vs. Rice—American Manhood against Asiatic Coolieism. Which Shall Survive?" With the Chinese Exclusion Act of 1882 on the verge of expiring, Gompers and other exclusionists renewed calls for harsh restrictions on Chinese immigration. Gompers used the metaphor of food to explain how unrestricted Chinese immigration would compromise the American way of life. Indeed, the American Federation of Labor's success depended on men functioning as breadwinners. Low-wage, immigrant labor threatened not only the livelihood of AFL members but also, in the eyes of most of the American labor movement, American identity itself. To drive this point home, Gompers's pamphlet draws a direct link between meat and male virility.[33]

The history of meat in America is a micro-history of industrialization and urbanization, and women helped create this narrative. [34] In the late 1700s and early 1800s, colonial women flexed their political muscle through consumer decisions. When public health concerns forced butchers to move to the outskirts of eastern cities, women protested the longer commute to shop. They bought meat from illegal meat wagons rather than trek across town. While New York butchers wanted to create markets only for meat vendors, consumers wanted convenience, which led New York City's city council to legalize meat sales in private stores. The result was easy access to butcher shops that numbered over 500 by 1850. [35] This neighborhood convenience also facilitated meaningful relationships between butchers and customers. In fact, these relationships often developed into intimate ones. Depending on the cut and type of meat a housewife purchased, she provided the butcher insight into her family's finances. Sometimes the butcher would protect favorite customers by lowering weights or slipping a nicer cut into their package. [36]

The link between meat and class was hardly unique to Hamtramck, Michigan. Meat functioned, as one historian put it, "as a symbolic expression of working-class aspirations for a better life." [37] This was evident in both popular culture and the daily experiences of working-class consumers. In Jack London's 1909 short story, "A Piece of Meat," first published in the *Saturday Evening Post*, the main character—an aging boxer named Tom King—returns to the ring, in a desperate last attempt to feed and house his starving family. On the night of the match against a young talented boxer, King sits down to a dinner of flour gravy and bread, after having spent the day "longing for a piece of steak, and the longing had not abated." [38] For King, his return to the ring is a "primitive . . . animal way" to provide meat for his family. In his mind, he is not a modern man; he is an animal. He cannot escape his hunger for meat, and his body grows weak, despite his superior skills in the ring. "He remembered back into the fight to the moment when he has Sandel [his younger opponent] swaying and tottering on the hair-line balance of defeat. Ah, that piece of steak would have done it! He has lacked just that for the decisive blow, and he has lost. It was all because of the piece of steak." [39]

For working families, consuming meat regularly represented attainment of an American standard of living. This was particularly true among immigrant families, but it also carried into second- and third-generation families. Meat consumption also represented masculinity on multiple levels. As the breadwinners of their households, men saw it as a matter of pride to feed their families meat on a regular basis. But for them as men, meat also reflected virility and strength.

In popular culture, simply choosing not to purchase meat inferred economic instability. In the 1941 pulp fiction novel *Mildred Pierce*, a recently divorced mother living during the Great Depression starts slipping down the class ladder. With scant income from baking pies for her neighbors, Mildred scrambles to pay bills and feed her children. In one scene, her estranged husband unexpectedly comes by to take their two children for the weekend:

> [Mildred] counted her money and stopped by a market, where she bought a chicken, a quarter pound of hot dogs, some vegetables, and a quart of milk. The chicken, first baked, then creamed, then made into three neat croquettes, would provision her over the weekend. The hot dogs were a luxury. She disapproved of them, on principle, but the children loved them, and she always tried to have some around, for bites between meals. The milk was a sacred duty. . . . She resented still more that Mr. Pierce had delayed his coming until she had spent the money for the chicken. But the prospect of having the children fed free for two whole days was so tempting that she acted quite agreeably about it.[40]

Mildred must take a waitressing job to support her family. She feels humiliated to be working for tips, even though the labor was similar to what she did as an upper-middle-class housewife. She hides her job from her children and family, eventually "confessing" to her best friend after she collapses from the exhaustion of her new job. Her friend, neighbor, and confidant tells a weeping Pierce that she would have most generously "brought over a roast or a ham, but you never would have accepted it." Even after Mildred becomes a successful restaurateur, her eldest daughter and the moneyed elite still see her success as tarnished by the stench of the fried chicken she serves. The ability to eat meat regularly was inextricably linked to class identity and the American standard of living; yet, the act of serving the meat created a class barrier between Mildred and her customers that could not be demolished.

The Streets of Hamtramck

Mary Zuk was already frustrated with the rising cost of living when she entered Polish Falcon's Hall. Along with hundreds of other neighborhood women, Zuk knew that it was the time to act. The immigrant Polish families of Hamtramck understood the impact a strike against local butchers could have on the local economy. But rather than jumping right into direct action, the wives—along with some husbands—opted to create a more coordinated campaign that would draw both local and national attention. They wanted to communicate the hardships experienced by working-class families in an industrial town located in the shadow of the sprawling Dodge plant. Hamtramck's working-class housewives realized that meat could become a weapon for a political cause. By controlling the resources that were nearby—the marketplace and the home—they could alter the trajectory of everyday life. Their strategic campaign took advantage of the tools of traditional labor organizing and used them to engage in a domestic politics that challenged the strict lines between public and private, shop floor and home.

The media's "generalissimo" of the 1935 meat boycott, Mary Zuk was among the wave of internal migrants seeking jobs in the auto industry.[41] In 1905, Mary Stanceus was born into poverty in the small mining town of Neffs, Ohio, near the West Virginia border.[42] After her father died in a 1915 mining accident, Zuk migrated to Detroit with her sister to find work.[43] Only fourteen, she lied about her age to secure work at the local Dodge plant to help support her family. By seventeen, she had met her future husband, Stanley Zuk, who arrived in the United States from rural Poland in 1912 and found a job at the Battle Creek auto plant. After returning to Poland for three years, Stanley came back to Michigan and he and Mary wed in 1922.

Michigan was hard hit by the Great Depression. In 1933, unemployment reached almost 50 percent. Most of the mines in the Upper Peninsula stopped production. A quarter of Michigan's banks failed, and the state was forced to borrow $21 million from the government—through the Reconstruction Finance Corporation—to provide relief to Michiganders. In 1932, unemployed Ford workers marched the almost ten miles from Detroit to Dearborn, demanding full employment and union recognition. Instead, they were met with police firing tear gas. Four marchers were killed. Over 15,000 people marched in the funeral procession.[44]

The Zuks were not immune to the Depression's hardships. Mary left her factory job to raise her two children. Stanley was out of work, and like almost half of Hamtramck's 11,000 families, they depended on government relief.[45] Hamtramck was home to migrants from Eastern Europe flooding the area seeking the promise of new jobs at the Dodge plant. The whole region's population was exploding, as European immigrants along with African Americans, looking to exchange the hopelessness of sharecropping for a job in Detroit's booming auto industry, made southeastern Michigan their home. Located north of the heavily Polish Ninth Ward and surrounded by the city of Detroit, Hamtramck was a tight-knit Polish immigrant community.[46]

In the early summer, housewives noticed the rising price of meat. Calling themselves the Provisional Women's Committee against the High Cost of Living, Hamtramck's housewives distributed leaflets door-to-door, asked people about their experience with the price of meat, and "explain[ed] the purpose of the [planned mass] meeting."[47] On July 19, 1935, 400 of Hamtramck's Polish working-class housewives—accompanied by some of their husbands—met at the Polish Falcon's Hall to take action against the cost of meat and other domestic goods, such as milk and heating fuel.[48]

By the end of the evening, neighborhood women had mapped out a boycott campaign with both local and national dimensions. Their strategy was slow escalation. The first step was to draft protest letters to be sent to local and national leaders. In their letter to President Franklin Delano Roosevelt and Secretary of Agriculture Henry Wallace, they criticized national agricultural policies and "demand[ed] action to reduce the cost of living."[49] Locally, they presented Mayor Lewandowski of Hamtramck and the local government's Common Council with a resolution, which stated their intention to boycott if the cost of meat was not lowered. While they waited for a response, the Committee organized another mass meeting. The housewives told local butchers that if they did not lower meat prices, the housewives en masse would boycott their shops. Their demands were met with silence and inaction.

The summer of 1935 was particularly hot, and by late July, temperatures were reaching into the 90s with high humidity. As 1,200 women gathered in the sweltering Copernicus High School gymnasium, emotions were running high.[50] These women were not seasoned activists; they were wives and mothers, most of whom had never spoken publicly before—let alone to a crowd of more than 1,000 people. Collectively the women of varying racial and ethnic backgrounds decided to boycott meat, targeting local butchers first.[51]

Mary Zuk was elected chairman of the Provisional Women's Committee against the High Cost of Living, soon renamed the Committee for Action against the High Cost of Living.[52] With no background in activism, Zuk attributed her convictions during the meat boycott to her daily experience of poverty. "The misery of my childhood, the struggles I had in later life to raise a family in Hamtramck as a worker in the Dodge plant all left their mark on me," Zuk told the *Voice of the People*. She mentioned in the interview that she did not think joining the meat boycott was "unusual," but she noted, "I knew that if I wanted to protect my children, I had to protect the children of my neighbors and fellow citizens."[53]

Nearly a month after the initial mobilization, hundreds of women gathered on Joseph Campau Avenue, the heart of Hamtramck's shopping district

FIG. 1.2 A children's picket along the streets of Hamtramck, Michigan, in support of the 1935 meat boycott.
Courtesy of Archives of Labor and Urban Affairs, Walter P. Reuther Library, Wayne State University, Detroit, Michigan.

and a commercial destination for many southeastern Michigan shoppers. With a streetcar running down its center, it ran the length of Hamtramck and was completely surrounded by Detroit. During this period, this single shopping district, with its streetcar service, was second only to Detroit in its statewide number of sales.[54] The street was narrow, lined with two-story buildings and dotted with signs in both English and Polish. Shoppers met all their needs on the thoroughfare, from daily food needs to long-term services such as funeral planning and buying real estate. As *The Guide to the Wolverine State*—one of the many state guidebooks written by the New Deal Federal Writers' Project—put it: "A chain drugstore advertised a huge *apteka* sign, and on the second floor windows were *adwokat* (attorney) and *dentysta* (dentist). There were many specialty shops, such as those selling feathers and quilts, and many 'bazaars,' their windows a melange of dream books, pictures of saints, razor strops, chewing tobacco, and first communion dresses. The windows of the white and gleaming *sklad wedlin* (delicatessen) were neatly packed with Polish foods that attracted shoppers from all parts of the Detroit district."[55] The women picketers focused on the larger meat purveyors in the community, such as Frank Jaworski's Sausage Company. Jaworski's and other stores were forced to close their doors early, due to poor sales, as the women picketed until sundown, despite the sweltering heat.[56]

The "fiery" energy of Zuk kept the media focused on Hamtramck, but it was hardly the only city attacking the high price of meat.[57] Across New York City, housewives picketed butchers demanding that shoppers boycott meat. In Brooklyn, six people were arrested for "minor disorders" such as physically preventing shoppers from entering butcher shops. The leaders of the City Action Committee against the High Cost of Living and the United Council of Working Class Women planned to urge Mayor La Guardia of New York City to support their case against the meatpackers.[58] In Chicago, housewives took their protests to the Polish butchers along Milwaukee Avenue crying "Don't Buy Meat!" and "Demand a 20 percent reduction" in English and Polish. The local committee also took advantage of the large number of packinghouses on Chicago's Southside and sent committees of women to meet with the heads of the companies.[59] In Detroit alone, both urban and suburban housewives were contributing to the momentum. For example, on the city's west side, Catherine Mudra, a Polish housewife and friend of Mary Zuk, organized the Women's Committee against the High Cost of Living, which picketed her community's butchers. Detroit's African Americans, along with other ethnic groups, organized picket lines in front of neighborhood butcher shops. Jewish and German housewives formed organizations, such as the Action Committee of the Twelfth Street Section and the Neighborhood Action Committee against the High Cost of Living.

Within the African American community, consumer issues were even more complicated. African American housewives involved in the Housewives' League of Detroit embraced what historian Darlene Clark Hine calls "a grassroots 'let's-keep-our-own-money-in-our-communities' nationalist approach more reminiscent of Marcus Garvey."[60] Throughout the Great Depression, African American women—like white working-class housewives—engaged in domestic politics that embraced the role of family manager, but they also pushed further to "engage in a practice of economic nationalism," which created a militant approach among some African American women. The Housewives League of Detroit mobilized their members to join the meat boycotts, but they also targeted their neighborhood's white-owned businesses for price gouging. Their efforts allowed Detroit to boast that it had "a greater per-capita volume of business controlled and patronized by Negroes that any other city in the United States."[61] In addition to support from area housewives, the meat boycott received community support from political, labor,

FIG. 1.3 A meat boycott picket along the streets of Hamtramck with Mary Zuk second from the right in the dark beret. This photo stands apart from other images of the 1935 meat strike because it included several African American picketers as well.

Courtesy of Archives of Labor and Urban Affairs, Walter P. Reuther Library, Wayne State University, Detroit, Michigan.

and social organizations. By the middle of August, the Detroit Federation of Labor endorsed the boycott and offered its support to the campaign.

As the boycott progressed, various neighborhoods, ethnic, and racial organizations formed the Central Action Committee against the High Cost of Living (CACHCL) to coordinate activities. The CACHCL was "composed of more than five hundred people elected at twenty five mass meetings in fifteen sections of Detroit, Hamtramck, and the vicinity."[62] Each of the 500 Central Action Committee members acted as block captains, and they met every evening to discuss "practical steps."[63] After these strategy sessions, the women would spread out to designated areas and host open-air meetings, which attracted 200 to 400 people.

With no sign of the boycott weakening, Hamtramck's city leaders began to clamp down on boycotters. Denied access to a public meeting space, protesters went to a Detroit meatpacking plant to demand a 20 percent reduction in the cost of meat. "The militant housewives ran into difficulties," reported the *Detroit Free Press*. "When they attempted to pour kerosene over the meats of a wholesale packer . . . three of them, in addition to a man, were arrested [and] charged with disturbing the peace."[64] Throughout August, the police arrested many housewives during rallies and picketing. After arresting five women during the day's picketing, the police were forced to release them when a crowd of "four to five hundred stormed the McGraw Avenue police station demanding their freedom." Those who attempted to torch the meats were eventually found guilty and received sentences of probation.[65]

For the CACHCL members, big business and government policies were at the root of the high cost of living. Having spent a month targeting businesses, the CACHCL turned their attention to the national government. On August 15, 7,000 people gathered in Perrien Park, in the heart of Detroit's Westside Polish community, to elect a delegation to take their demands to leaders in Washington, DC.[66] Their primary targets were President Franklin D. Roosevelt, Secretary of Agriculture Henry Wallace, and policies these men supported, like the Agricultural Adjustment Act (AAA). The CACHCL believed that government policies—such as the forced destruction of livestock; the new processing tax, which was "gobbled up by the bankers, loaners, and mortgage holders"; and the "refusal to aid the farmers during the drought, compelling them to sell their cattle for practically nothing"—needed to be repealed. Under these policies, the meat trust—dominated by Armour and Company and Swift and Company—was continually increasing its profits. In their talking tips for speakers, the CACHCL cited Department of Labor statistics showing that meat prices had risen 54.9 percent since 1933. The rising prices, according to the CACHCL, were the result of stockmen stockpiling meat to keep prices inflated as well as to "store away meat for war purposes to feed future military armies while at the same time the boys in the CCC [Civilian Conservation Corps] camps received inadequate food."[67] They demanded an immediate investigation of the packers and the "prosecution of the Packers for profiteering," citing the salaries of company executives that went as high as $125,000—the equivalent of $2.2 million in 2016.[68]

The Roosevelt administration had implemented the 1933 Agricultural Adjustment Act (AAA) to allow government agencies to enable administrative controls over the production of farm goods, in conjunction with farmers. The issue around farm production arose during World War I, when export production rose dramatically during the war and its aftermath, but dropped off as European production stabilized in the 1920s. As a result, American agricultural production exceeded export demand. The AAA wanted to restore farm purchasing power to pre–World War I levels, through subsidies and a voluntary reduction of production. It also regulated marketing and the food processing industry and licensed processors to eliminate unfair taxes.

By having farmers not plant on part of their land, destroy surpluses of cotton and tobacco, and kill off excess livestock, surpluses could be eliminated and prices would go up. The products named in the original act were wheat, cotton, corn, hogs, rice, tobacco, and milk. These were chosen because they had surpluses, required additional processing before consumption, and strongly affected other commodity prices. Amendments to the act added rye, flax, barley, cattle, peanuts, sugar beets, potatoes, and other products. The goal was to raise farm prices to "parity," or prices in a comparable ratio to industrial prices, similar to prices before World War I.

The government wanted to help farmers struggling with mortgages. Prior to the act, there were frequent foreclosures on farms, and Roosevelt urged creditors to hold off on foreclosures, at least until the act could have an impact. From the perspective of American consumers, however, the AAA benefited the agricultural elite by increasing local meat prices. The AAA was also criticized by other groups, such as southern sharecroppers and the Wisconsin dairy industry. During the mid-1930s, the Roosevelt administration dealt with a barrage of letters, petitions, and delegations, all of whom represented large swaths of the American public that were excluded from many of the New Deal's transformative policies, such as American housewives, agricultural workers, southern sharecroppers, tenant farmers, and migrant farmworkers in the West. Thus, the 1935 meat boycott—which spread throughout the industrial North—was not an isolated incident, led by a "fiery" young mother and a bunch of "militant housewives," but part of a systematic movement among both the agricultural and industrial working classes.

The Washington, DC, delegation garnered significant media attention. Mary Zuk, along with four other boycott leaders—Catherine Mudra, a housewife of Polish descent and close ally of Zuk; Elizabeth Moss and Pearl Alterman, two white housewives; and Irene Thompson, an African American housewife—were elected to the delegation.[69] In addition to this delegation, a second went to Chicago to challenge the meatpackers in their own backyard, Chicago's Packingtown.[70] Upon arriving in Washington, the delegation met with Secretary Wallace. Zuk confronted him about the AAA's policy to pay farmers to destroy livestock and the inflated meat costs that resulted:

> "Is the government going to see that meat prices are reduced 20 percent?" Mrs. Mary Zuk, leader of the delegation, demanded of Wallace.

"Under drouth [*sic*] conditions it is impossible to guarantee future meat prices," Secretary Wallace replied.

"Why does the government pay farmers not to raise little pigs?" Mrs. Zuk countered.[71]

Wallace's response was a hasty departure from the meeting. The women handed their petition to Calvin Hoover, the AAA's consumers' council. Next to a photo of Zuk with Hoover, the *Detroit Free Press* headline read, "Wallace Beats Hasty Retreat before Irate Detroit Women." The *New York Times* and *Chicago Tribune* also reported on this delegation's trip to the nation's capital. Three months later, Wallace found himself defending his decision to destroy millions of little pigs to stabilize pork prices. Wallace gave a speech outlining the economics of over-production. "People who believe that we ordered the destruction of food are merely the victims of their prejudices and the misinformation that has been fed to them by interested persons."[72] Wallace's categorization of boycotters as "victims" fueled the gendered stereotype that the housewives could not organize a boycott without the influence of "interested persons."

After delivering their petition to Hoover and failing in their attempt to meet with Roosevelt, the delegation met with Michigan's Representative Dingell who, earlier in August, had submitted a House Resolution requesting an investigation into the "spread between the prices paid to the Producer for hogs, cattle, and sheep and the prices paid by retailers and consumers for meat and meat products."[73] Initially, Representative Dingell's resolution went nowhere. While it sparked colorful debate on the congressional floor, the resolution failed to win funds for the investigation. In a September 1935 letter to Zuk, Otis B. Johnson, secretary of the Federal Trade Commission, reported that "the appropriation bill providing money for this inquiry failed to pass," and he argued that an inquiry into the high prices of meat in Hamtramck was unjustified, given the spike in prices nationally.[74] In the end, however, the federal government did begin an investigation, "behind closed doors," which frustrated Zuk. "Shouldn't we demand that this investigation be held in the open, so that everybody could see and listen to it?" Zuk cautioned. "In my thinking, the federal investigation should not be carried out in order that a few officials had an opportunity to kill time somehow."[75]

In Hamtramck, the boycott quietly faded as the summer came to a close, and by September there was little news coverage of Zuk and her band of fiery housewives. Beyond Detroit, there was a different story. In Minneapolis, Milwaukee, and Chicago, housewives were starting their own boycotts. In

Minneapolis, the Women's League against the High Cost of Living picketed for four days and planned to send a delegation of women to Chicago to meet with packinghouse owners. The league noted that they were funding their organizing through "public subscriptions."[76] Perhaps taking a hint from their wives, the National Restaurant Association (NRA) passed a resolution to boycott pork and "such other foods as have been exorbitantly raised in price by artificial control under the . . . AAA program." Frank O. Sherill, the NRA's new president, noted, "It means we are joining in the housewives' fight with all the force we can command." Sherill estimated that the NRA's boycott had the potential to impact the 20 million meals served daily in restaurants across the country.[77] Boycotts continued throughout the fall but seemed to abate by the start of the holiday season. While the demand of a 20 percent price reduction was never met, neighborhood butchers were pressured through the boycotts to lower their prices in order to bring their customers back. In 1936, the US Supreme Court ruled that the AAA violated states' rights and was deemed unconstitutional.[78]

Councilwoman Zuk

As the meat boycott ended, Zuk turned her attention to local politics. In a speech on the local Polish language radio program, she compared the housewives' efforts to two Polish American war heroes. "Same as [Tadeusz] Kosciusko and [Casimir] Pulaski, who were declared heroes because they fought for freedom of this country, so we, the women should be remembered for our efforts to free ourselves of shackles imposed by profiteering trusts."[79] Embracing an ideology of domestic politics, Zuk invoked women's responsibilities as mothers and household managers in her appeal to women to join the Hamtramck People's League, a new local political party. "Women! You, who carry on your shoulders [the] heavy duty of bringing up your children and managing your households, you, who must work very hard for a living, rise to action, support the work of our League against High Prices."[80]

Zuk channeled this momentum into a successful run for the Hamtramck Common Council on the Hamtramck People's League ticket, which was affiliated with the Michigan Farmer Labor Party. The same year, delegates to the United Automobile Workers union (UAW) voted at their national meeting in Indiana to support the formation of a national farmer-labor party. At that same gathering, the delegates voted down a resolution to endorse President Roosevelt for a second term. And, in the time preceding the UAW's national convention, Hamtramck's Local Union 229 passed multiple resolutions call-ing for a farmer-labor party.[81]

The influence of leftist politics in Detroit was nothing new. As one histo-rian argues, Detroit—along with Toledo and Cleveland—formed a "reform triangle" dating back to the start of the twentieth century. With the election of progressive mayors, these industrial cities were critical to the "emergence of [a] new urban politics," embodied in a "municipal socialism," which pro-moted programs beneficial to the working class. These programs included improved city services; union wages for city workers; and consumer pro-tections, such as food inspections.[82] The grassroots social reformer leg-acy of Hazen Pingree—Detroit's mayor in the last years of the nineteenth century—lasted well into the twentieth century.[83] Consequently, Detroit was a progressive urban center, in which community organizing flourished. The city's strong, working-class communities were built on vibrant social and religious organizations largely dominated by individual ethnic and racial groups. These communities helped the growth of domestic political action, such as the meat boycotts.

Zuk built a strong friendship with legendary union organizers Stanley Nowak and his wife Margaret, who lived only a few blocks away from her home. An organizer with the UAW, Nowak was charged with organizing the Polish autoworkers into the UAW Polish Trade Union Committee. Using his community and union connections, he won a seat in the Michigan Senate, representing the Twenty-First District. Margaret became an active leader in union women's committees, which would later form the basis of the UAW Women's Auxiliaries.[84] Zuk, probably through her friendship with the Nowaks, developed a relationship with Charles C. Diggs, a progressive leader in Detroit's black community and a fierce ally of Nowak. Diggs won a seat as a Democrat in the state's Senate for a district with a mix of African Americans and Polish Americans. As Zuk's circle of acquaintances gained power, she likely gained a new sense of confidence. With a broad base of support from organized labor, the Communist Party of America, a variety of ethnic organizations, African American religious leaders, and the Farmer Labor Party, Zuk's election to Hamtramck's Common Council was a turn-ing point in leadership among citizen housewives. Zuk could capture not just the imagination of housewives but that of working-class male leaders as well.

Zuk's time within the halls of power was brief. In 1938, Zuk lost her re-election bid. A number of factors possibly contributed to her failed re-election campaign. Two years after the meat boycott, she filed for divorce from her husband. In a close-knit Polish Catholic community, her decision to divorce could not have been made lightly. The public scandal that followed her filing revealed a common story: Mary testified that Stanley beat her "every weekend of their 15-year marriage." Eight years earlier, in 1930, Zuk told the judge that she started divorce proceedings, only to withdraw them when Stanley pledged to be a good husband. When the judge estimated that she would have endured 700 beatings, Zuk responded, "It was more than that."[85] She went on to state that Stanley failed to be a successful breadwinner. "For the last two years he has failed to support me and I've had to go to work to provide for my children," recounted Zuk.[86] The judge granted the divorce, but the alimony he ordered Stanley to pay was nowhere near the cost of raising a family. Circuit Court Judge Robert M. Toms demanded that Stanley pay $2.50 a week in alimony in contrast to an earlier ruling that he pay $5 a week. Based on the average salary of an industrial worker in the last 1930s, this amounted to less than 10 percent of Stanley's potential take-home salary at the Ford Motor Company.[87]

The public fight over the Zuk's divorce demonstrates several social tensions. Mary's claims against Stanley were countered by his statements that she was likely having an affair and would not care for him appropriately. "She spends much of her time in the company of another man." Stanley continued, "She is frequently absent from home, especially when I was in the hospital recently." In his eyes, she was not fulfilling her duties as a wife and homemaker. He went on to red-bait her by claiming that she donated $20 a week to the Communist Party of America, carefully noting that "I am not a Communist and I strongly object to her belonging to any such organization."[88] Whether Mary was a member of the Communist Party (CP) is impossible to determine. Stanley's efforts at red-baiting her were nothing new. Newspapers were consistently attributing the widespread meat boycott to "communist agitators" with headlines declaring "Reds Blamed for Housewives' Meat Boycott."[89]

The CP's involvement in the Detroit area boycotts and those elsewhere is, however, indisputable. With active boycotts in Cleveland, Chicago, Pittsburgh, and New Jersey, the CP was calling for a nationwide campaign to curb the high cost of living—including the price of rent and gas as well as sales taxes. *The Working Woman*, a monthly magazine for "working women, farm women and working-class housewives," published by the Communist Party, printed a call for women to make the "Action Committees against the high price of meat permanent Action Committees against the high cost of living."[90] This Communist influence was not unusual, especially in industrial epicenters like Detroit, home to a vast array of political parties committed to the working class.[91] When media and public officials accused the boycotters of Communist Party involvement, spokeswomen and delegation members Zuk and Mudra consistently responded, "There may be some Communists among us. There are also a lot of Republicans and Democrats, too. We do not ask the politics of those who join the strike. All we want is to get prices down where we can feed our families."[92]

At the time of the divorce proceedings, Zuk was earning a living wage through her work with the labor movement and the Common Council. Stanley argued that she was bringing home approximately $67 a week, totaling $3,500 a year, while he earned only $45 a week.[93] Stanley's assessment of Mary's salary was undoubtedly inflated. A federal employee working in an executive capacity earned $1,183 annually, while someone working in the insurance and real estate field was earning on average of $1,632 a year.[94]

In addition, the newspapers that once vilified Mary as a "Communist menace" now helped Stanley promote an image of her far removed from the struggling mother of the 1935 boycotts. The *Citizen* published a photograph of a well-groomed and plump Mary Zuk wearing a dress hat, jewelry, and a fur coat.[95] While the court granted Zuk full custody of their children as well as alimony from Stanley, damage to her reputation had been done. In a religiously conservative community of Polish Catholics, a divorce would certainly undermine the support of some 1936 voters. In fact, the *Detroit News* commented, "the menfolk of Hamtramck are convinced that if ever there is another woman elected to the council, it will not be Mrs. Zuk."[96]

Zuk, on the other hand, "dismissed the divorce as a negligible factor in her defeat."[97] She believed that her re-election bid was weakened by the "defection of the city's communists from her cause."[98] However, it is unlikely that there was a single reason. Zuk's gender—along with widespread accusations that she left the welfare rolls for "a position of comparative affluence"—certainly contributed to her loss. After 1938, her political influence faded. This did not, however, keep the US House of Representatives' Special Committee on Un-American Activities from listing her as a communist while investigating communist influences in industrial Michigan. Noting that she was working in one of Hamtramck's city departments, William Odell Nowell—a former "labor spy" for the Ford Motor Company who also engaged in undercover work for the Immigration and Naturalization Service—testified, "she is still there and is still an active Communist."[99]

The local focus of early twentieth-century protests—such as the 1902 kosher meat boycott—do not diminish their historical significance, but it does set them apart from the 1935 meat boycotts. The politicization of women's networks, the reawakening of the labor movement, and the increased cost of meat, a food that was not just nourishment but also symbolic of class identity, combined to create an intensely militant atmosphere. To many of the Detroit housewives, the boycott represented an opportunity to insert an agenda of domestic politics into the political process more permanently.

2

"Women—The Guardians of Price Control"

WORKING-CLASS HOUSEWIVES, CONSUMER ACTIVISM, AND THE STATE

IN SEPTEMBER 1943, Beatrice Seimeincic, a foundry worker and wife, attended the monthly meeting of the local Labor Advisory Council (LAC) of the Office of Price Administration (OPA). She explained to Pittsburgh OPA Director Alvin J. Williams that avoiding the black market was virtually impossible, given the current rationing program. Wives were pushed to shop on the black market because their husbands demanded more meat than rations could provide. Citing her husband's "strenuous job" as a coal miner and her daughter's work at a war plant, Seimeincic felt she had to turn to the black market. She explained that the rationing program was causing a decline in the health of women war workers. Helen M. Minear, secretary of the Pittsburgh Newspaper Guild, also spoke up to object that the rationing program was putting basic food like canned peaches and peas out of reach for workers. C. A. Blanchett, a union member, disclosed in a letter to Walter Reuther, the leader of the United Automobile Workers union (UAW), "This is the most painful and hungry day I have ever experienced in my 45 years in this . . . working class district where I live. No meat, no butter, no sugar, no soap. Most people are without coal." In "this land of plenty and over-production," said Harry Travis, vice-president of the AFL's Pittsburgh Central Labor Union, the OPA should collaborate with local consumer organizations. Travis concluded, "Labor and business and all others should throw away their prejudices," in favor of collaboration to keep prices down.[1]

This meeting was just one of many held when the Office of Price Administration introduced their wartime rationing program: the Home Front Pledge Campaign. In 1943 alone, the OPA hosted meetings in 171 cities. The plan was to mobilize housewives "in helping [to] hold prices in line."[2] J. Paul Leonard, the OPA's chief of Group Services Branches, called this effort "the most important and extensive programs [the OPA] have prepared yet."[3] The OPA's two-part program included introducing its price control plan at mass meetings and then scheduling follow-up meetings with local organizations to check on their progress. The OPA believed that its program would succeed only "if every woman assume[d] this individual responsibility."[4]

This chapter explores how working-class housewives used labor union auxiliaries to mobilize a consumer movement that linked the workplace and the home using the language of "domestic politics." Labor union auxiliaries had the potential to reach the homes of millions of working-class families. The women's auxiliaries of the newly organized industrial unions affiliated with the Congress of Industrial Organizations (CIO) developed a coalition to pressure the government to protect the American standard of living for workers as businesses profited handsomely from wartime production. The auxiliaries' leadership intentionally crafted an identity rooted in domestic politics that pushed housewives beyond the traditional responsibilities associated with the strike kitchen, such as feeding strikers and soliciting donations, and into the public sphere. Their strategic use of the term "housewife" was as much a political tool as it was a requirement of auxiliary membership. From the 1935 meat boycott through World War II, the image of a cadre of citizen housewives developed in the public's consciousness.[5] Race and class played a critical role in the creation of this public image. By the time the United States entered World War II, the government's Rosie the Riveter campaign reinforced the perception that a working-class white woman was America's citizen housewife.[6] While mainstream media continued to reinforce this characterization, a study of consumer activism during this time revealed a more accurate portrayal of real citizen housewives.

Building a Movement of Housewives

"What price milk?" Hester LaDuke asked a room full of housewives in 1938. A member of the United Auto Workers Women's Auxiliary Board from Flint, Michigan, La Duke called on these working-class housewives to educate themselves about the complexities of consumerism and advertising. "The

American standard of living. What is it?" LaDuke continued, "Educators have defined it, economists have analyzed it, liberals have said we must have it, but it has remained for labor to go out and fight to get it. . . . Food."[7] From their founding, women's CIO-affiliated auxiliaries used consumer issues to defend a standard of living they believed was the product of labor's growing power.[8] As war production catapulted the United States out of the Great Depression, working-class housewives of industrial labor unions—such as the United Automobile Workers (UAW)—tried to define and defend the American standard of living through consumer activism.

While there is a long tradition of women using their consumer practices to reduce prices, these protests rarely resulted in substantial organizational influence or access to the halls of power. Although they achieved an array of neighborhood victories, the Detroit-led boycotters in the mid-1930s failed to gain any institutional power. The rise of a more militant working-class supported by the CIO, combined with the United States' entry into World War II, created an environment ripe for a collective working-class women's voice.[9]

The auxiliary movement provided the infrastructure that earlier consumer organizing by working-class housewives had lacked. The housewives' affiliation with labor unions provided ready-made auxiliary members in the wives, daughters, and girlfriends of the male union-affiliated workers. The auxiliaries made direct financial contributions and in-kind donations, and they established a more explicit link between home and the shop floor. The CIO auxiliary movement was centered on the principle that the home belonged at the center of the labor movement.

Two women led the early organizing of the UAW auxiliary, creating the momentum for working-class housewives to move beyond the strike kitchens and childcare centers and directly into the public sphere. In 1936, Catherine "Babe" Gelles's husband went on strike at Detroit's Bohn Aluminum plant. He, along with 450 other workers, occupied the plant for twenty-eight days. Gelles, a former Bohn worker, was not sold on the strike. "Maybe it was for selfish reasons," she recalled years later. "But having worked at Bohn's I [knew] there were quite a few good looking women working there and I wondered if they would be sitting down too."[10] Noticing her reservations and perhaps a tinge of jealousy, Gelles's brother suggested that she go to the union hall to voice her concerns. Walter Reuther—then a local union president who would ultimately lead the UAW into its heyday—explained to Gelles and other weary wives why their husbands were striking.[11] By the end of the meeting, Gelles "was thoroughly sold on the union."[12] When Reuther asked for volunteers to set up a strike kitchen, Gelles jumped at the

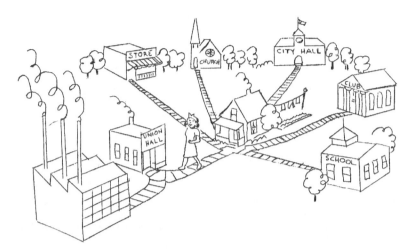

FIG. 2.1 This cartoon from the September 1945 issue of the *Women's Auxiliary News*, the monthly newsletter of the UAW Women's Auxiliary, illustrates the organizing vision of the auxiliary. They believed that the home rather than the workplace should be the focal point of organizing (UAW Women's Department, Women's Auxiliary News, 1940–51, Box 3N-D-6, Folder 1945, v.5).

Courtesy of Archives of Labor and Urban Affairs, Walter P. Reuther Library, Wayne State University, Detroit, Michigan.

opportunity. "I rolled up my sleeves and worked all during the strike."[13] The UAW Women's Auxiliary was permanently established during this wave of sit-downs from 1936 to 1937.

Born in St. Joseph, Missouri, and raised in Colorado, Gelles moved to Detroit with her family when her cattleman father got a job with a packinghouse. She soon found work at the Bohn Aluminum and Brass Company. "The wages were low, we worked long hours, and the working conditions were not too good."[14] Within a year, Gelles met her husband, married, and left the plant. The Bohn strike was not Gelles's first experience with labor unrest. As a child, she took part in a 1919 streetcar strike, during which she "helped to stop the cars so the older girls could throw rotten eggs at scabs."[15] Still, it was her work at the Bohn plant and her early involvement with the UAW Women's Auxiliary that propelled her into union life.

Shortly after the Bohn sit-down, on December 30, 1936, workers in the Fisher Body Plant at General Motors in Flint, Michigan, went on strike. The sit-down there lasted for forty-four days during the harshest months of winter. As with other strikes, the wives and some female workers were asked to leave the plant to avoid bad press about men and women spending nights together inside the plant. Frustrated by their second-class role, the women workers—together with the wives of the male workers—organized the first UAW Women's Auxiliary. They set up a strike kitchen, a childcare center, and a first aid station. Still, many women—including Catherine Gelles and the better-known Genora (Johnson) Dollinger, later nicknamed "the Joan of Arc of Labor" by the French press—wanted to move beyond the traditional care-giving roles.[16]

Born into a prominent Methodist family in Flint, Michigan, Dollinger rebelled at a young age. Reacting to the class upheaval in her industrial home-town, Dollinger joined the Young People's Socialist League and attended meetings of the League of Industrial Democracy, a militant socialist organi-zation. By the time she was sixteen, Dollinger was an avowed socialist who espoused the philosophies of Leon Trotsky. She ran off to Ohio to elope with her high school boyfriend, Kermit Johnson. After a quick civil ceremony, the couple drove back to Flint. Genora and Kermit both returned to their respec-tive homes as though it was any other date night. They kept their marriage a secret for weeks, until Kermit let it slip one night at dinner. Dollinger's father was furious that his daughter had married secretly and without his permis-sion, but in time, her father gave his blessing. Within a year, Dollinger was pregnant and dropped out of high school. Kermit was working as a general laborer.[17] Her married life was about as far from the comforts of her upper-middle-class life as she could have gotten had she not eloped. She threw her-self into socialist politics with even more gusto. The Flint sit-down strike offered the perfect training ground.

Believing that women had more to offer than making sandwiches in the strike kitchen, Dollinger, Gelles, and their allies established the Emergency Brigade, military-style flying squads to aid the picketers. Using the strike kitchens and childcare center as recruiting sites, brigade members built a network of women willing to put themselves between the workers and the Pinkerton strike-breakers. The recruiters did not sugarcoat the dangers of bri-gade participation. In an auxiliary meeting, Dollinger explained, "It can't be somebody who's weak of heart. You can't go hysterical if your sister beside you drops down in a pool of blood." Dollinger recalled that brigade members "didn't pressure anyone to join. We made it very difficult." Yet, after expe-riencing grinding poverty and watching a labor movement that was largely uninterested in organizing industrial workers, these women were ready to embrace militant action. During the meeting, a woman in her seventies stood up and said, "You can't keep me out. My sons work in that factory. My hus-band worked in that factory before he died and I have grandsons in there." After her lengthy speech, she—along with dozens of other women—signed up for the brigade.[18] Within two weeks, more than 400 women had joined. For Dollinger and other brigade members, the picket line was the front line of battle, and they were "the women's battalion." Dollinger demanded that women "be prepared to stand in front of men if shooting broke out."[19] Armed with rolling pins, brooms, mops, and clubs, these women took their duties seriously.

During the Flint sit-down strike, the Emergency Brigade functioned as a twenty-four-hour crisis response corps. Members embraced their new identity by wearing military-style uniforms, including berets, and developed a color-coded system to identify the brigade's affiliation. For example, Flint Brigade members wore red; Detroit, green; Lansing, blue; and Pontiac, orange.[20] In addition to uniforms, many women carried concealed weapons, such as wooden clubs, "with handles carved to fit a woman's grip."[21] The brigades became the face of the UAW Women's Auxiliary movement in the late 1930s. With their faces on the front page of the *New York Times* and other national newspapers, brigade members helped the auxiliaries to establish both a relevance and a militancy that exceeded previous auxiliary activity.[22]

Participation in the Emergency Brigade proved a transformative experience for many of the women. According to one member involved in the Flint sit-down, "a new type of women was born in the strike. . . . Women who only yesterday were horrified at unionism, who felt inferior to the task of organizing, speaking, leading, have, as if overnight, become the spearhead in the battle of unionism."[23] Many women were motivated to support their husbands and families. However, the housewives' involvement also created a self-confidence that was channeled into the growing organization. So, while the impetus was to "protect our husbands," the growth of the organization demonstrated a motivation that was personal as well. While the brigades were critical during crisis moments, it was the daily work of the local auxiliaries that proved to have resilience, as the auxiliaries matured into organizations with a national vision for organizing working-class women.

As the sit-down strikes ended in victory, the Emergency Brigades' militancy on the picket lines was no longer needed. For some women, like Dollinger, the auxiliary movement's future appeared too staid.[24] For women like Catherine Gelles and Faye Stephenson, however, the sit-down strikes were only the beginning. Like Gelles, Faye Stephenson had joined the UAW Women's Auxiliary during the 1936 sit-down movement, in her case at the Fisher Body strike in Cleveland, Ohio. In 1908, at the age of thirteen, Stephenson had left school to work in a cigar factory. During the Great Depression, her leadership skills were evident. She worked with "Relief Agencies for the Unemployed" and led a delegation to Washington, DC, to campaign for unemployment insurance.[25] As a forty-year-old mother of three, Stephenson helped organize UAW Women's Auxiliary No. 35 during the Fisher Body strike. She also played a leading role in the 1939 film, *United Action: Story of the GM Tool and Die Strike.*

Because of their early leadership in Detroit and Cleveland, Gelles and Stephenson were among the first elected leaders of the UAW Women's Auxiliary. Faye Stephenson, the CWA president, ascended from the ranks of Cleveland's UAW auxiliaries. In 1943, Catherine Gelles, a Detroit auxiliary leader, assumed a national role as the director of the national childcare program for all CIO auxiliaries.[26] At one of the first auxiliary conferences, Stephenson, chairman of the UAW Women's Auxiliary National Coordinating Committee, noted, "We had very little to speak of in the way of a Women's Organization."[27] Yet, within a year, sixty-nine "functioning chartered auxiliaries" were organized, mostly in the Midwest.[28] Stephenson added, "we have not only increased in numbers, but we have increased the political and economic consciousness of the women in the Auxiliary movement."[29] The UAW Auxiliary membership numbers continued to grow on both coasts and throughout the industrial Midwest. They soon became the largest and most influential auxiliary affiliated with the Congress of Industrial Organizations.

The UAW Women's Auxiliary leadership wanted to keep local auxiliaries from becoming "introverted." Leaders encouraged them to develop relationships outside of the UAW—especially with local community and political organizations, such as parent-teacher groups, churches, and the League of Women Voters. As the auxiliary movement expanded across the nation, the auxiliary transformed itself from an internal UAW group to a community organization with an identity "distinct and individual" from the UAW International Union.[30] While the auxiliary continued to organize within the UAW and to support job actions, the auxiliary leadership also worked to drive down the cost of living and to support legislation to improve the lives of the working class, including wage-earning women and African Americans.

In January 1941, the *Women's Auxiliary News* (*WAN*), the monthly newsletter of the UAW Women's Auxiliary, reported their first victorious battle against the high cost of rent. With Gelles at the helm, the Detroit-area Auxiliaries' Council appealed to the Detroit Common Council and demanded that the aldermen begin to study Detroit housing. The council representatives pointed out to the aldermen that Briggs and Chrysler, two

FIG. 2.2 The International Executive Board of the United Automobile Workers Auxiliaries demonstrating its support for the Allis-Chalmers strike. Left to right, seated: Maxine Lewis, Flint; Dorothy Keene, international president, Rockford, Illinois; Catherine Gelles, international secretary-treasurer, Detroit; Mable Mayne, Ontario. Standing: Mildred Falls, Evansville; Florence Kasper, Detroit; Joyce Newton, Rockford. Courtesy of Wisconsin Historical Society.

Detroit manufacturers, were benefiting from government aid by renting new defense plants at a dollar a year while the government invested $20 million dollars into the plant. Couching her argument in the language of domestic politics, Gelles urged the Detroit Common Council to see national defense from the perspective of working-class families:

> Not one dollar of that twenty million will go to housing the new employees in those plants. We believe in national defense, but we also believe that national defense should begin with the defense of a decent standard of living for workers and their families.[31]

The entry of the United States into World War II created an opportunity for auxiliaries to demonstrate their maturity as community organizations. With networks based in both workplaces and neighborhoods, auxiliaries could help raise awareness about wartime programs. The vast Office of Price Administration was eager to capitalize on this.

A National Voice for Working-Class Housewives

The Office of Price Administration launched the Home Front Pledge Campaign in 1943, the same year the Congress of Women's Auxiliaries (CWA)—the umbrella organization of CIO-affiliated women's auxiliaries—held its first national gathering. [32] In their eyes, the meeting set a precedent not just for the labor movement but for the women's movement as a whole. The leadership remarked to the audience that this is "the first time in the history of the labor movement of the United States that organized wives of organized workers from all fields of industry have met in a formal conference to consider a national program that will meet their needs and embrace their interests as women and as part of the labor movement. . . . For it is an historic fact that every step forward in the struggle for *women's* rights has occurred simultaneously with some larger struggle for *human* rights."[33] The CWA's mission was closely tied to the objectives of organized labor, but its mission and programs reached beyond the scope of the shop floor. The CWA behaved much like other national women's organizations which they collaborated with and supported, such as the National Council of Jewish Women, National Council of Negro Women, Parent-Teacher Association, League of Women Shoppers, and Young Women's Christian Association.

The auxiliaries called on women to challenge the fact that the wages of women entering large manufacturing industries "lag far behind those of men," citing this as "one of the most important problems which the Unions must solve." The auxiliary leadership understood this issue from two perspectives. First, by paying women "less than the lowest average for men," the union wage scale would eventually be at risk. Dorothy Bellanca, vice-president of the Amalgamated Clothing Workers of America, said it best during a CIO Political Action Conference: "The idea of women going back to their homes some day is outworn. . . . No one has the right to question the right of women to work. Women belong everywhere, wherever they want." She went on to warn that if unions did not organize and support women workers "they'll be faced with an army of trained scabs."[34] Lower wages for women and the threat of wage ceilings also translated into weaker purchasing power for families. In a statement presented to Congress by a national delegation of UAW auxiliary members, one woman demanded:

> The women we represent . . . are rallying to the call for . . . strengthening of the defense program by raising the living standards of their families and communities. . . . We ask . . . that Congress make it possible for

us to do this important job by legislating against sky rocketing prices which are impoverishing . . . the well-being of the people.[35]

The links between women's rights and the "sky rocketing" cost of living permeated the work of the CWA throughout the 1940s.

Headquartered in Washington, DC, the CWA was staffed by Eleanor Fowler, a member of the National Newspaper Guild's Women's Auxiliary. She was married to C. W. Fowler, a writer for the *CIO News*; he would become the editor of the *FTA News,* the newspaper for the militant Food, Tobacco, Agricultural and Allied Workers Union of America (FTA) that was committed to organizing a multi-racial labor movement throughout the southern United States.[36] Far from a "typical" auxiliary housewife, Fowler had a pedigree that more closely resembled that of Progressive Era reformers and settlement house leaders.[37] Educated at Bryn Mawr, the London School of Economics, and the Sorbonne, Fowler used her education to publicize the needs of working-class housewives. Her weekly column "Women in War," gave her a national platform and made her one of the most nationally recognized auxiliary leaders.[38] Her essays connected the minutiae of housekeeping to the pressing social needs of working families. With articles entitled "Indiana Women in Political Drive," "Women's Stake in Reconversion," "Negro Women Finding Freedom in PAC Work," and "Childcare to Keep Women on War Jobs," the CWA educated a large number of working-class housewives and called them to action. The Home Front Pledge provided the ideal opening for auxiliary leaders to set an agenda for their local members to work with the OPA, the nation's largest governmental agency. The potential for broadening their political voice was not lost on Fowler or other national leaders such as Gelles and Stephenson.

Among labor union auxiliaries, the CWA led the lobbying efforts, and, not surprisingly, Eleanor Fowler, the relentless voice of the CWA in Washington, DC, helped to lead the charge. As a regular wartime columnist in the *CIO News*, she trumpeted the need for auxiliary women to mobilize on issues related to the war as well as broader issues of racial equity and citizenship. In her *CIO News* column Fowler called on auxiliary members to support a host of legislative initiatives, chief among them childcare funding, the Fair Employment Practices Commission, school lunch programs, and cost-of-living policies.[39] Fowler also represented the CIO auxiliaries' interests in a variety of committees, such as the Consumer Clearing House and the Office of Price Administration's Consumer Advisory Committee, giving voice to working-class interests within predominantly middle-class coalitions.

Furthermore, Fowler regularly testified before congressional committees to represent the interests of working-class housewives. During one trip to Capitol Hill to lobby against the Equal Rights Amendment, Fowler recalled the "smooth talk" of a National Woman's Party lobbyist as she was "honored with a two-hour monologue . . . when I incautiously sat down in the Senate waiting room."[40] With the CWA functioning as a national lobby group and women's auxiliaries scattered throughout both rural and urban areas working as local community groups, working-class housewives used the auxiliaries to shape their political voice and assert their citizenship rights.

Fowler's residence in the nation's capital and her educational background made her the ideal candidate to lobby on behalf of the auxiliaries. She was one of only six paid auxiliary staff nationally, and she earned a small stipend intended to cover the cost of a "maid for . . . [her] children."[41] Like many middle- and upper-middle-class white women, especially in southern cities, Fowler employed an African American housekeeper to help care for her children, but nothing more is known about this woman.[42] In a 1943 letter to Mary Anderson, director of the Women's Bureau, Fowler referenced her reliance on a paid childcare provider. Apologizing for her slow reply to an earlier letter from Anderson, Fowler explained that "my family has all had the flu and my housekeeper has left so that I have to stay home with the children."[43] Fowler's personal engagement of the housewife identity illustrates the power of the theater and rhetoric of the housewife in the political sphere.[44] Still, the majority of the auxiliary leadership remained under the control of working-class women like Faye Stephenson and Catherine Gelles.

As most women's organizations were staffed by volunteers, Fowler's salary stands out. The other five paid workers included Catherine Gelles, who was paid as secretary-treasurer by the largest and most successful auxiliary, the UAW Women's Auxiliary. Gelles remained on staff until her retirement in the 1970s. District 3 of the United Electrical Workers also paid a full-time auxiliary staff organizer, and in Los Angeles, the auxiliaries combined resources to employ a regional Los Angeles Auxiliary organizer. The American Newspaper Guild and the Mine, Mill, and Smelter Workers' Auxiliaries both paid an organizer to work part-time, and the CWA employed Eleanor Fowler as its secretary-treasurer on a part-time basis.[45] While six paid organizers were a far cry from the fully staffed labor unions, the auxiliaries benefited from their ability to focus exclusively on the work of building the auxiliary movement.

CIO auxiliaries relied heavily on both the monetary and in-kind support of their international unions and the dues paid by their membership. Yet despite the advantage of paid organizers, the movement's ability to handle diverse programming reflects the commitment of the local auxiliary members on the ground. It also reinforced the weight of the CWA's concerns over some auxiliary members' decision to pour their energy into their neighborhood organizations rather than maintain involvement in their auxiliary. Without an army of volunteers dedicated to the auxiliary movement, the ability to build a national movement of housewives would fade. This fear foreshadows changes that came after the 1955 merger of the AFL and CIO when the organization chose to focus on building its political action work through a new structure rather than relying on the existing auxiliaries.

Five months after the nation's entry into war, President Roosevelt laid out a domestic plan that highlighted the patriotic duty of "sacrifice."[46] His economic policy combined the regulation of spending and wages with the maintenance of a high tax base for individuals and corporations. Roosevelt's ambitious Seven Point Plan was an administrative labyrinth. For the average consumer, the program was meant to "stabilize wages," while "fixing ceilings on prices and rents" through price controls and rationing of "all essential commodities."[47] Controlling food costs was particularly urgent, since families typically spent up to half their income on food.[48]

Established in 1941 as a department within the Office of Emergency Management, the Office of Price Administration worked to oversee and to regulate the cost of living through price controls, rationing, food grade labeling, and monitoring rent control. With a budget as hefty as the Social Security Board's and a staff of over a quarter million, including a volunteer army consisting largely of housewives, the OPA was a massive government organization that "touched the daily lives of ordinary citizens more than . . . any other agency."[49]

The experience and language of sacrifice was the common dominator that brought housewives together. For many grassroots activists—such as the housewives affiliated with the Congress of Women's Auxiliaries—the needs of the OPA offered the link between the CIO membership's focus on economics and a greater vision of women's equality. The UAW Women's Auxiliary—the largest within the CWA—used their 1942 membership drive to demonstrate the importance of women's rights. Hoping to increase their dues-paying members to 20,000 women, the UAW Auxiliary leadership urged women no longer to think "in terms of small groups—we are an integral part of a mighty organization of hundreds of thousands . . . a part of a larger community which is America."[50] This message encouraged members to see themselves as parts of a collective body.

Fighting the High Cost of Living

The impact of food rationing was felt so strongly in most households that musicians began weaving the struggle into their music. Rhythm and blues artist Louis Jordan's song "Ration Blues" hit number one on the Rhythm and Blues and Country charts and reached number eleven on the Pop charts in 1943.

> *I got to live on forty ounces*
> *Of any kind of meat*
> *Those forty little ounces*
> *Gotta last me all week*
> *I got to cut down on my jelly*
> *It takes sugar to make it sweet*
> *I'm gonna steal all your jelly, baby*
> *And rob you of your meat*[51]

As the popularity of Jordan's song attests, accessing affordable food was an issue that impacted all working-class families. Widespread concern over the cost of food opened doors for collaboration among organizations of working-class housewives, particularly on a national level. With a national office in Washington, DC, the CWA could represent the interests of working-class housewives in diverse legislative and coalitional settings. Their participation in the Consumer Clearinghouse (CCH) most clearly reflected the leadership's recognition of domestic politics' importance to their membership. Established in 1943 by Caroline Ware, a New Deal activist and historian, and Donald Montgomery, a former New Deal staffer and legal counsel for the UAW, the CCH was founded as an activist coalition with a mission to influence policy at the OPA. The CCH drew attention to price control by focusing on issues like grades and standards, school lunches, food stamp proposals, and other matters related to stabilization.[52] Like Fowler, Caroline Ware was a well-educated woman born into a privileged and socially conscious family of Unitarians. Growing up in Brookline, Massachusetts, she attributed her class-consciousness to her childhood observations of the class divisions between the "top of the hill," represented by professional and business Protestants, and the "bottom of the hill," primarily Irish Catholic blue-collar workers.[53] Educated at Vassar, Ware trained as a historian and applied her craft to her organizing and education work. Her leadership at the CCH was a natural fit;

she moved among working- and middle-class communities with ease as she facilitated trust between many organizations.

With Eleanor Fowler as their representative, the CWA—along with the UAW Women's Auxiliary—shared the CCH table with progressive organizations representing women, workers, African Americans, farmers, and educators, just to name a few.[54] This role in the CCH set the CWA and their affiliate auxiliaries apart from earlier auxiliary efforts by the AFL and even the spontaneous meat boycotts of the early twentieth century. As a coalition-based organization, the CCH was made up of a large network of organizations, but a core group met monthly during the war years.[55] Operating on a shoestring budget, the CCH was dedicated to bringing a diverse collection of like-minded organizations together to influence governmental policy.[56] While the CCH sought recognition from Capitol Hill as a unified national consumer voice, it did not attempt to speak on behalf of all the member organizations. This work would be left to the individual organizations or smaller coalitions.[57]

Throughout the 1940s, the CWA and other auxiliary representatives attended the CCH's regular meetings in Washington to strategize about regulating the cost of living and keeping it in line with wages. These women wanted to make sure that the OPA and other government agencies did not bow to the "selfish interests of an infinitesimal minority" rather than seeking to improve the "welfare of the people as a whole."[58] Thus, two of the CCH's top issues were preserving the OPA and rent control.

By fall 1943, high food prices were to blame for 80 percent of the increased cost of living. In response, the OPA worked to return prices to their September 1942 rates by reducing meat and butter prices and implementing "weekly ceilings" on the highest-selling fresh fruits and vegetables, which were to blame for 60 percent of the food cost increase. The OPA had to contend with the lure of the black market, to which consumers turned when they became frustrated with the non-availability of goods and the lack of local enforcement of OPA policies. For example, at a Labor Advisory Council (LAC) meeting of the OPA, Beatrice Seimeincic explained that housewives were afraid to question the price of foodstuffs because they feared someone might shut "off her source of supply." As Seimeincic pointed, this was of particular concern for women in small communities who could only "shop in their immediate neighborhood."[59] This was true not only in Pittsburgh but also throughout communities in which housewives had long-standing relationships with their local food vendors. The anonymity of big box grocery stores was still decades away.[60]

Consumer Clearinghouse coalition members drove the agenda, and they hoped that by expanding beyond the beltway, they would be able to "stimulat[e] the development of local consumer clearing houses composed of branches of the national organizations."[61] In collaboration with Gerson Levi of the National Council of Jewish Women (NCJW) and Jeanetta Brown of the National Council of Negro Women (NCNW), Eleanor Fowler began to work on engaging local collaboration in a way that mimicked the efforts of the CCH on a national level. Within a few months, the subcommittee of three women gave a report to the CCH that strongly encouraged building local networks. They identified several cities they believed would benefit from local CCH committees: Washington, Baltimore, New Orleans, Indianapolis, and Los Angeles. In addition to organizing new groups, the CCH wanted to reach out to existing consumer groups in New York, Cincinnati, St. Louis, and Chicago.

As the women pointed out, this work would put "an additional work burden" on the national officers of the organizations, and they suggested that a CCH organizer be hired to organize these local groups. Still, despite this encouraging local news, the national coalition lacked the funding to make its next move and was forced to put the project on hold.[62] This lack of funding made the local networks all the more important in the fight to keep food prices low.

Yet it proved a missed opportunity for cross-ethnic and racial organizing. The diversity of the CCH coalition enabled many organizations concerned with consumer issues to collaborate on strategy. Businesses and advertisers began appealing to the expanding African American communities in northern industrial cities in earnest in the 1940s when the purchasing power of African American consumers grew. Threatening to march on Washington, African American community and labor leaders pressured Roosevelt to address employment discrimination of African American workers in the war industry. In June 1941, Roosevelt signed Executive Order 8802 banning discrimination "in the employment of workers in defense industries or government because of race, color, or national origin."[63] The Fair Employment Practices Commission (FEPC) was established to enforce Roosevelt's order. While still earning a fraction of what many white workers were earning, African American workers were gaining access to new job opportunities throughout the industrial North. According to one study, African American consumers had $7 billion in disposable income in 1946, and food purchases were at the top of the list of expenditures, with clothing and housing much further down. Despite the expansion of job opportunities, the high cost of food persisted in gobbling up $2.5 billion, or over one-third, of African American disposable income.[64]

The Congress of Women's Auxiliaries (CWA) was one organization that would allow the OPA to quickly build grassroots networks through alliances with housewives. While the CWA recognized that "no existing organization or combination of organizations represents all of the women who must be mobilized for this job," the CWA was a formidable network that could reach into the homes of CIO members.[65] With war production at full speed, CIO membership soared, reaching 3.9 million by 1944. In unions with strong, well-organized auxiliaries, membership increased almost eight times over pre-war numbers. For example, membership in the United Electrical, Machine, and Radio Workers of America (UE) leaped from just under 50,000 in 1939 to 432,000; the Mine, Mill, and Smelters union membership jumped from 30,000 to 98,000; and the UAW increased its members from 165,000 to over 1 million.[66] With labor union density at a national high, the OPA's program could potentially reach into as many homes through the organization's alliances with both CIO and AFL union auxiliaries.[67]

The OPA, however, was clumsy in its execution of this plan. Among the vast list of potential collaborators—including women's organizations—they neglected to list the AFL and CIO, despite pressure from OPA staffers who especially understood the organizational force of the CIO auxiliaries. Some OPA staffers grew exasperated with the slow-moving bureaucracy. Flora Y. Hatcher recognized that stalling a localized campaign would negatively affect the OPA's efforts to enforce price controls. There are "endless possibilities," she noted to J. Paul Leonard, director of the Consumer Division of the OPA. "It seems urgent to work with this group as soon as possible,—otherwise we will lose ground already gained."[68] Hatcher understood the utility of allying with powerful organizations, and she worked to establish relationships with women's groups, African American organizations, and labor unions.

To facilitate its outreach, the OPA established regional and local advisory committees to address labor, women, and consumer issues. For auxiliary members, there was overlap among the three committees, as they engaged in activities that touched on all of these issues. This crossover provides further evidence of the CIO auxiliaries' ability to use domestic politics to bridge organizations. The local OPA councils functioned to "carry out regulations" and to "administer price control and rationing on the local level," but they were not "empowered to act on matters of national policy."[69] They interacted with the community, but they held few decision-making powers. Still, local OPA staff members often fell prey to the politicking of the DC beltway. Their power was limited by Congress's appropriations, which cut sharply the number of local OPA enforcement personnel. The OPA's power was further hindered by seemingly random governmental decisions, such as the comptroller-general's ruling that forbade the OPA from buying samples of rationed goods for "evidence to use in prosecution of violators."[70]

Despite their limited authority, the OPA staffers did express a willingness to share recommendations and concerns from local community members. In Philadelphia, for example, OPA staff met with representatives from labor unions, auxiliaries, and the Communist Party.[71] Claiming to represent 27,000 community members in the Philadelphia area, the organizations pushed the OPA to create meaningful price controls and to explain the growing disparity between wages and the cost of living. Community delegates to the OPA's Labor Advisory Council argued that wage freezes and price controls needed to be "consistent." With limited local staff, the OPA needed organizations such as the auxiliaries to motivate consumers to act in their own interests.

Auxiliary members understood that the union wages of their husbands and fathers meant little if high costs put home essentials out of reach. In their review, the government was obligated to intervene and ensure access to an American standard of living. As household managers, housewives were the experts in this field. The auxiliary leadership quickly took up the challenge when the Office of Price Administration announced its new system of volunteer price checkers and its desire to partner with organized labor. Dorothy Keene, president of the UAW Women's Auxiliary, "urged each and every member of the UAW-CIO Women's Auxiliary to volunteer and work for what we believe in and have fought for."[72] The CWA appealed to their memberships' patriotic duty and demanded that "the housewife in every union household must be enlisted."[73] These calls to arms were pervasive throughout the war. The Office of Price Administration's appeal to housewives and the nationwide mobilization of CIO auxiliaries was notable, however, in giving working-class women a link to the state through domestic politics that had evaded them for decades. In turn, the OPA finally understood that its success depended on the regular involvement of American housewives across the country.

The OPA sought the early support of the CIO auxiliary members. Attending the first CWA convention, Helen Gregory, a field representative for the Consumer Division of the OPA, used the language of the labor movement, emphasizing that a higher cost of living was "a wage cut for you."[74] Gregory encouraged the CWA to support the OPA as it established national "experimental consumer information centers" and asked for the women's "wholehearted cooperation."[75] At the same conference, more than 100 delegates representing 100,000 CWA members mapped out a program for the coming year, citing the "protest of [the] rising cost of living" as one of their "most important tasks." They also amended the "consumer pledge," which "commit[ed] the housewife to buy carefully, to take care of the things she has and to waste nothing," and concluded with an anti-profiteering commitment: "I will cooperate with all other consumers to guard against profiteering."[76] Just as Mary Zuk and the housewives of the "meatless summer of 1935" attacked the profits generated by high meat prices, auxiliary members also sought to regulate the profits that businesses could earn while families struggled to meet their basic needs.

Knowing the proper price of foodstuff and household goods was not always easy for the citizen housewife. The regulation of many products lacked transparency for the consumer. The CCH complained to the OPA, "It is hard to see how the public can be expected to respect regulations, let alone help to enforce them, when the Government puts it beyond their reach either to understand them or to comply with them."[77] The government banned the grade labeling system designed to set prices in line with quality of foodstuff, which made setting clear prices more difficult. In Los Angeles, seven auxiliary women from the CIO Women's Auxiliary Council brought seven packages of hamburger to the local OPA office to clarify the relationship between the price and the quality of the hamburger, a staple in most working-class homes. Many vendors were selling lesser quality hamburger—"pale" and high in "beef fat"—at prices above the ceiling. Auxiliary members who understood the minutiae of OPA pricing policy had many questions: "What is hamburger?" "Don't you have regulation regarding fat content?" "How many [ration] points [per pound]?" and "How can a housewife tell about fat content?" In response to the last question, the women were met with an astounding answer. "If you think it has too much fat, you should buy at least ¼ lb.—get a receipt—and take the meat *unopened* to the Laboratory in City Hall for chemical analysis. If hamburger is found to have more than 28% fat report this to your Local Rationing Board and the OPA will act on it."[78] The fat regulations in ground meat varied between city regulations and OPA regulations, which often contradicted one another. Yet food rationing was so restrictive that less than half of American housewives actually exchanged their recycled fat for ration cards.[79]

This issue was as much about the patriotic duty of Americans to salvage fat as it was about price controls. According to the US military propaganda machine, one pound of salvaged fat could provide one pound of glyceride, a staple ingredient in building bombs. The Greater New York Council of CIO Women's Auxiliaries reminded their members that "your can of waste fat can blow up a Jap."[80] Despite the CIO auxiliaries' efforts at multi-racial organizing, their anti-war materials consistently reminded their members of the evils of Germany and less frequently Japan. There was no discussion or mention in auxiliary publications of the internment of Japanese Americans and Japanese immigrants.

There was a shared benefit to working together for the CWA, their affiliates, and the OPA. The OPA, however, seemed to be overwhelmed by these possibilities. Hatcher was frustrated by the lack of attention paid to building relationships with women's organizations—such as the AAUW and the CWA—within the OPA's Women's Activities Branch. In a memo to Ruth Ayers, who was charged with setting up the branch, Hatcher offered four pages of detailed comments about policy. In particular, she expressed concerns about communication between the national and local levels. As Hatcher noted, a letter arrived from the CWA "urging OPA to set prices at retail level." While the letter was sent before the announcement regarding the General Maximum Price Regulation policy, it was still several weeks after the "price control program was underway" before the staff answered it. For Hatcher, this was a critical oversight, since she believed that the Women's Activities Branch staff did not "recognize [the letter's] importance," thus undermining a critical relationship between the OPA and a national women's organization.[81]

Despite the muddled OPA bureaucracy, the organization's reliance on local housewives empowered consuming women—middle- and working-class alike—to act as "experts" on quality and price controls. By allowing housewives to make "test purchases" in the marketplace, they gave ordinary women new authority as "uniquely qualified advocates."[82] The first priority for women's organizations was to give current price lists to members of the community. Katharine Armitage, president of the League of Women's Shoppers (LWS), a well-established militant consumer organization, urged LWS branches to "get behind this program 100%" and to put "the weapon of the price list in their hands."[83] Armed with current price lists, housewives were the frontline monitors at their neighborhood markets. Unlike the earlier meat boycotters—who had protested the high cost of meat from the sidewalks with minimal impact—the OPA's program depended on the intervention of housewives. In Minneapolis, for example, members of the North Star Auxiliary of the CIO volunteered to price check twenty-five staple food items.

Despite the CCH's decision to postpone the formation of local coalitions, the CCH staff members poured their energy into supporting the OPA. Using slogans such as "Price Control or Panic" and the "OPA Must Be Defended," CCH leaders coordinated support for a price-control week, as members worked with the bipartisan Congressional Committee for the Protection of the Consumer to renew price controls.[84] In May 1944, more than 200 organizations representing the "AFL, CIO, Railroad Brotherhoods, consumers, women's auxiliaries, farmers, white collar, religious, veterans and businessmen" focused attention on the importance of maintaining price controls, which were due to expire in June 1944.[85] In hundreds of cities, individuals asked their congressional representatives to support price control extensions.

Testifying before the Senate Banking and Currency Committee, Mrs. Richard King, the wife of a steelworker, shared copies of her grocery receipts as evidence that the Bureau of Labor Statistics was out of touch with working-class families. The 1943 AFL-CIO cost of living study revealed that it took $1.43 to buy what $1.00 would have bought in 1941.[86] The United Steelworkers of America's (USWA) also conducted a study showing that the average steelworker family was not "making ends meet. They're running in the red 79 cents each week."[87] To illustrate further the significant increase in the cost of living, Eleanor Fowler conducted her own study to chart the change in price of fourteen of the most common household items between the years 1941 and 1944, using her receipts from the Rochdale Stores, cooperative grocers that flourished during the 1930s and 1940s. Rochdale Stores were based on the Rochdale principles, which emphasized "active consumer ownership" through democratic management and the belief that the consumers were "the true owners" of the stores.[88] Fowler's study found massive price increases for foods like potatoes, apples, grapefruit, and carrots as well as household items such as scouring powder and toilet tissue. The price increases "ranged from 8 to 171 per cent, with six of 14 foods or household necessities above the 132 per cent mark!"[89]

Consumer activism was a highly segregated activity. The OPA engaged with African American organizations (such as the National Urban League, the National Council of Negro Women, the YWCA, the National Housewives' League) and labor union auxiliaries (such as the Ladies' Auxiliary of the Brotherhood of Sleeping Car Porters) but the organizing remained largely separate from other outreach efforts by the OPA to what they categorized as labor and women's organizations.[90] In New York City, for example, the National Urban League held mass meetings of housewives to encourage the neighborhood and block organizations to use the *OPA's Market-Basket Price Book*. The National Housewives League's Fannie Peck arrived in Detroit in the midst of martial law. For three days in June 1943, African Americans and whites in the city clashed over the lack of housing and the integration of jobs brought on by Executive Order 8802 and the establishment of the Fair Employment Practices Commission. Throughout the spring of 1943, wildcat strikes kicked up at plants when white workers protested the hiring of African American women or the promotion of African American men. The tensions came to a head by mid-June when violence broke out between the city's whites and African Americans.[91] For Peck, price controls were galvanizing tools for organization in the midst of the racial tensions. "The riot would increase rather than lessen people's interest in price control."[92] "Informed People Are Strong People" declared the *Chicago Defender*, one of the most influential African American newspapers, as it called on African American consumers to turn their attention to issues of economic security, emphasizing the importance of education.[93] The rising cost of food was a universal concern, and the OPA's dependence on volunteer price-checkers made it possible for every neighborhood to engage in consumer activism.

With growing frustration over the political nature of the Bureau of Labor Statistics (BLS) numbers, the CIO conducted its own research. Thus, the CIO was able to provide separate statistical frameworks and offer a more complete picture of the domestic economy of the working class. In a joint study, the AFL and CIO argued that the cost of living had jumped by more than 40 percent between 1941 and 1944.[94] In the *CIO News*, C. W. Fowler— labor journalist and husband of the CWA's Eleanor Fowler—argued that the Bureau of Labor Statistics' cost-of-living estimates between 1941 and 1944 were highly inaccurate.[95] By not including a broad spectrum of goods, the BLS's claim that the cost of living had increased only 23.4 percent was viewed as a slap in the face to the working class. Fowler pointed out that the BLS "resolutely refuses to survey rent costs in boarding houses, trailers, rooming houses, etc.—despite the fact that hundreds of thousands of workers are living in such places."[96]

Phillip Murray, president of the CIO, announced to the executive board, "If I am compelled to take my choice between [the BLS] and some steel worker's wife . . . my inclinations will naturally run to the facts presented to me by the housewife."[97] The dispute between labor and the BLS ultimately forced President Roosevelt to appoint a special committee to resolve the questionable statistics.[98] These battles turned labor's attention away from the shop floor and toward the marketplace, reinforcing the weight of domestic politics and the housewives' influence in the public sector.

The OPA soon discovered, however, that an army of housewives was not sufficient to monitor prices. While urban areas could take advantage of pre-existing networks of women—such as the League of Women Voters, which boasted 550 communities—who "will . . . work for public understanding and the support of the Price Control Act," there were still not enough networks to monitor prices reliably.[99] By 1945, the OPA only had 3,500 investigators—or approximately one investigator per county.[100] As the black market grew, OPA staff called on the leadership to hire an additional 2,500 investigators and an additional 4,500 price clerks. In a memo to Oliver Peterson, the director of the OPA's Group Services Division, there was concern expressed that without "much greater enforcement, funds will be needed to make the clothing program work, as well as wipe out the growing menace of the black market."[101]

The persistence of the black market worked to the advantage of price control opponents. The CWA and affiliated auxiliaries spent the first half of 1945 organizing for the renewal of price controls that were going to expire at the end of June. In the Senate, there was a fierce campaign to "junk price controls." Eleanor Fowler dedicated many of her *CIO News* columns to debunking the legitimacy of the Senate's "food probe," arguing that hearings were "put-up jobs . . . engineered by the meat packers . . . to get higher ceilings."[102] In the report "Keep Your Eye on Congress," the *CIO News* monitored the status of price control renewal, placing much of the blame on Senator Taft's use of the Agriculture Committee for the legislation's defeat.[103]

The beginning of the end for New Deal liberalism started with a battle over the OPA and the retention of price controls. In 1946, the National Association of Manufacturers—along with other business interests—launched a media campaign to undermine price controls. Even during the war, the influence of business was substantial. As veteran organizer Florence Wycoff recalled, consumers, labor, and women were each represented by three separate OPA groups, while businesses found favor in over seventy different OPA councils.[104] Wyckoff, born into a liberal California family and educated at the University of California, Berkeley, was politicized by the 1934 San Francisco General Strike and joined San Francisco's YWCA Industrial Committee. Eventually, she left San Francisco for Washington, DC, to work part-time in the mid-1930s for Food for Freedom, and by 1944, she was active in the National Consumers' League.[105] She was an ally to both Fowler and Ware in the battle for price controls.

When World War II finally ended, opposition to price controls was mounting from trade associations, the farm bloc, and merchants. The public's embrace of the Office of Price Administration soon began to dwindle, and the OPA was criticized as anti-American. Senator Robert Taft attacked Chester Bowles, the "hero of housewives," and the OPA leader: "What you are doing is organizing consumers against business. . . . It is absolutely un-American and contrary to law and contrary to the Constitution."[106] Taft, alongside US Representative Fred Hartley, was not only focused on price controls but also on weakening the 1935 National Labor Relations Act through the passage of the Taft-Hartley Act. As labor historians often note, Congress's override of President Truman's veto of Taft-Hartley marked the beginning of the decline of organized labor.[107]

Still, historians too often overlook the effects of Congress's refusal to maintain price controls and a post-war version of the Office of Price Administration. Two years earlier, the Federal Works Agency (FWA) announced the closure of publicly funded childcare centers established during the war through the Lanham Act. This decision came only six days after Japan's surrender, leaving working mothers without affordable and accessible childcare.[108] This was the government's first post-war swipe at working families. The simultaneous congressional battle to pass Taft-Hartley and to shutter the Office of Price Administration was the next one-two punch by industrialists and legislators to quell the growing influence of working families.[109]

As union members walked out on massive strikes to gain wage increases, working-class housewives pursued a domestic politics agenda that married the fight for higher wages with state price controls. With price controls on the verge of extinction, a delegation of "irate citizens . . . descended on Washington to voice their protest against lifting of Price Controls."[110] The *Women's Auxiliary News* reported that the UAW Women's Auxiliary made up the largest contingent and was "militant." On the way to Washington, the auxiliary members "voiced their protests over a loud speaker from every town and hamlet."[111] Yet, despite pressure from consumers, the OPA was shuttered in May 1947, and only a handful of its functions were absorbed by other government agencies.

Within days of the OPA's shutdown, prices shot up. From June 15 to July 15, 1947, "the cost of living went up 5.5 percent, the single highest one-month jump ever recorded by the BLS."[112] Meat immediately jumped $.05 in one week, and by September 1947, the cost of meat had doubled from $.35 to $.70 a pound.[113] Just as in previous years, consumers would not tolerate these higher meat prices. "There's no difference," Josephine Lerner of New York City angrily wrote President Truman on June 25, "between the man with a mask on his face and a gun in his hand, and the man who, as happened today, wanted to sell me a pound of hamburger for $1.20 [before the war a pound of hamburger had cost less than $.20]. When I protested, he said that he couldn't stay in business unless he charged such a price. He said that the meat packers were waiting for the OPA's funeral and then they would do it legally and I couldn't even raise my voice. . . . What's the little guy going to do then?"[114]

Despite wartime rationing, meat consumption had increased among Americans—from 127 pounds to 150 pounds per capita—during the 1940s. And "thanks to larger incomes and the equity of rationing, the poorest third of the population increased their protein consumption by nearly seventeen percent."[115] After years of effective price controls, working-class housewives did not want to return to uncontrolled pricing. In 1946 and 1947, working-class housewives mounted meat boycotts with the backing of organized labor, consumer groups, and the American public. The cross-coalitional support for the OPA was reminiscent of the 1935 meat boycotts. Price controls were widely accepted and embraced by citizens. From the start of the war until 1946 almost 75 percent of Americans had approved of price controls. In Brooklyn, the Brownsville Consumer Council, led by Clara (née Lemlich) Shavelson, the legendary young garment worker who helped launch the New York City 1909 uprising of 20,000, called for the renewal of the OPA and threatened another boycott of meat. After her marriage, Shavelson and her husband moved from the overcrowded Lower East Side of Manhattan to Brownsville, a well-established Jewish community. Shavelson's continued community organizing in Brownsville reflected the essence of domestic politics. According to Shavelson's friend Rae Appel, Shavelson believed that housewives "shouldn't feel that they have to stay in the kitchen and cook . . . that picketing for the staff of life is just as important [as] picket lines in the needle trades."[116] While Mary Zuk, the leader of Detroit's 1935 meat boycott, did not re-emerge during this time, the involvement of the Brownsville Consumer Council as well as other community groups such as the Washington [DC] Committee for Consumer Protection, a "spirited . . . ad-hoc group" according to Annie Stein, a militant working-class activist and organizer with the group, focused on bringing down the price of meat through a pledge system to not "buy high" or more than a set price. Stein recalled, "I learned something in that. . . . When people sign a pledge, they mean to carry it out."[117] Detroit area auxiliaries reported that they were "seriously alarmed by the lifting of price controls," but they did not commit to a full boycott of meat. Instead, they promised "to buy as little as possible of consumer goods until price control is restored."[118] In addition to the meat boycott that gained national momentum, a coalition of working- and middle-class white and African American women organized a milk strike to protest high prices.[119] Despite the appearance of an integrated organization, Stein recalled that African Americans in the group "bitterly resented" their lack of voice in the group and inability to raise their own demands. For Stein, it was "one of the reasons I got out of the consumer movement."[120]

Meanwhile, the conservative National Association of Manufacturers (NAM) continued their campaign against price controls, spending $3 million to defeat the OPA.[121] The closed butcher shops and the media campaign denouncing price controls began to chip away at the vast majority of Americans who had supported price controls in 1946. Consumers thereafter began to regard the OPA as "ineffectual" and "no longer able to control inflation."[122] Despite the incremental collapse of the OPA, the CCH and its coalition partners still believed that price controls were critical to a post-war economy.

With price controls gone, CCH member organizations sought ways to maintain influence within the government. These organizations were committed to institutionalizing their agenda on a national scale rather than just reacting in a piecemeal way on a local level. At the January 1947 meeting of the CCH, the CWA and other activist groups discussed the importance of supporting consumer-oriented agencies, such as the Food and Drug Administration, the Bureau of Human Nutrition and Home Economics, the Federal Trade Commission, the Federal Communications Commission, the Anti-Trust Division, and the standards work of the Departments of Commerce and Agriculture. The CCH agreed to draft a description of services to consumers that these federal agencies offered as well as to maintain contact with the leaders of the agencies. The CCH noted that "any organizations which . . . establish[es] or maintain[s] close contact with any of these agencies is adked [sic] to inform the Consumer Clearing House Chairman in order to serve as a lookout for the group."[123]

The dismantling of the OPA was a critical loss of a key government ally for working-class housewives. This loss undermined the political influence that auxiliaries had acquired from the founding of the CIO and through the war. Conservatives sought to tie the hands of many New Dealers by expiring price control legislation and pushing through the Taft-Hartley Act, which in turn undermined the power of organized labor by outlawing closed shops, regulating strikes, and placing restrictions on organizing. The auxiliaries were not immune to these attacks. While most groups remained steadfast in their commitment to the governmental control of the cost of living, some auxiliaries appeared defeated by the upheaval at the OPA. Not surprisingly, this split mimicked the political and racial divisions with the national auxiliary movement. Clara Bradley, the president of the Ladies Auxiliary to the Brotherhood of Railroad Trainmen in Ohio—an AFL auxiliary of all-white railroad workers with a tradition of conservativism and exclusion—rejected OPA information for her organization, claiming, "I hardly feel with the unsettled conditions at present and the O.P.A. offices closing, that the circulars mentioned should be sent."[124] In contrast, Verna E. Bell, national president of the National Women's Auxiliary of the United Transport Service Employees of America—an African American union affiliated with the CIO—sought to reassure Chester Bowles at the OPA that her auxiliary intended to offer "the same support you received in the past . . . in the fight to combat inflationary pressures and maintain price control." Bell concluded her letter with the hope that "all those who so faithfully served your office . . . be just as determined in the unsettled future."[125]

While the story of price controls during and after World War II is ultimately one of decline, the organizing efforts of working-class housewives demonstrate the national influence of domestic politics. During this period, CIO auxiliaries partnered with the OPA and the CCH—in the words of Catherine Gelles—to defend themselves "when the enemies of labor are plotting to destroy the Union."[126] Auxiliary members viewed themselves as the "double experts, for we know both the impact of the removal of price controls on us as trade unionists and the impact on us as consumers."[127] The perception of themselves as "experts," along with the belief that the state was obligated to ensure an American standard of living, pushed working-class housewives to organize their members and communities to become political activists. Not only did auxiliary members see themselves as activists, but the state did as well. For this moment in time, domestic politics were front and center. Yet a post-war atmosphere that was growing colder to policies perceived to be "communist" dealt a harsh blow to national political participation.

3

"Without Any Suspicion of . . . Communism"

DOMESTIC POLITICS DURING THE COLD WAR

THE COLD WAR took its toll on working-class activism. Perhaps most telling was the slow decline of the Congress of Women's Auxiliaries and their affiliates. With the passage of Taft-Hartley over President Truman's veto in 1947 and the failed campaign to extend the Price Control Act, organized labor went on the defensive. The leaders of the Congress of Industrial Organizations, along with the leaders of the largest CIO-affiliated unions, tied their political future to the Democratic Party and purged the more radical rank-and-file unions.[1] At the 1947 UAW Women's Auxiliaries annual conference, President Dorothy Keene affirmed the damage that Taft-Hartley and "other anti-labor bills" would have on organized labor. She called on "wives, mothers, sisters, and daughters of autoworkers to take especial cognizance of the fact that one of the most important and immediate jobs which our Auxiliaries must participate in is the 1948 election. [We] must get into the campaign and mobilize the housewives in each community, to elect a people's Congress."[2] But Keene went a step further in her speech. "This is my own personal opinion . . . that we would have had no Taft-Hartley Law in our country if labor were united today; and not only UAW but labor as a whole, the AFL, CIO, and all organized labor. . . . It [Taft-Hartley] has taken away the democratic rights of the people as a whole."[3] The tone of Keene's speech sent a clear message to the assembled women that organized labor should not fall prey to the fear of the congressional investigations to ferret out communists and communist sympathizers. Keene exhorted, "If you want to see a dictatorship of any form of a government committee, it will pay you at your own expense to go up to Washington and see the Thomas-Rankin Committee in action. And the next investigation is going into the labor ranks."[4]

Congress was not the only place in which housewives experienced a post-war backlash. Because of Taft-Hartley's required anti-communism pledge, the CIO began to retreat from their radical, grassroots origins and purged eleven unions suspected of communist influences. Within the UAW, the newly elected union president Walter Reuther began a reorganization of the union that put the auxiliaries out in the cold. While some historians have argued that the consumer activism during World War II prompted organized labor to engage consumers in their organizing, organized labor did the opposite during the post-war period.[5] Rather than embracing the auxiliaries' domestic politics approach, CIO unions—such as the UAW—cut support for women's auxiliaries after the war, essentially putting a halt to effective consumer organizing.

Within the UAW, there was a notable decline in the women's auxiliaries' political and organizational involvement in the union. While the UAW helped to lead the movement for gender and racial equality in the labor movement, its supposed commitment to gender equality for all women (not just women workers) was compromised by its actions to reorganize and cut funding for the auxiliaries. By the end of World War II, the UAW was strictly regulating the structure and activities of the auxiliaries.

As post-war reconversion pushed many women out of the workforce and out of their unions, auxiliary membership jumped 51 percent, as the women turned to the auxiliaries for their union activism once many of them were no longer working in unionized factories.[6] The UAW began to take a renewed interest in the auxiliary as its membership ticked upward. Under Walter Reuther's leadership, the UAW more closely regulated membership standards and folded the auxiliary into a department within the union. In 1947, the union cut the auxiliaries' budgets in half, severely limiting members' ability to travel and organize new chapters. At the 1949 Constitutional Convention, the International Women's Auxiliaries lost their semi-autonomous status, which had allowed them to function as community organizations. This change allowed union officials to more directly supervise the auxiliaries.

Article 51 of the 1949 UAW Constitution stipulated that the president of the International would "appoint the director to direct, coordinate, and supervise the activities of the Women's Auxiliaries."[7] This type of hands-on oversight was common in AFL auxiliaries but not in CIO auxiliaries, and UAW auxiliary members balked. At the 1949 UAW Constitutional Convention, Emil Mazey, director of the Women's Auxiliaries and UAW Secretary-Treasurer, stated:

I want to dispel some rumors that have circulated in some sections of the country that these changes in the auxiliaries are designed to weaken, destroy, or limit the auxiliaries. That is not so; they are designed to strengthen its functions and tie them more closely to the International Union.[8]

Mazey's claims proved weak at best. At the 1951 UAW Constitutional Convention in Cleveland, delegate Herman Steffes, a member of Local 75 in Milwaukee, urged the officers to revive the women's auxiliaries. "We have taken a position in this International union a year or so ago technically abolishing women's auxiliaries, and I am just wondering if something could be done in reorganizing the women's auxiliaries. . . . I know the service we got from them in the last election, that we have to get our people educated, and there is no better way of getting them educated than telling a woman, because she can really get around and do it."[9]

As the United States went to war again, this time in Korea, women were once more entering the workforce, generating another decline in auxiliary membership. For the first time, the UAW Executive Board relaxed the by-laws and allowed members to hold dual membership in the auxiliaries and the union. An exchange of letters between Emil Mazey and Catherine Gelles underscores the reason for the need for dual membership. Mazey wrote:

It has been brought to my attention that a number of our Auxiliaries are faced with a tremendous loss in membership as a result of members of the Auxiliary obtaining jobs in plants under the jurisdiction of the UAW-CIO. I have been advised that unless we relax the interpretation of . . . the International Constitution, many of our Auxiliaries will be forced to discontinue their operations.[10]

The auxiliaries' demand for dual membership further illustrates the politicization of the housewife identity. Domestic politics organizing was in the realm of the auxiliaries and not the union.

The exception for dual membership proved temporary. Furthermore, it was distinctly uncharacteristic of the union. The UAW normally resisted any exceptions to union policy. At the end of the war, the UAW executive board had returned to their original policy forbidding dual membership. Despite the end of both World War II and the Korean wars and the job losses for women, many auxiliaries continued to see a decline in membership. This is evident in an exchange of letters between Catherine Gelles and Ruth M. Gladow, an auxiliary president from Lockport, New York. Gladow wrote:

> Our membership now numbers approximately 15 active members. At one time, we had a membership of 70, but as a result of the ruling of the [UAW] International Convention prohibiting dual membership in both the Local Union and the Auxiliary, we decreased in size about 25 almost overnight, and since that time, others have become members of the Local Union and have, thereby, ceased being affiliated with our Auxiliary.[11]

Gelles's response reflects a regret at the loss of membership as she proposed that women workers should sponsor their female relatives to maintain auxiliary memberships. Gelles wrote, "It is a little more difficult to organize an amalgamated local, especially when most of the members of the local are women, altho [sic] these women can sponsor their mothers, sisters and daughters into the Auxiliary."[12]

The UAW auxiliary leadership faced not only a decline in membership but also an overall lack of support from the International union. In a memo penned to the UAW International Executive Board, Gelles argued that wives deserved their own organization just as women workers deserved union representation. "When the change was made in the structure of the Auxiliaries back in 1947, when we agreed to change from an International Auxiliaries organization with our own officers and our own convention, we held conferences in the various regions, pointing out some of the disadvantages and the problems that we were faced with under than structure," reminded Gelles. "We agreed to change our status . . . and although there were some who didn't wholeheartedly agree with the change nevertheless were willing to work under an Auxiliaries department."[13] In one last ditch effort, Gelles penned the 1955 memo in an attempt to preserve the auxiliaries as substantial and relevant organizations. In order to maintain the same level of influence in their communities, however, the Auxiliary needed the infrastructural support provided by the International.

By 1955, the International had established a Women's Department, and with the AFL-CIO merger on the horizon, the executive board wanted to merge the Auxiliary and the Women's Department into one. The leaders of the UAW Auxiliary firmly objected to this merger fearing that they would "lose [their] identity as an Auxiliary organization."[14] Gelles stated:

The women in the union have their organization—the union. We have our organization—the Auxiliaries, and this is the only close tie with the union that the wives have—and we want to keep this tie. . . . Far from being absorbed in another department the International should help us enlarge, increase and strengthen our department . . . where we, as wives of union members helped build this organization and right-fully belong.[15]

Despite both organizational and ideological objections by auxiliary leaders, the International folded the auxiliaries into the UAW Women's Department.

The impact of anti-communism infiltrated both AFL and CIO auxiliaries throughout the 1950s and 1960s. While the AFL auxiliaries were more top-down and conservative that their CIO counterparts, they still played a role in the community and political engagement of working-class wives—both white and black, especially in the Detroit area. The Detroit and Wayne County Women's Auxiliary of Labor, one of the region's most active AFL auxiliaries, decided to "disband" in 1952 when they struggled to "get any cooperation for anyone." Anna P. Kelsey, the president of the national American Federation of Women's Auxiliaries of Labor (the CWA's AFL counterpart), reported that "members have lost interest, and no one comes out anymore." More significantly, Kelsey's letter reported that the membership believed that Mrs. Bradley, the president of the Detroit and Wayne County Women's Auxiliary of Labor, "belonged to the Commies . . . no doubt we can reorganize them some day, perhaps without any suspcision [sic] of 'communism' involved."[16] The decline of auxiliary activism was a bonus for the advocates of Taft-Hartley. The fear of communism was certainly one reason for the decline in auxiliary membership and activity. But there was also another lesser-known cause that contributed to the slow demise of auxiliary influence.

The development and expansion of the AFL-CIO's Committee on Political Education (COPE) program drove a wedge into women's activism in the labor movement. In the 1950s, as the labor movement solidified its social, economic, and political standing, it turned its focus toward its political program and promoting the union label, a long-time program of the AFL auxiliaries that encouraged consumers to buy union-made products marked with a union label. In December 1957, Anne P. Kelsey, the head of the AFL Auxiliaries, became president of the newly merged AFL-CIO Auxiliaries. Rather than using the existing women's auxiliary networks—whose units had previously functioned largely as separate entities—the union leadership established the COPE Women's Activities Department (WAD) to engage the union membership's female family members and women political workers. Nationally, the women chosen to lead WAD often had no prior auxiliary experience, but they were still put in charge. Locally, auxiliary members expressed confusion when WAD leaders would attend or direct an auxiliary meeting. Rather than build an existing women's organization through the auxiliaries, the AFL-CIO opted to disengage from the auxiliaries and develop a new organizational structure through COPE's WAD.

The tension between the local auxiliary leadership and the COPE WAD program was obvious from the beginning. To prepare for the 1958 AFL-CIO convention, Lillian Sherwood, the state auxiliary leader, called on the state's local auxiliaries to each bring "one new member" into the organization.[17] Sherwood and her husband were longtime leaders within the UAW. She organized Michigan's Kent County CIO Council Auxiliary and served as the last elected president of the Congress of Women's Auxiliaries. She was active in politics, eventually running for Michigan state representative on the Democratic ticket, but she would lose this campaign in a Republican stronghold. As a leader, Sherwood was also obligated to recruit for the COPE's Women's Activities Committee. The Michigan State AFL-CIO noted, "This is not to be construed to be a part of the ladies' auxiliaries which are now functioning. This committee is to be composed primarily of <u>wives</u> of union members." Sherwood's retort to the request expressed her offense: "I am sure you realize that if all of the womenfolk of our union members were auxiliary members and active in COPE activities, it would be unnecessary to set up this special committee."[18] In short, the transition was not smooth.

Among the UAW auxiliaries the tensions seemed to run particularly deep. In Michigan, the Traverse City Industrial Union Council (IUC) Auxiliary voted to disband and discontinue their relationship with the AFL-CIO National Auxiliaries. Yet within a matter of months, a new UAW auxiliary was organized and remained unaffiliated with the national office. The secretary of the newly formed auxiliary went so far as to request that the national office transfer the remaining funds from the IUC Auxiliary into the account of the new auxiliary indicating that the disbanded membership was likely reorganizing as an independent auxiliary. The national office rejected the request and urged the auxiliary to affiliate with the national organization.[19] In Ohio, a Columbus area UAW auxiliary reported to Catherine Gelles, the sole staffer working in the UAW Women's Auxiliaries, that despite their growing membership their offers to assist with local political work and promoting the union label fell on deaf ears. In her response, Gelles noted, "I was very surprised to hear this as help is so badly needed. . . . You didn't say to whom you offered your assistance, was it COPE or the Local Union?"[20] The lack of coordination between the local union auxiliaries and the National AFL-CIO Auxiliaries appeared to be chronic.

There was also a marked shift away from explicit social concerns such as racial and gender inequality by the national office. Prior to the merger, the CIO auxiliaries were engaged in building a new auxiliary network throughout the South as Operation Dixie, the organizing campaign launched by the CIO during the 1940s, gained momentum. For the UAW auxiliaries, the leadership gauged their power by "the strength of our women in the different communities and all over the country." In particular, the auxiliaries focused on the organizing progress among oil workers in the South. "We have a Negro Auxiliary of the oil workers in Port Arthur [Texas], over a hundred members that are going around raising funds in their neighborhood, in their blocks, and in the communities as a whole, to pay for the votes that they can get out." The auxiliaries focused significant time educating auxiliary members about poll taxes and the subsequent disenfranchisement of black voters in the South. In her fiery speech at the 1947 UAW Women's Auxiliary conference, Dorothy Keene explicitly marked out organized labor's responsibility to challenge the poll tax system and end voter suppression. "You know there are 11 million people, colored and white, that are disfranchised. That is nothing new to us . . . but now the women have taken it upon themselves to do this pioneering and historic job of getting people out to vote." By June 1947, thirty-five new auxiliaries were organized across the country including the South.[21] This burst of organizing began to dwindle as the Cold War sent shivers of fear throughout the CIO and AFL leadership. The 1957 merger of the AFL and CIO auxiliaries put an end to the more radical vision embraced by UAW Women's Auxiliary leaders like Keene and Gelles. Instead, the new National AFL-CIO Auxiliary leadership embraced a short-sighted vision focused on immediate gains through electoral politics and a well-established AFL union label program.

While the national office focused inward, the civil rights movement gained momentum in the 1950s as the vicious lynching of fourteen-year-old Emmett Till by a gang of white men in Mississippi drew national attention and the 1955–56 bus boycott in Montgomery, Alabama, challenged the legal segregation of public spaces. While employment for African American workers—both men and women—grew during and immediately after World War II, they still remained far behind the gains of white workers. In manufacturing, an industry that was heavily unionized in the post-war period, employment rates for black men grew from 24.7 percent in 1940 to 38.3 in 1950. Meanwhile, black women's domestic employment declined significantly from 67.2 to 34.0 percent while they made major gains in manufacturing employment, jumping from 9.3 to 30.0 percent during this same period. Despite their entry into manufacturing jobs, black workers were still relegated to the jobs that offered the least opportunity for advancement and training. As the economy began to decline in the late 1950s and early 1960s, African American workers were the first and hardest hit, with rates of unemployment as high as 20 percent in the Chicago area.[22]

The 1950s did not have a wave of meat boycotts that gained national attention, but the decade was still marked by consumer protests, especially on the local level within African American communities. As domestic politics languished in the auxiliary movement, African American women defied Cold War threats and created a counter-narrative to McCarthyism, which they called "familialism," a renewed focus on the importance of family as a social unit that was in direct contrast to McCarthy's efforts to create an atmosphere charged with fear and insecurity. The Sojourners for Truth and Justice, a short-lived organization, embraced the "dignity of black womanhood" to fight for civil rights and against racism and Jim Crow laws.[23] The Sojourners worked collaboratively with many of the same Popular Front organizations that the CIO auxiliaries had joined with in the 1940s. If the auxiliary movement had not been both internally and externally worn down by the Cold War, the CWA would have likely supported their efforts for racial and economic justice.[24]

In New York City, black housewives protested inflated housing costs through rent strikes and community meetings when a proposed statewide bill threatened to increase rent costs by 15 percent. More than 400 housewives "raised their collective voices" during a community meeting in an appeal to lawmakers to defeat the bill. The mass meeting brought together representatives of the National Association for the Advancement of Colored People (NAACP), local parent-teacher associations, several churches, local politicians, and other community leaders including an organizer from the Brotherhood of Sleeping Car Porters.[25] During a rent strike, tenants of four "dilapidated and rat infested tenements" chose July 4 to picket outside of their apartment buildings to protest housing violations with placards that read "Act Like Landlords: They Do Nothing, We Pay Nothing" and "My Child Is Too Pretty to Die." The picketing housewives reported "no hot water for month at a time and this terrible plague of rats. Babies can't sleep at night."[26] In suburban Long Island, African Americans were confronting the redevelopment and elimination of black communities altogether. Between 1940 and 1960, the population of central Long Island (Nassau and Suffolk counties) grew from 604,000 to almost 2 million residents. The view by developers and white homeowners alike was that established black communities were a hindrance to the new residential communities. In the town of Freeport, Long Island, the historically black community of Bennington Park was one such place and was characterized by overcrowding and landlord neglect. This neighborhood, located along the Long Island Railroad, was considered the "worst rural slum in the state." A vigorous campaign was mounted to demolish the neighborhood and redevelop it. In the end, low-income residents were forced down the road into subsidized housing while the rest of Bennington Park was converted to light industrial use.[27]

As the Civil Rights Movement employed consumer tactics throughout the 1950s, advertisers focused on constructing an image of the American Dream that was decidedly white, middle-class, and suburban. The government's public Rosie the Riveter campaign was replaced by print and radio advertisements encouraging housewives to embrace a domestic ideal that celebrated a white, patriarchal, and heterosexual norm. Advertisements extolled the virtues of the perfect foundation garment, the modern kitchen, and the joys of suburban living. The coordinated consumer activism of the 1930s and 1940s faded into the background, but this did not mean an end to domestic politics. Cold War politics, however, did open a political space that embraced "individualism, selfishness, and national strength."[28] When domestic politics of the 1950s are examined through a labor history lens, the impact of American business leaders' efforts to steer the post–World War II nation away from European-style social democracy and pursue a strategy to "re-privatize the meaning of security" becomes clear. The AFL-CIO merger and businesses' aggressive bid to keep collective bargaining solely between the employer and the employee without any connection to social welfare programs generated an environment closed to women activists; in this atmosphere, the domestic politics of the working-class housewives suffocated under organized labor's willingness to depart from an earlier vision of shared "economic management and working-class political power."[29]

The Education of Esther Peterson

The anti-communism witch-hunt within the federal government put additional pressures on the future of domestic politics. Activists with ties to or influenced by American communism began to retreat from the public eye.[30]

This becomes quite evident in the lives of Esther and Oliver Peterson. Well-established progressives who traveled in many of Washington's leftist political circles, the Petersons left the nation's capital with their children in tow when Oliver was offered a state department job in Europe.[31] Despite their distance from the increasingly anti-communist rancor of the United States, the Petersons could not completely avoid the witch-hunt. In 1952, Oliver was called back to Washington to testify before the House Un-American Activities Committee. The Petersons' circle of friends was vast and included people affiliated with the Communist Party of America, yet no evidence suggests that the Petersons ever joined the party, despite their left-leaning sympathies. Having been cleared by the committee, Oliver returned to Sweden and kept his diplomatic post. However, he was investigated two more times, in 1955 and 1960.[32]

With a motherly demeanor and "a halo of white braids pinned atop her head," Esther Peterson appeared an unlikely heroine for housewives.[33] Born in Utah and raised in the Mormon faith, she was brought up in a community steeped in traditional values and conservative politics. Peterson attended Brigham Young University (BYU) in part because her parents expected it and also as a means of finding a husband. Having spent years nursing her ill father, Peterson longed to become a doctor. At college, however, she was told "women don't do that." Her time at BYU reinforced the church's prevailing social norms. She recalled, "I had been discriminated against. . . . We were taught at BYU that women were to be wives and mothers. Professionally we could be teachers, nurses, secretaries. I had wanted to go into medicine" but was discouraged by her professors.[34] Frustrated by the limitations of life in Utah, Peterson headed for New York, where she enrolled in Columbia University Teachers College. There she fell in love with Oliver Peterson, a fellow student at Columbia from a working-class immigrant family, committed to economic and social equality. Esther introduced herself to his circle of friends and colleagues, which helped her to commit to a life of activism and advocacy. They married in 1932 and spent their honeymoon traveling through Norway and Denmark, searching for their familial roots.

After their honeymoon, the Petersons moved to Boston where Esther taught gym at the Windsor School—an elite private school for girls—and Oliver studied at Harvard University. During her time off, she volunteered with the Boston Young Women's Christian Association (YWCA) where she developed an understanding of class inequality. As a child, she had witnessed railroad workers on strike for an eight-hour day. Holding fast to her conservative upbringing, she saw the union and the labor leaders as troublemakers, and she had little sympathy for the workers. Unlike Caroline Ware and Eleanor Fowler, Peterson's political education came after she moved away from the cocoon of her Mormon upbringing, which she later said was the thing "that did shape a lot of my feeling," but she also said that "the very thing that the Mormon Church gave me is one of the reasons I've broken from the Mormon Church now."[35]

In the 1930s, the Petersons taught summer school to women workers. These were among the most formative years of Peterson's political development. At the prompting of M. Carey Thomas, longtime dean and president of Bryn Mawr College—a small women's college outside of Philadelphia—the Bryn Mawr School for Women Workers opened in 1921. With Hilda Worthington Smith at the helm, the Bryn Mawr School became a model of workers' education. The mission of the school was "to offer young women [workers] of character and ability a fuller education and an opportunity to study liberal subjects in order that they might widen their influence in the industrial world, help in the coming social reconstruction and increase the happiness and usefulness of their own lives."[36] The school provided both a comprehensive education for young working-women including literature, history, economics, theater, and physical education and a much-deserved respite from the rigors of urban industrial labor. Esther was in charge of physical education. The Petersons developed close relationships at the school with activists who would later face scrutiny when Oliver was called before the House Un-American Activities Committee. During one of the first summers, Esther recalled using a racially derogatory slur with her students. The students grew quiet and explained to Peterson why her "off-the-cuff" remark was racist. Peterson realized at that moment that she, too, had a lot to learn.[37]

During World War II, Oliver worked for the Office of Price Administration and Esther worked for the Amalgamated Clothing and Textile Union (ACTU) while raising their children. As the war ended, the Peterson family moved to Europe, as Oliver was appointed the labor attaché to Sweden and later Belgium. The family spent ten years abroad. During this time, Esther worked with Sweden's labor movement. She was particularly interested in how Swedish public policy approached domestic labor. She authored a report on the Swedish policies for the US Women's Bureau, while also working with the Swedish Trade Union Federation and the International Confederation of Free Trade Unions (ICFTU) to organize the first international summer school for union women.[38] While she was likely to have thrown herself into working with the European labor movement under any conditions, there was a specific reason for her work. By allying herself with the ICFTU, she was crafting a political identity that set her (and by default Oliver) apart from the radical politics of their American friends in an effort to send a message that the Petersons were not communists or communist sympathizers.[39]

Within a year of the family's return to the United States, Peterson was working full-time in the labor movement as the first female lobbyist for the newly merged AFL-CIO's Industrial Union Department. While working at the AFL-CIO, Peterson experienced explicit gender discrimination, an indication of the more conservative path the labor movement took during the Cold War:

> When we discussed the terms of my employment, Carey asked me to accept a salary that was $2000 less than that of the man who held the job before, even though the job was identical. He has the audacity to say, "Oh Esther, you don't need the money. Oliver has a good job." I was appalled. I asked, "Is that the way you negotiate for all your people in the union?"[40]

Peterson was assigned to lobby John F. Kennedy, the junior senator from Massachusetts. They became fast friends. This brief but significant relationship would set Peterson on a path that would define the rest of her life. Upon winning the 1960 presidential election, Kennedy named Peterson director of the Women's Bureau and assistant secretary for the Bureau of Labor Standards. Consumer activists celebrated the appointment of Peterson, since her new position allowed them to gain insight into the future of consumer representation. Colston E. Warne, head of the Consumers' Union, sent warm congratulations that also nudged Peterson to pressure the "adminstration['s] plans . . . on the Consumer Counsel front."[41]

While at the bureau, Peterson won Kennedy's approval to establish the President's Commission on the Status of Women. Kennedy appointed former First Lady Eleanor Roosevelt as chairwoman, and Peterson worked closely with Roosevelt as executive vice-chairwoman. After Roosevelt's death in 1962, Peterson became chairwoman and helped finish the commission's final report, *American Women*, delivered to Kennedy in October 1963. The commission's work, the publication of the report, and the endorsement of President Kennedy all advanced a national conversation about women's rights, with Peterson at the center of the debate. Peterson's close friend, lawyer Pauli Murray, wrote a decade later that Peterson "appears to [have] inherit[ed] Mrs. Roosevelt's mantle as the Dean of American Democratic Women—not through age but through your standing in the party."[42]

President Kennedy sent a message to Congress calling for the protection of consumer interests in which he laid out a call to action including four essential consumer rights: the right to safety, the right to be informed, the right to choose, and the right to be heard. He noted that "all of us are consumers. All of us deserve the right to be protected against fraudulent or misleading advertisements or labels . . . [and] the right to choose from a variety of products at competitive prices."[43] Kennedy's consumer program was among many initiatives that were cut short by his untimely death. Shortly before he was killed, his administration was in the process of appointing Peterson as the first Special Assistant for Consumer Affairs. With a familiarity born of her work with Eleanor Roosevelt and her time as a lobbyist for labor unions, Peterson displayed a passion for the legislative process and her pragmatic political perspective. As Kennedy thought, who was better to be the voice of the American consumer than a woman who looked just like an American consumer? Within a month of Kennedy's assassination, President Lyndon B. Johnson appointed Esther Peterson the first Special Assistant to the President for Consumer Affairs (SACA). This was the first time that consumers had had the potential for direct access to the president. Peterson's appointment made her the first woman to hold the position of Special Assistant to the President.

The political engagement of working- and middle-class housewives before and after Peterson's appointment challenges the commonplace belief that suburban women were struggling with "the problem with no name."[44] Many housewives used their role in the home and as consumers to engage in political action. For some of these women, their entry into grassroots political activism was the steppingstone to higher education and political leadership.[45] Peterson embraced her new role and sought to create a space in the White House that allowed consumers—typically housewives—to voice their concerns. However, Peterson often met roadblocks within a White House that did not know how the American consumer fit into Johnson's Great Society. Despite these internal barriers, she cultivated a national reputation as the voice of the American consumer.

The White House Years

Within four days of her appointment as Special Assistant, Peterson received 3,000 consumer letters, explaining how they had been "duped" by the food industry. The number one complaint—according to the *New York Times*—was misleading prices. Believing an item was "3 cents off," consumers would arrive at the checkout line only to be told the item was a higher price. For many consumers, Peterson was seen as "a latter-day Joan of Arc, armed with a sword of righteousness and protected by the armor of her indignation, fighting the dragon of big business until it begged for mercy." [46] They poured their hopes into Peterson.

To build continuity within his new administration, President Johnson kept working on some of Kennedy's programs, including the consumer platform. The Kennedy administration's style was to "have a white paper on everything," recalled David Swankin, a young activist and Peterson's sole staff member in the White House. "The Peace Corps, the Job Corps, all those things had thought-through white papers that had been prepared by task forces."[47] The Johnson administration did the exact opposite. Johnson simply called Peterson to his Texas ranch and asked her to be the first Special Assistant to the President for Consumer Affairs. Johnson wanted to guarantee "the voice of the consumer will be heard loud, clear, uncompromising, and effective in the highest councils of the Federal Government."[48] To this end, he established the President's Committee on Consumer Interests. Peterson was working as the assistant secretary of the Bureau of Labor Standards and was expected to take on a second role at the SACA. Peterson "once quipped that she divided her time 'two-thirds at Labor and two-thirds at the consumer job.' "[49] Indeed, the office of the SACA was obligated to function like a guest in the West Wing. Aside from David Swankin, who had been part of her staff at the Department of Labor, Peterson had no staff. As Swankin remembers it: "We ended up . . . borrowing people from other agencies. . . . We never had a dedicated staff of our own. . . . And that's how this thing began, with no particular agenda."[50]

Consumers wrote to Peterson on issues ranging from the high cost of meat to misleading packaging to games and gimmicks offered by supermarkets with claims of savings. An Oklahoma housewife wrote, "The housewives of the nation should be grateful. . . . There's something wrong when the ranchers are protesting about what they are getting and the majority of people can afford a decent cut of meat only on Sunday." A housewife in Ohio wrote, "I am furious. I walked into the market for groceries, picked up my usual box of cereal, and was astonished to see that the price has risen from 37¢ one week ago to 43¢ today. . . . A price rise of almost 20%." Another housewife in California complained about the misleading packaging of meats at her local market: "You will lower the blood-pressure of women like myself who market at respectable stores (meats, especially) to find a thread of lean through the cellophane, adroitly wrapped—and a plethora of fat and bone. I've made complaints to local market managers without effect."[51] Not since the Office of Price Administration during World War II had consumers had an official office to which to send their complaints.

Peterson began her White House tenure with a regional listening tour. Interested in the concerns and grievances of the average consumer, Peterson held meetings in St. Louis, Detroit, Salt Lake City, and Atlanta. Peterson wanted housewives to "be able to express their views—and receive directly from government officials information on government programs."[52] In each of the four regions, she was welcomed by consumers, as well as by representatives of business, labor, and local government. In the end, her office drafted a report to the president, outlining five recommendations to move forward with the consumer agenda:

- The adoption of Federal information on performance standards of consumer goods—information developed at the taxpayers [*sic*] expense—for use by the general public;
- The establishment of a special interdepartmental subcommittee on consumer information to develop a detailed, up-to-date index of Federal consumer services and information;
- Action by all appropriate agencies to create more and better informational materials for the poor, and elderly, the non-English speaking and the poorly educated;
- Action by the Office of Education to assist schools in instituting consumer economics courses;
- Encouragement of interested private organizations to conduct new or expanded consumer education and information programs at the community, State and regional levels.[53]

This report reflected Peterson's political pragmatism. At her core a New Dealer, Peterson believed that local, state, and federal governments were obligated to protect consumer interests.

While most consumers were thrilled with their newfound soapbox, others were less than enthusiastic. In an effort to curtail the consumer program, business interests and the advertising industry issued statements of veiled flattery, such as, "The modern housewife is too intelligent and wise to fall for that stuff," referring to gimmicks such as grocery store bingo.[54] Peterson retorted, "Of course, the modern housewife is intelligent, and she is wise to the ways of the marketplace. That is why she is determined to clean up some of the practices that have grown out of hand."[55] Peterson was often at odds with the

advertising industry over the demands of consumers. She recalled that her
"advertising friends" once asked her, "Every time I hear the word consumer,
I think of Henry VIII gorging himself on a piece of choice mutton! What
in the world *is* a consumer, Mrs. Peterson?" Peterson responded by noting
that advertisers may not believe in consumers as a constituency, but "they are
[here] all the same."[56]

Businesses and advertisers persisted in their objections to a public campaign among consumers. In particular, they objected to representatives of the
executive branch advocating for a comprehensive consumer economics program in public schools. At the 10th Annual AFL-CIO Community Services
conference, Peterson spoke in favor of a consumer education program, "I am
suggesting . . . that our children must have training in consumer economics
in our schools—today. I suggest that if we, as a Nationa [*sic*], are going to use
our resources and productive facilities in a wise, efficient, and tasteful manner,
such training is an absolute necessity."[57] One advertising agency declared, in
Peterson's words, "war" on her vision. "There is grave danger in the kind of
economic education which the 'consumer protectors' favor, education which
begins with the premise that business is a big bad wolf, ready to devour its
own customers," commented the Grey Advertising Company in their August
1965 newsletter.[58] These sentiments feed the Cold War business ethos that
sought to "keep themselves sufficiently outside the bounds of the state."[59] The
threat of having a consumer advocate with the national presence of Peterson
was a threat to the post-war campaign to construct a system of welfare capitalism that relied on a strict division between business and the state. Peterson's
role smelled too much like European-style capitalism.

Business people and advertisers were not the only ones concerned about
the proximity of Peterson to the Oval Office. The FBI was also critical of
Peterson's consumer advisors. Two women in particular stood out. In 1965,
Persia Campbell was head of the Department of Economics at Queens
College; however, her early years with what the FBI termed the "ultra left"
Consumers National Federation certified her as a "veteran in the left wing
ranks of the consumer movement." Indeed, Campbell was a life-long consumer activist who spent much of the 1930s lobbying Congress.[60] In 1938,
Campbell noted that Washington was "an 'open sesame.' . . . I never have
the least difficulty in making appointments in or out of the government."[61]
Caroline Ware, Peterson's longtime friend, was also highlighted in the FBI's
report. Despite what the FBI called an "impressive career" as a university
professor, Ware's time at workers' schools such as Brookwood Labor College
and the Southern Summer School for Women were considered suspicious.

Both workers' schools were seen as sympathetic to "Communist causes," and they were suspected to be communist organizations.[62] Like Peterson (and Catherine Gelles and Eleanor Fowler), Campbell and Ware were well-regarded New Deal leaders and had dedicated their lives to domestic politics. Women leaders lobbying against business interests made ideal candidates for investigation. Peterson was under the microscope before she even set foot in the White House. Unsurprisingly, she often felt "marginalized" during her tenure as Special Assistant to the President.[63]

In 1966, Peterson drafted a comprehensive revision of the Department of Labor that she believed would be "responsive to the needs of workers and their families" that she called a "Working and Living Conditions Program." Her hope was that by reorganizing the Department of Labor, it could respond in a more comprehensive way to the needs of workers both at work and home.[64] In the introduction she wrote, "Working and living conditions reflect society's conscience. . . . They should be alive and ever-changing. The norms, or standards, of 1966 differ from those of 1936." Peterson believed that the intersections of work, leisure, community, and family life should not only be "governed by economic values" but also by "personal and social values as well."[65] Her ten-page plan addressed concerns such as workers' compensation, training and career ladders that promoted a "craftsmanship concept" for service sector workers, increasing volunteer time in the community by allowing for more leisure time, and the "promotion of personally satisfying and socially and economically effective work arrangements."[66] By broadening the scope of the Department of Labor, Peterson was embracing a policy of domestic politics that directly conflicted with business interests, who hoped to keep the government out of their boardrooms as much as possible. She was determined to "put 'politics in the pantry.' "[67] While Peterson's new Department of Labor never came to fruition, the issues she raised in her 1966 memo mirror many of the struggles workers and worker organizations have continued to address to the present day.

The 1966 Food Protests and the "Militant Petticoat Brigades"

In the spring of 1966, Peterson sent a telegram to seventy-nine of the country's major women's organizations, asking them to "hold the line" on prices and quoting President Johnson, who said that housewives should "substitute" high-priced products for lower priced items.[68] Two weeks later, Peterson remarked that while "government cannot order prices down," if consumers "resolve to substitute lower-prices goods for higher and to speak up against high prices, I am confident we will see price improvement."[69] Peterson's statement was read by many as the endorsement of consumer action by the White House. By the fall of 1966, Denver housewives were picketing supermarkets, and new cities joined the first national meat boycott since the end of World War II.

For many consumer activists, the 1966 boycott was an innovation that brought "new and original form[s] of action to the American scene." As one consumer activist noted, "Widespread support grew out of the suggestion that a nationwide consumer organization is needed to help defend and protect the consumer."[70] The shot heard round the world—or at least the suburbs— showed up as a photo in the *Christian Science Monitor*. This photo featured Esther Peterson embracing Denver's boycott leader at the Denver airport, as she arrived to offer her support. "I just think it's so beautiful that the gals are waking up," Peterson told the media.[71] According to research conducted by Monroe Friedman, a psychology professor at Eastern Michigan University, most boycotters were young, with limited experience in activism. This revival of the meat boycott signified a reappearance of consumer protests, but the context was different.[72] In 1902, the public perceived the kosher meat boy-cotters as a "dangerous class of women."[73] In 1935, the boycotters had become more visible to the American public, and they took their fight to Washington, DC. In 1966, Washington, DC, was coming to the protestors.

Soon other urban areas joined in the call to boycott meat. From Peterson's own backyard, north to Boston, and south to Atlanta, consumers were calling on housewives to respond at the supermarket to the high cost of living. In an attempt to diminish the political influence of the boycott, a headline read, "In Texas, they call it a Ladycott." In Washington, DC, 200 people gathered at the Lincoln Memorial Congregational Temple, which had been founded as a refuge for newly freed slaves in the African American Shaw neighborhood. They came to listen to Joyce Thomas, a young African American organizer with the Washington Area Shoppers for Lower Prices. Thomas told the crowd, who were fed up with gimmicks and "excessive advertising," to begin boycotting the following day at seven local food stores in the District.[74] The Washington Area Shoppers for Lower Prices was a coalition of neighborhood organizations along with consumer and civil rights activists. The co-chairwomen included Joyce Thomas and Shirley Gray, two young, married African American women, and Geraldine Sears, a single older white woman. This diversity—of race, age, and marital status—reflects the fact that the 1960s and 1970s boycotts were led by a

FIG. 3.1 Esther Peterson, Special Assistant to the President for Consumer Affairs, greets Mrs. Paul West, leader of the housewives' food shops boycott in Denver, 1966. This photo sent White House officials into a tailspin when it appeared in the papers. They were concerned that Peterson's embrace implied that the White House supported the actions of boycotting housewives. Private collection.

more representative group of women than those of a generation earlier.[75] Having the backing of religious leaders and civil rights activists, the meat boycott reflected a blend of traditional consumer activism with some civil rights tactics, such as "don't shop where you can't work" campaigns used to divert black consumers away from stores that engaged in discriminatory hiring practices. Thomas promoted a "unique strategy," including "buying clubs," an informal neighborhood based consumer co-op, and the coordination of transportation to help all consumers—including the poor—boycott large chain stores, such as Safeway, A&P, Kroger, and Giant. While these tactics were new to consumer activism, they found their roots in the Montgomery bus boycott's elaborate carpooling system and the formation of local food-coops to give under-served communities access to affordable groceries.[76]

The Federal Trade Commission (FTC) launched an investigation into the use of "promotional schemes," such as grocery store sweepstakes and other games of chance. The FTC was concerned with the "increased . . . cost of food to the housewife," and whether or not "these schemes involve any deception or 'rigging.' "[77] Business leaders criticized the FTC investigation, arguing that housewives should stop playing these games if they found them offensive. One newspaper editorial told housewives not to "fall" for the schemes, and then, the " 'gimcrack stunt' will cease."[78] Housewives across the country boycotted grocery stores, demanding lower prices and an end to gimmicks that claimed to save shoppers money. In Miami, housewives picketed outside grocery stores—children in tow—with signs that read, "Give us a break," "We won't buy," and "Let's Play a New One: Cut Food Prices."[79]

In Washington, DC, protesters used the grocery store games as theater. The Washington Area Shoppers handed out flyers on the corner of Columbia Road and 18th Street NW—in the largely African American Adams-Morgan neighborhood—calling on shoppers to play "Bonus Boycotts." Paul Kutzner, the manager of the neighborhood Safeway, was irate with the protesters leafleting his store. Kutzner declared, "They aren't housewives. They're a bunch of professionals. It's the same bunch that pickets for civil rights and against the war in Vietnam." While Kutzner was wrong that the protesters were "professionals," the Area Shoppers group reflected the diverse coalition behind the DC protests. On this particular Saturday, picketers included Jane Schroeder, a recent graduate of Wellesley College who was in charge of public relations. A reporter covering the event—obviously smitten with the red-headed Schroeder—noted that she looked "attractively non-subversive to the male and middle-aged press."

Schroeder believed that this issue was "apolitical." In her press comment, she noted that this was not only an urban issue, "The women in the suburbs feel the same way. It's a more serious problem for the inner city where so many of these stores charge higher prices and the food is so bad. If you were an indigenous leader on a block, wouldn't you boycott?" Other protesters included a housewife and her two-year-old; a young male lawyer who was active in the Civil Rights

Movement in Mississippi before he had been "driven out of the state"; and Thomas, the head of Area Shoppers, with her one-year-old son.

While Thomas was pleased with this day's turnout, Topper Carew, a young African American "neighborhood artist and architect" who coordinated the day's picket, was less pleased with the involvement of "intellectuals," claimed the former community organizer and provocative newspaper journalist Nicholas Von Hoffman. In Hoffman's reporting, Carew called out Schroeder, telling her she "should be over in the basement mimeographing." Standing her ground, Schroeder replied that she was "doing more here."[80] Decades later, Carew recalled the action but not the interaction with Schroeder. Given Von Hoffman's inclination to use his news reporting to provoke conflict, it is difficult to know the full meaning and context of Carew's comment. However, the tensions of gentrification in the Adams-Morgan neighborhood were very real. At the time of the protests, Carew was a student of architecture at Howard University and was committed to preserving Adams-Morgan by saving the homes of elderly black families in the area and keeping longtime merchants in business by helping protect them from the encroachment of white professionals looking for good investment properties. The neighborhood was largely run by the local Black Panthers chapter and a group of "powerful matriarchs" who advocated local school control, helped feed families, provided childcare, and pushed for community control.[81]

As housewives targeted the food industry, the industry redirected the blame toward both the government and the housewives. According to Clarene G. Adamy, president of the National Association of Food Chains, housewives should "practice good buying habits—stick to the bargains until increased supplies lower the prices of other items."[82] Adamy's faith in the invisible hand of the food market reflected the industry's frustration with the boycott actions spreading across the country. Mrs. Charles Lundstrom, president of the Greater Miami Consumers Civic League, challenged Adamy's claims that the housewives' organizing efforts would not lower prices. In a quote that captured the national imagination, Lundstrom declared that her organization would "battle on the streets, in the stores and in the legislative halls of city, county, state and nation."[83] At sixty-five, Lundstrom was much older than the average boycotting housewife. She was a veteran boycotter, and her first consumer action was in response to the high price of milk in 1937.[84]

To dismiss the boycotters' accusations of profiteering, one industry leader embraced the popular characterization of boycotting housewives as irrational and hysterical. These stereotypes date back to the tea boycotts of the American Revolution, during which women were lambasted for try-ing to mount a consumer campaign that supported independence.[85] Citing a study by the National Association of Food Chains showing a decline in annual profits, Seymour D. Simpson, executive vice-president of the New York–based Daitch Shopwell Supermarkets, noted that "this report won't go into the heads of the housewives. They are very emotional. The logic of our balance sheets does not interest them. They wouldn't even bother to study it."[86]

Some media outlets fingered Peterson as the central figure in a left-wing conspiracy and framed groups of housewives as "militant petticoat brigades." The *New York Times* cited former senator Barry Goldwater, who claimed that Peterson enlisted "left-wing groups" to foment rebellion among housewives over high prices. The *Times* noted that Peterson's trips around the coun-try to discuss food prices seemed to be followed by boycotts. "After several of [Peterson's] visits . . . boycotts of grocery stores have begun." Peterson responded by explaining, "The boycotts are 'a spontaneous reaction to mat-ters of genuine concern' by American housewives, who 'are not a left-wing group.'"[87]

With a message couched in neutral language that diverted attention from inflation, Peterson urged women to hone their shopping skills by looking in multiple stores for the best deal. "Many women don't know how to shop. . . . If one store charges too much, do alternate shopping—shop in an alternative store in the neighborhood, or pick an alternative item. Learn which brand and which size is really your best buy."[88] While this comment was likely a favorite in the White House, housewives found it irritating. For example, Kathleen Harrington of the Pantry Pennypinchers, a consumer activist organization in Flushing, New York, challenged that housewives' time is "too valuable to spend in lengthy shopping." She went on to ask, "And what about areas that have only one store?"[89] When confronted with these comments, Peterson let her guard down a bit, noting that boycotts had been "most effective," but she was also careful to add "I can't go so far as to urge boycotting. That's up to the individual housewives."[90]

As the boycott continued, both Democrats and Republicans responded. In an election year during which Republicans were moving away from Goldwater-esque conservatism, the focus on rising inflation during a Democratic administration was a gift. In Florida, Republican candidate Mike Thompson creatively embraced the boycott by diverting housewives away from supermarkets. Thompson enlisted fifty "women on the Warpath" to picket the Miami office of Representative Dante B. Fascell, a Democrat, holding signs that read: "Dante—We Can't Afford to Feed Our Kids," and "Food Prices Swell with Dante Fascell."[91] Meanwhile, Democrats—including Peterson—reinforced their claim that retailers and processors were partly to blame for the high cost of living. Citing a newly released Federal Trade Commission report that supported the Democrats' position, Peterson declared the paper "is what we've needed; we've needed the facts." Eventually, the boycott faded, but it initiated a generation of consumer activism.

"A Special Assistant in Name Only"

It would be an oversimplification to attribute Peterson's resignation to the 1966 meat boycott and her public embrace of Rose West, the leader of the Denver boycott, and the boycott action in general. Instead, Peterson spent much of her time debating whether to stay in the White House, as evidenced by the numerous resignation letters she drafted during her tenure. Swankin places blame on the power of the advertising industry and "the ongoing dispute with advertising. . . . None of them liked her. . . . The advertising industry would have liked to see her go from day one."[92]

Peterson's support of the 1966 Denver meat boycott is often cited as the reason for her resignation. Media outlets questioned how long Peterson would last as the voice of consumers in the White House. Historians have also treated her support of the boycotters as the impetus for her resignation. Yet a careful study of her papers reveals that Peterson wrote numerous resignation letters, many pre-dating the 1966 boycott. In her words, she felt that she was "a Special Assistant in name only." Her grievances were plentiful, and she often grew "tired of the bickering." In one set of notes that Peterson made for her talk with the president's special assistant Bill Moyers, her list of reasons for resigning all focus on her physical and intellectual exclusion. Peterson said that her views were not "given any consideration at all by the various people who . . . held [her] 'account,'" most significantly Johnson's special assistants Jack Valenti and Joseph Califano, who advised him on domestic legislative issues. She explained that the gatekeepers were assigned to "'reassure Esther' while the ground was being knocked out from beneath her feet."

Peterson struggled to be treated as an equal in the White House. While consumers were thrilled to have a "voice" so high up in government, the reality was that Peterson had to "raise hell to get even an invitation to a White House party." She saw her place in the West Wing as "superficial," with no actual influence and power. There was a push by those closest to Johnson to move the consumer program to the Department of Labor. Peterson vehemently opposed this move:

> Labor is the wrong place for the program to go. The consumer movement will rightfully raise hell—and so will the business community, with whom we have worked so hard. All our plans for cooperation with business will go down the drain with the labor transfer. I could never suggest a move—nor will I. The "housekeeping purposes" argument doesn't work either. Everyone will know that's a phoney.[93]

Peterson's rejection of the move harkens back to Catherine Gelles's outrage when the union leadership threatened to eliminate the Women's Auxiliary department and placed it with the UAW Women's Department. It was not long before the UAW Women's Auxiliary lost its national voice as an influential women's organization. Peterson witnessed these shifts as World War II came to a close, and as a seasoned civil servant, she knew the impact that this move would have on the legitimacy of the consumer program. In the end, Peterson felt that the consumer program was "something that must be suffered."[94]

Peterson's politics were deeply pragmatic. She sought to equal the playing field across gender, race, and class lines through legislative change. As she told President Johnson, "My first love is legislation," yet her position in the White House removed her from the mechanizations of Capitol Hill.[95] Because of this, she often found herself lost in the political labyrinth of the White House. Peterson reflected, "How can I retain self-respect while being cajoled. Both friends and enemies know how 'far-out' I am. They wonder why I take it—and so do I."[96] Peterson had little patience for the politicking of the White House, and she also realized that Johnson's appointment was likely a knee-jerk reaction to Kennedy's assassination.

Peterson's resignation caused a public outcry. As one housewife wrote to President Johnson, "Consumer[s] don't have a highly financed lobby. . . . We only had Mrs. Peterson."[97] Given the timing, many believed that Peterson's support of the 1966 boycotts caused her resignation. One housewife from Boulder, Colorado, wrote to Peterson: "I'm sure your support earned you the enmity of those who had to get rid of you, as you were doing your job only too well."[98] Housewives were not the only people mourning Peterson's departure. She did have some allies in the business world, among them executives at Giant Foods. Paul Scott Forbes, public relations manager at Giant, wrote, "I knew it had to happen eventually, but things won't be the same without

Esther Peterson. . . . In my mind (and I am sure, in the mind of the public) the person and the function have become synonoymous [*sic*]."[99]

In anticipation of her resignation, Peterson drafted a short list of candidates to succeed her. It "stunned" many when Johnson announced Betty Furness, a former model, actress, and most famously, the face of Westinghouse refrigerators during the early days of television ads, as her replacement. "I cannot keep from feeling that this is a slap in the face to women," wrote Chloe Gifford at the University of Kentucky. "It makes one question the President's real interest in women in government." The *Louisville Times* penned an editorial questioning the appointment of Furness. "One of the symbols of advertising's prowess," according to the *Louisville Times,* Furness appeared ill-equipped to take over for Peterson, a woman described by the Advertising Federation of America as "the most pernicious threat to advertising today."[100] Comparing Peterson to the late Eleanor Roosevelt, the editorial questioned Johnson's commitment to protecting the interests of consumers.

After her resignation, Peterson returned full-time to her position in the Department of Labor and then to legislative work at the Amalgamated Clothing and Textile Union (ACTU). It was not long before Giant Foods president Joseph B. Danzansky began courting Peterson. They offered her a new position as the first consumer advisor in the grocery industry. Looking to change their image as a consumer-friendly grocery store, Giant urged Peterson to advise them on what consumers wanted. Peterson recalled, "I had been yelling about the supermarket prices. . . . Danzansky offered me the job [and] he said, "Well, Esther, put up or shut up. If you know so much, come and tell us what to do." She joined their staff in 1970. "[Giant] met my terms. . . . I had to be independent, I had to represent the consumer to the corporation, not [be] the ambassador of the corporation to the consumers. . . . So when I sat in those meetings, I was the one who pushed the supermarket cart. And I had to have the understanding that I could be independent and I could say what I thought."[101] Peterson would remain at Giant until her return to the West Wing as President Carter's Special Assistant for Consumer Affairs.

4

"What Do Housewives Do All Day?"

THE SUBURBANIZATION OF MEAT BOYCOTTS
AND SUPERMARKET PROTESTS

AS THE NEWLY elected Richard Nixon took office as president of the United States, working- and middle-class housewives were aware that when they filled their shopping carts, their pocketbooks were lighter than in previous years. Many women could not afford the most basic foodstuffs, and others were forced to buy less expensive items and cheaper cuts of meats. In 1960s suburbia, shoppers had far fewer options than today, as most communities had only one or two primary grocery stores. Unlike their mothers, these women were no longer shopping at locally owned, neighborhood stores. Moving from the city to the suburbs not only changed women's housing and neighborhood life but radically shifted their shopping patterns as well as. As this chapter demonstrates, however, the suburbs were not bubbles of complacency and homogeneity.[1] In fact, they were home to grassroots activism driven by the same housewives Betty Friedan characterized as trapped by the "feminine mystique," in which "there is no other way for a woman to dream of creation or of the future. There is no other way she can even dream about herself, except as her children's mother, her husband's wife."[2]

Housewives were angry not only over the high cost of meat but also by its packaging. By the 1960s, consumers were shopping more often at one-stop supermarkets, especially true for the new suburban middle class. In places like Levittown, New York, the local grocer and butcher were gone. Instead, housewives drove to shopping centers where they could stock up on everything they needed.[3] Many shoppers lost personal relationships with the people who sold them groceries. The shopping process became depersonalized, as housewives scanned the meat aisles full of chicken, pork, and beef, sitting in Styrofoam and wrapped in plastic. As one Illinois housewife complained:

> There are times when new housewives who can't make their paychecks stretch . . . get tough meat with bone and fat wrapped up in their package they can't see until they get home. By the time all the waste is removed . . . the price becomes very expensive.[4]

A California housewife frustrated with the packaging of meats lamented the consequences of tearing into the packaging at the grocery store:

> Is there a possibility I could be arrested if I tear off the papers to inspect the hams before making my selection? Any laws against seeing what I am buying?[5]

In post-war suburban communities, there were no Main Streets included in community development plans. Instead, developers constructed shopping centers close to the local highway system to serve the surrounding community. On Long Island, Levittown consumers were dependent on their cars to shop. Even in pseudo-suburban areas like Queens, where shoppers could reach their local markets by walking, shopping patterns in the city drastically changed. One architecture magazine referred to these new shopping centers as "markets in the meadows."[6]

Weekly grocery shopping was among the most time-consuming tasks for all women. As one historian of American supermarkets suggests, regardless of whether a woman worked outside the home, she was the default purchaser of groceries, and this was no small task. Grocery stores added gimmicks and promotions in an effort to lure shoppers in, a practice most women resented. As one woman put it, "It is difficult enough to watch the children, check how the bags are being packed . . . and count the change. But to add stamps, games, and coupons to all this is only insulting the shopper."[7] Despite the labor-intensive nature of shopping, the isolation of suburbia was often broken for housewives by the social interaction at the grocery store.

Just as consumption was gendered female, grocery stores were gendered female. Grocery shopping, an essential duty for the family manager, became also a social activity, and these social interactions gave shoppers the opportunity to express to one another their concerns over products, packaging, and pricing. Thus, protests over rising meat costs and misleading food labels, in the words of one protester, were incredibly "subversive."[8] Direct action was in

itself subversive. In the post-war period, grocery store developers had sought
to transform their spaces into "an emblem of smooth-running consumption
and domesticity," like the suburban landscapes that surrounded them.[9] But
in doing so, they inadvertently created political spaces.[10] While the grocery
industry sought to create an atmosphere of leisure and comfort in every store,
housewives viewed grocery stores as a public space of protest, where they
could articulate their disapproval of food costs and quality. This behavior conflicted with the Cold War–era vision of domesticity and femininity. Unlike
the housewives enlisted by the World War II Office of Price Administration
who were fulfilling their citizenship obligations by holding grocers accountable for the quality and price of goods, housewives in the 1960s were upend-
ing notions of gender roles and expectations; they were putting at "risk their
femininity and access to the benefits of postwar shopping."[11]

"I Don't Know Where I Got the Guts"

In August 1969, Mickey DeLorenzo got a call from her sister who had recently
relocated from Brooklyn to Long Island. Struggling to make ends meet, her
sister was finding it difficult to deal with rising prices. "Everything is so expensive and there is nothing you can do about it," Mickey's sister fretted. Ross
DeLorenzo, Mickey's husband and a union electrician, "cavalierly" asserted,
"Of course, there is something you can do about it. . . . Boycott something!"[12]
Mickey and her sister tried to figure out what food item their families could
do without before arriving at the decision many women had reached before
them—meat. Just three years after the 1966 meat boycott, which drew
national attention and prompted Esther Peterson to declare, "I just think it's
so beautiful that the gals are waking up," two housewives from Long Island
again called on the meat industry to lower prices.[13]

   Both DeLorenzo and her husband were sixteen years old when they met
in their Brooklyn neighborhood. Mickey's grandparents were Jewish immigrants who settled in the Lower East Side neighborhood where the 1902
kosher meat boycotts took place. Following the migration patterns of so
many other immigrant families, Mickey's parents moved to the quieter streets
of Brooklyn, working long hours at white-collar jobs that enabled her family
to achieve some financial stability. Her father worked in the composing room
at the *New York Times*, and as Mickey recalled, when her father "allowed"
her mother to work, she found a job as a bookkeeper. Eventually, her parents saved enough money to open a small soda shop in their neighborhood.
After a few years of marriage, Mickey and her husband left their childhood

neighborhood for the promises of Levittown. One of three communities that Levitt and Sons built after World War II, Levittown was a "planned community" for GIs returning from the war. In the mid-1960s, it remained a white middle-class community due to the initial housing covenants restricting homes sales to non-whites.[14] The community was built around close-knit social groups of young families.[15] Mickey's husband drove twenty-five miles to and from Manhattan to his job as a union electrician. They were living the dream: a single family home, two children, and a stay-at-home mother.

By 1969, meat was a staple in the working- and middle-class American diet. Between 1947 and 1972, the weekly earnings of non-supervisory workers increased 62 percent, and the consumption of meat was symbolic of this success.[16] Working-class families could afford meat daily—albeit cheaper cuts such as hamburger. Many middle-class families transformed by union wages could afford sirloin and porterhouse steaks. Regardless of the cut, per capita meat consumption rose from "57 pounds in 1955 to 70 pounds in 1965, reaching a peak of nearly 80 pounds of beef per American in 1970."[17] Translating this into servings per year, Americans were consuming an average of around three, eight-ounce servings of beef a week. With the inclusion of cheaper meats, such as chicken and pork, the average American might have sat down to one serving of meat every night of the week.

During the summer of 1969, meat was becoming more expensive. The "For and About the Family" section in the *Long Island Press* reported that the retail meat bill was up 3.7 percent over the previous year, according to the US Department of Agriculture (USDA).[18] Middle-class families like the DeLorenzos were choosing to buy cheaper cuts, and many working-class families—as well as senior citizens—were finding it impossible to afford even the least expensive meat. As DeLorenzo emphasized throughout the boycott, "The housewife we were most concerned about was not the one who had been able to afford sirloin and porterhouse before the prices rose, but rather the woman who is working within a fixed budget."[19]

Despite having no prior political involvement and having just given birth to her second child, DeLorenzo—and her sister—made the decision to boycott meat and they set into motion a national consumer action. Placing an invitation in the local *Levittown Journal*, Mickey called a meeting at the Levittown Hall, a community space in the town center. Not knowing how many people to expect, Mickey's father-in-law, a UAW organizer, advised her to set up a limited number of chairs. He explained, "If you have a lot more chairs and . . . people don't show up, it's going to look as it people aren't concerned." Lack of interest proved not to be a problem. The room filled with more than 150 people upset over the high cost of food.[20] Confronted with the number of her neighbors concerned about this issue, DeLorenzo became aware that she was "unprepared in every way."[21]

The meat boycotts were not the only grassroots organizing in Nassau County, Long Island. Only seven miles southwest of Levittown, students in Freeport had spent the past school year engaging in non-violent civil disobedience—in sit-ins and walk-outs, for example—to confront racism in the school system. Freeport in the 1960s was more diverse and integrated than Levittown, but racial stereotyping persisted in the high school and in the segregated bus system. With a growing African American middle class, the parents—including some white liberal parents—came together to challenge the system. In the spring of 1969, these protests culminated in violence that broke out after a student council meeting called to heal the community. Racial tensions escalated in Freeport, as conservative white families began to fight back against integration. These tensions would continue into the 1970s, as they did in urban areas throughout the country.[22]

With no shopping centers in Levittown, 100 housewives gathered to picket the grocery store at the Hempstead Turnpike shopping center on August 12, 1969. They named their group For Lower Prices (FLP). Handing out menus for "tasty fish dishes," the women chanted "Let the Meat Rot," "Down with the Greedy, Corrupt Meat Industry," "Give Us More for Our Dollar and We Won't Holler," and "Prices Too High, We Won't Buy!" At their first stop, the women split up and targeted three supermarkets in the shopping center.[23] With her two children, including her newborn son, in tow, Mickey organized pickets around Nassau County. The picketers enraged the supermarket management, and FLP members were repeatedly threatened with arrest. Trained by Mickey's father-in-law, the women knew "the ins-and-outs of walking the picket line," and Mickey carried the telephone number of her father-in-law's attorney in her back pocket as protection.[24] By October, DeLorenzo estimated that 1,500 housewives on Long Island were participating in the boycott activities from Great Neck east to Southampton.[25]

The boycott generated media coverage beyond the New York area. Within a month of organizing their first picket, FLP members were putting together FLP Kits, starter packets to help other communities organize meat boycotts. With no national coordination, meat boycotts sprang up in Virginia, Connecticut, Colorado, and Florida.[26] In Arlington, Virginia, organizers met at a local Lutheran church to garner support for a Washington area boycott. Like the Long Island housewives, women in Virginia organized other housewives by passing out leaflets in several shopping centers.[27]

DeLorenzo's regular contact with about twenty leaders across the country left her with little time to do much else. Her home became the epicenter of the 1969 boycott, and her phone rang off the hook. With some local political pressure, the DeLorenzos jumped to the top of the waitlist for an additional phone. Arriving on a Saturday to install the new line, the telephone worker commented that he did not understand the rush. As he plugged in the new phone, it rang.[28]

Like Mary Zuk, DeLorenzo and the other members of FLP were concerned about more than just the price of meat in their local stores. In fact, DeLorenzo demanded a federal investigation into the pricing of meat. Placing the blame on the packers and public policy, she was careful not to get angry at the farmers, since she believed that the blame lay with the policymakers and the packers. Despite her carefully crafted messaging, she attracted the attention of Eddie Collins, a farmer and radio personality from Red Oak, Iowa. On September 7, 1969, a truck pulled up in front of the Long Island home of Mickey and Ross DeLorenzo and dropped off a 400-pound steer, as the neighbors stared in amazement. Sent as a challenge by Collins, the steer was a publicity stunt to draw attention to the struggles of small family farmers. Furious that boycotting housewives were claiming that prices were too high, Collins declared: "Long Island suburban housewives don't know what it takes . . . to bring a calf from birth to slaughter. . . . [And] you don't understand what is going on here [Ames, Iowa]."[29] Collins threatened to send the steer to DeLorenzo after they argued on a national radio program about the meat boycott she had started over the summer. Mickey bit back, declaring, "I can tell you this much. That calf will never be slaughtered." Mickey and her husband accepted the steer as "a living symbol of the boycott movement" and appropriately named him FLP (pronounced "flip"), in honor of the consumer organization DeLorenzo founded.[30] True to her word, FLP was never slaughtered. Instead, he spent part of his life in a Long Island petting zoo, later retiring to upstate New York.

While DeLorenzo was raising the ire of midwestern cattlemen, local political leaders were expressing support for the work of DeLorenzo and FLP. On Long Island, William "Monk" Larson, a Democratic candidate for the position of Hempstead Town Supervisor, pledged to create a "homemakers' advisory board," not unlike the local advisory councils of the OPA during the 1940s. Nassau County Executive Eugene H. Nickerson not only offered his endorsement but also encouraged the protests, calling on "concerted action by large numbers [as] necessary to achieve fair and realistic prices."[31] The

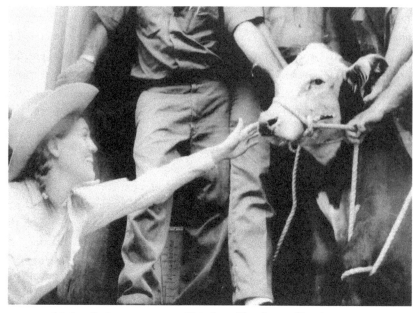

FIG. 4.1 Mickey DeLorenzo petting FLP the calf in front of her home in Levittown, New York. FLP was delivered to her home by Eddie Collins, a farmer and local radio personality from Red Oak, Iowa. Collins wanted to make a point that raising cattle was not an easy or inexpensive venture, September 9, 1969. DeLorenzo made the most of the media attention going so far as to don a cowboy hat. Private collection.

FLP protesters knew they were having an impact when Congressman John S. Monagan of Connecticut contacted DeLorenzo to testify on Capitol Hill before the House Subcommittee on Government Operations. Excited by the potential to influence public policy, DeLorenzo and her husband escaped to upstate New York to draft her testimony. However, she quickly grew leery when Monagan's staff firmly requested that her testimony not include the word "boycott" and sent a legal aid to her home to read her statement.

Just as Zuk had demanded a transparent investigation in 1935, only to be rebuffed and met with a closed-door hearing, DeLorenzo realized this investigation was a "whitewash."[32]

At the hearing, DeLorenzo presented two testimonies—the Monagan-approved version and her own statement. In her testimony before the House Subcommittee on Government Operations, Mickey DeLorenzo expressed her frustration with the media, which implied that housewives were angry with farmers. Commenting on her gift of FLP the Steer, DeLorenzo pointed out that raising a calf in suburban Long Island was "an unrealistic experiment." She commented,

It was . . . [a] false assumption that the housewife blamed the farmer and ranchers for the high retail cost of meat. In truth, the housewife does not feel that the small cattleman, operating on a marginal profit is to blame. . . . [W]e do know that after our first meeting with supermarket executives, retail meat prices in local stores of supermarket chains dropped by 20 to 30 cents per pound without a corresponding decrease in wholesale prices.[33]

Months later, during a trip to Indiana organized by local farmers, DeLorenzo discovered that some media outlets in the Midwest were misquoting her statements by implying a lack of support or awareness for the small farmer. This further confirmed for DeLorenzo that the issue of meat pricing was a complicated, intrastate affair in which many people had a stake. DeLorenzo recalled that she went into the boycott "as an innocent and came out of it unfortunately a bit cynical."[34] Shortly after the boycott ended, a local community leader called to ask if she would be interested in running for public office. DeLorenzo said she was "exhausted" and had no interest.

The Code Breakers

Rising food prices were not the only issues impacting grocery stores and consumers. Shoppers were growing weary of a lack of transparency concerning the goods they were purchasing. This issue was not new, as evidenced by the quantity of consumer protection legislation passed between 1960 and 1970. During this period, Congress passed twenty-eight pieces of legislation, including the Color Additive Amendment (1960), the Fair Packaging and Labeling Act (1966), and the Truth-in-Lending Act Amendments (1970).[35] Still, housewives often found food items to be inaccurately priced or, even worse, when they returned home they found items were spoiled. When they inquired about the lack of labeling or the price discrepancies, they were typically rebuffed by the clerk or store manager. For a group of housewives in suburban Chicago, honest pricing and transparent labeling became a mission.

In 1968, Jackie Kendall was living in Washington, DC, with three young children, while her husband worked full-time as a lawyer. In the lead up to the Poor People's Campaign march, a local civil rights organizer came to the Kendalls' church asking for volunteers. With only a few weeks left in the district before moving her family to Chicago, Kendall volunteered. Her husband was already engaged in draft counseling for conscientious objectors, but neither had been involved in grassroots organizing of any kind. With their pending move, Kendall did not feel able to do more than help finding free housing for out of town marchers. As she recalls, "Maybe I found housing for two or three people max."

The purpose of the Poor People's Campaign was to highlight the endemic problem of poverty in the United States. A year earlier, while organizing for the campaign, the Reverend Martin Luther King Jr. had told a Los Angeles congregation, "We aren't merely struggling to integrate a lunch counter now. . . . We're struggling to get some money to be able to buy a hamburger or a steak when we get to the counter."[36] With the passage of the Civil Rights and Voting Rights Acts, King focused on combating poverty and achieving economic justice for African Americans. Noting that the passage of the civil rights legislation cost the government no money, King and others believed that the government needed to direct billions of tax dollars to defeat poverty among African Americans, poor whites, immigrants, Native Americans, and others. The Washington gathering has largely been understood as a failure, with the assassination of King, lower than anticipated turnout, dismal weather, and little media attention. On a grassroots level, however, the campaign was transformative for many. On the day of the Poor People's Campaign march, it rained. Kendall gathered with thousands of other people in the muddy conditions. She thought to herself, "Oh my God! I can't believe people came here. . . . Wow! I helped make this happen." It was then that she promised herself that she would get involved—"whatever get involved meant"—when she got to Chicago.[37]

Upon settling in north suburban Chicago, Kendall volunteered for a local congressional special election. The congressional district campaign was waged between the Democratic Party candidate State Representative Edward A. Warman, a War on Poverty liberal, and Republican nominee Philip Crane, a former history professor and early supporter of Barry Goldwater. As Kendall remembers it, Crane was "a far right guy . . . and everyone kept saying—'We hope Phil Crane wins, because he will be easy to beat.'"[38] The Warman campaign was a big flop, and Crane won despite long odds, spending his entire political career holding that congressional seat.

The campaign may have put an end to Warman's political aspirations, but it opened up a social network for Kendall. "It was during that campaign that I ran [into] Lynne Heidt." Heidt—who was already politically active with the United Farm Workers (UFW) grape boycott and Jesse Jackson Jr.'s Operation Breadbasket—asked Kendall to join her on the grape boycott picket line. With three kids at home and no knowledge of the boycott, Kendall put Heidt off until after the election, when "she shows up and invite[s] me to a picket line down in Chicago." Still reluctant, Kendall went to check it out the picket line. "So I'm standing on the sidelines and I'm watching these people walking around," Kendall remembers. This was her first picket line. "And there was a woman with two little kids, one in a stroller, and she was carrying another one . . . and I'm looking at her and going, 'Hmmm. If she's doing that, I guess I could do that.'"[39] The picketing mother Kendall watched was Heather Booth, the founder of the Abortion Counseling Services of Women's Liberation, more commonly known as the Jane Collective—a Chicago-based underground network of women to help women find access to safe abortions. The trip to the grape boycott picket line solidified the friendship between Heidt and Kendall, who lived close to one another in the northern Chicago suburbs. Itching to do something more, Kendall said to Heidt:

> Think about it. We have all of these women like us who are housewives, young mothers. We're home with kids, educated, and [have] time. . . . I said let's think about where do we go the most? The two places we came up with were church or synagogue, right? Or the supermarket. Those were the two places we went every week. . . . It's like a Richard Scarry book—"What do housewives do all day?"

For suburban housewives, this was their reality. Many predominantly white, working- and middle-class housewives had time on their hands. By the late 1960s, only 30 percent of the full-time workforce was made up of women, and they were working largely in low-wage, entry-level jobs or service jobs.[40] Many housewives were capitalizing on their housewife identity to attract attention to issues of food affordability and packaging transparency.[41] For Kendall and her team of housewives, the supermarket offered a stage to test their political voice. The world around them was changing rapidly, but in suburban America, there was often an imagined simplicity that was out of sync with the outside world. Once Kendall discovered that she had a knack for street theater, the stillness of Chicago's north shore was shattered.

The 1969 meat boycott was over, but consumer issues were on the national stage. Nader's Raiders—Ralph Nader and a cadre of recent law school graduates—had just released their report on the ineffectiveness of the Federal Trade Commission. The combination of Rachel Carson's 1962 book, *Silent Spring,* and the national attention paid to California farmworkers' working conditions exposed the environmental and physical violence of the agricultural industry. President Nixon was unable to handle inflation, and wages were stagnating. Johnson's War on Poverty may have been over, but the nation was cognizant of the growing economic divide, despite the passage of civil rights and consumer protection legislation.

Heidt and Kendall did not have a plan the first time they visited their local supermarket intending to conduct consumer research. With clipboards in hand, they wandered the aisles, looking for a problem. This problem presented itself in the form of a stock clerk. After inquiring about their clipboards, he said, "If you really want to do something, get rid of the codes." Heidt and Kendall looked at one another and then the clerk. "What codes?" they asked. It was not uncommon for consumers to wonder how long a packet of bologna or a loaf of bread had been sitting on a grocer's shelf. Rather than a "use by" stamp, consumers found a code that meant nothing to them. Heidt had noticed the code one time when her milk delivery was spoiled. She complained to the delivery driver, who twisted the bottle around and looked at a code. Use of the coding system turned out to be an industry-wide practice, unintelligible to the uninitiated.[42]

Despite their inexperience and lacking an official organization, Heidt and Kendall were featured in a two-page article in the *Daily Herald* right after their first trip to the supermarket.[43] A local journalist saw their clipboards and wanted to know what they were doing. Thinking quickly on their feet, the two women explained the coding system and expressed their concerns about food safety and packaging transparency. With the persistent urging of Kendall's lawyer husband, the women decided to incorporate themselves. But first they needed a name. As Kendall recalls, there were four or five people trying to come up with a name. Deciding to be bold, they called themselves the National Consumers Union.[44] They wanted the name to reflect something beyond their community, and they also liked the idea of linking the name to the labor movement.

No sooner was their stationery printed when they received a call from Esther Peterson, who insisted on meeting with them. Peterson and a colleague flew to Chicago to meet with the new NCU. Kendall recalled a tense lunch, during which she finally blurted out, "Okay, so what's the problem?" Peterson informed the women that the organizational name—National Consumers Union was already in use. In Kendall's words:

> "Wait a minute. So, you already have a thing called the National Consumers Union?" And they're like, "Oh, please." And I think they thought they were going to have a lawsuit on their hands and all this stuff. . . . "Look, the only thing we've put out so far is we've printed letterhead."

Expecting to receive support and encouragement from Peterson—a consumer activism legend—they instead found themselves looking for a new name. Peterson's concern about organizational competition revealed the lack of a cohesive national vision within the consumer movement. It also reflected a disconnect between Beltway politics and localized consumer movements that dated back to the work of the Consumer Clearinghouse in the 1940s. Kendall, Heidt, and the others decided to change their name to National Consumers United so they did not have to give up their logo design.[45]

"This Was Clearly More Exciting Than Just Being a Housewife"

Several weeks later, Janice Schakowsky, with her two kids in tow, went to do her family shopping at a local grocery store. However, what she encountered at the butcher counter was anything but business as usual. A group of housewives, including Heidt and Kendall, were demanding information about the age of the meat behind the counter. Having been rebuffed recently for asking the same question, Schakowsky sidled up to the group. "If you don't like our meat or think it is good enough, then I can throw you out of here on your fannies, you geeks!" the butcher yelled at the women. Schakowsky thought to herself, "This was clearly more exciting than just being a housewife."[46] The women were "outraged" that they could not get a straight answer out of their local grocery store about the condition of the food they were feeding their families.

In 1969, Janice Schakowsky was a newlywed with two young children living in Mount Prospect, Illinois. Like Levittown, Mount Prospect was a town built to accommodate the baby boom. Only 9 percent of its housing was built prior to 1940, with 79 percent built during the 1950s.[47] In 1960, the median value of the homes was $25,000, or the equivalent of $406,000 in 2010 dollars.[48] Based on a 1971 sociological study of suburban Chicago, several women interviewed indicated "a strong prejudice against the neighboring farm-field community of Rolling Meadows." Because of Rolling Meadows' lower socioeconomic bracket, the women felt that Mount Prospect was "losing prestige and declin[ing] as a result of its proximity."[49] Schakowsky, along with her fellow boycotters, did not share the views of the more conservative housewives of Mount Prospect. In fact, all of them moved out of Mount Prospect and the surrounding suburbs during the 1970s. Schakowsky was born in Chicago and grew up in Rogers Park, a heavily Jewish neighborhood on the north side of the city. She attended the local neighborhood school, and—unlike

DeLorenzo, who did not complete college before having children—went on to the University of Illinois, earning an education degree in 1965. Soon after graduating, Schakowsky married, moved to Mount Prospect, and had two children.

The core team of the Code Breakers, as they named themselves, included Schakowsky, Heidt, Kendall, and Marian Skinner, whose husband was a union steelworker and who had been involved in the 1966 meat boycott in Denver, Colorado.[50] They were, in the words of Schakowsky, "authentic" in their desire to do their jobs as housewives and feed their families healthy meals. "We were so suburban housewife in our little polyester outfits and our kids [and] our starter houses," she recalled.[51] Yet their authentic representation of the accepted portrait of the suburban homemaker did not preclude them from sharing in the excitement of the social and political upheaval of the late 1960s. While their grassroots activism was limited, the opportunity to use domestic politics as a route to greater political participation was exciting to Schakowsky and the others.

With national attention on the meat boycott waning, the women called for a "consumer independence day" in the fall of 1969. Invoking the language of organized labor, the National Consumers United (NCU) used this day of action to affirm that consumers have the "right to collective bargaining, to limit the mounting costs of goods and services, and to expect that purveyors have the authority and obligation to stand behind the goods they sell."[52] With this mission in mind, NCU members focused their attention on the local grocer and encouraged the media to cover their activities. With clipboards in hand, the housewives returned to the supermarket and conducted store inspections. They examined food items—such as Oscar Meyer bologna, loaves of bread, baby formula, and baby food, recording the codes on the items. In order to understand the codes, the women turned to the stock boys. Calling their actions "subversive," Schakowsky remembers that they "push[ed] the stock boys against the shelves . . . [to] make them tell us how they knew to rotate the [stock]."[53] To avoid the sale of potentially expired goods, the women stabbed pencils through packs of bologna and loaded up carts of expired foods to deliver to the store manager, often visiting the stores on Saturdays. Kendall remembered one example of the coding system and Peter Pan Peanut Butter:

> Peanut butter is 12 letters. If there was a notch above the label, it meant it was manufactured in an even-numbered year; if there was a notch below, it was an odd-numbered year. Peanut butter, 12 letters, so one for each. So, they'd put the notch above one letter, and that was the

month. I mean, it was goofy, really goofy. So, we started cracking codes, and sometimes somebody would know and they'd sneak it to us. . . . So, we were compiling the codes, and then, we could go to the supermarket and check. So, we'd go. It was always on a Saturday because of the kids. So the kids would stay home with the husbands, and we'd all traipse off to the supermarket.[54]

The National Tea Company felt so threatened by the organizing efforts of the National Consumers United that they hired Kirkland and Ellis, one of the world's largest corporate law firms, to investigate the group's members. "Can't you control your wife?" Lynne Heidt's husband was asked during a call to his offices at Montgomery Ward. Jackie Kendall's husband, then a lawyer at Abbott Labs, received a similar call.[55] In 1970, National Tea operated 950 stores in 20 states, including 250 stores in the Chicago area. It was a regional supermarket chain similar to Kroger and Piggly Wiggly with annual sales of $1.5 billion.[56] Yet a group of suburban housewives and their clipboards posed a threat to one of the nation's largest grocery chains.

By August 1970, National Tea's anxiety increased after the women purchased a share of their stock and showed up at a shareholders' meeting in Wilmette, Illinois, a wealthy enclave on Chicago's north shore. They came to voice their anger about the lack of transparency to consumers. The NCU's shareholder action was part of a new strategy to make corporations answerable to consumers. The shareholders' rights movement was a response to the lack of corporate accountability and transparency that fueled the 1929 stock market crash, but not until the early 1970s would organizations use shareholder activism for social causes.[57]

NCU's strategy for the shareholder meeting was to create a scene so it could generate press about food labeling. At the meeting, the women used their one share of stock to nominate Mike Royko—a Chicago muckraking newspaper columnist to the board of National Tea.[58] This stunt generated such an uproar that other shareholders began to ask for the proxies back. During the chaos, the women lobbed questions at National Tea's president Norman Stepelton. The women demanded to see the company's records and wanted to know how much money the company had spent to spy on them. Stepelton lost his temper and yelled at the women, "I don't know who you people are! Are you communists? Or spies from Jewel [a competing grocery chain]?" The next day, Stepelton dropped dead of a heart attack at his home in Winnetka.[59]

Media played a critical role in the success of the NCU's campaign. While the women were anything but media savvy, they made a good story.

Schakowsky penned press releases drawing attention to their actions, but it was Ralph Nader's comment about their "spontaneous consumer movement" on national television that trained the spotlight on them. "We were so suburban housewife," Schakowsky remembers. She believed that this was the appeal for the media. Jackie Kendall made an appearance on a national radio show in New York City, and Lynne Heidt was interviewed by Barbara Walters and Hugh Downs when the *Today Show* came through Chicago. Both Kendall and Heidt announced to the nation that they had developed a "codebook" to decipher the expiration codes on foods. Pricing the books at 50 cents, the women soon began to receive orders from across the country. They found themselves opening sacks of mail and sorting thousands of coins. In the end, they received over 30,000 requests for books.[60]

With no institutional support, the NCU (like Levittown's FLP) was funding its own activities. The production costs for the codebook was too rich for their pocketbooks. They applied for a grant from the Chicago-based Playboy Foundation. Beginning in the late 1960s, pressure from women's rights groups caused the foundation to fund feminist causes and women's rights organizations. Specifically, the Playboy Foundation funded support for abortion access and organizations that helped rape victims.[61] While food labeling and expiration dates were not quite the same hot button issues as abortion and rape, the domestic politics that drove the NCU's campaign clearly appealed to the foundation. The small grant enabled the women to produce 50,000 bound copies of the codebook to fill their orders. Housewives across the country were now armed with a set of codes to decipher the age of the goods they purchased. Realizing how big this issue had become, Jewel grocery stores—National Tea's competitor—ran ads stating that their store brand had freshness dates. This campaign became an extension of the women's jobs as housewives. For Schakowsky and the others, the lack of transparency in food packaging was a gendered assault on their ability to do their jobs. "Would your husband buy a car from a dealer who refused to tell him what year it was?" Schakowsky and the other women would ask shoppers. Schakowsky and her colleagues believed that because grocery shoppers were predominantly women, the industry thought it could take advantage of them. However, the NCU's shoestring campaign succeeded in rattling the grocery industry to its roots and forcing it to make changes to benefit consumers.

The grassroots activism of suburban housewives in Long Island and Chicago was a response from those who were confronted most intimately with the rising gap between the cost of living and the ability to earn that marked the late 1960s and 1970s, and it demonstrates the willingness of

ordinary women to become deeply involved when an issue affects them pro-
foundly. After the end of President Johnson's War on Poverty and the election
of President Nixon, domestic politics became a motivating force for many
working- and middle-class housewives, especially among white families who
saw themselves as the American Dream generation as they moved out of urban
areas and into the suburbs of the industrial North. By the 1960s, people self-
identified as "consumers" more than any at time previously.[62] Inspired by the
political actions of the civil rights movement and the United Farm Workers'
nationwide boycott against table grapes, politically progressive housewives
saw opportunities to channel their energy into a cause that benefited their
families directly. For some women such as Jan Schakowsky, this was a jumping
off point into the world of political organizing, as she later decided to run for
local political office. For Jackie Kendall, it meant helping to establish community organizations and training programs for additional progressive causes.
Others, such as Mickey DeLorenzo, left the limelight but were inspired to
pursue careers outside the home. After the meat boycotts subsided and FLP
closed their imaginary doors, DeLorenzo returned to school and earned a
graduate degree in social work. She turned down requests by local political
leaders to run for office, citing her frustration with the lack of transparency in
the political process.[63]

The relevance of domestic politics to the growing focus on women's rights,
however, was missed by many. In the winter of 1971, the American Home
Economics Association (AHEA) invited radical feminist and women's rights
leader Robin Morgan to facilitate a conversation about "the whole big question of women's rights and responsibilities in this changing world."[64] Morgan
was asked to give a five-minute opening statement to launch the panel, "Rights
vs. Responsibilities in Women's Changing World." She would then share the
stage with three other women who would address "a cross-section of contemporary thinking on women's rights," including a "traditional approach"
in contrast Morgan's expected "radical" approach as well as the viewpoint of
African American women.[65] The AHEA got an earful on that summer day
at the Denver Hilton—likely more than they bargained for. Morgan's best-
known and most often cited quote from that speech—"as a radical feminist,
I am here addressing the enemy"—exemplifies the tension between the 1970s
women's movement, popularly referred to as "second wave feminism," and
the mission of home economics. Morgan claimed that the radical women's
movement was "out to destroy" the holy grail of home economics—marriage,
family, and consumerism, and that the "institutions are dying even without
the feminist revolution."[66] Morgan and her peers proved to be misguided.

5

Organizing in the 1970s

THE RISE AND FALL OF DOMESTIC POLITICS

BY 1973, WAGES were at a standstill, and food prices continued to climb. Calling the increase in the cost of meat "a serious drain of the average American's take-home pay," three thousand AFL-CIO delegates set aside time during their collective bargaining convention to endorse a weeklong meat boycott in April 1973.[1] Between 1968 and 1973, housewives in urban and suburban areas felt the effect of stagnating wages on the family economy. Meat was not the only grocery item becoming unaffordable. Shoppers also saw the price of instant coffee and onions increase. "You can't even afford to have a decent cry anymore," one shopper commented about onions, which had gone from 5 cents per pound to 35 cents per pound in mere months.[2]

The high cost of food became a national issue, and elected officials began to call for a boycott and price controls. Congressman William R. Cotter of Connecticut urged consumers—meaning housewives—to organize a national boycott of meat. In a speech to the House of Representatives, Cotter noted that Washington, DC, housewives had organized a rally to be held on the Ellipse on April 1. Noting that the march was to occur on April Fool's day, Cotter commented that women will "no longer be fooled by a price control program that simply does not work."[3] As President Nixon's efforts had failed to curb the rising cost of living, Cotter was not the only politician who questioned the president's financial policies. US Representative Ogden R. Reid of New York introduced legislation days before the April Fool's meat boycott, calling for a "roll back" of food prices to January 1, 1972, levels and a limit on future increases to 3 percent.[4]

The housewives' boycott dominated the national news.[5] In New Hampshire, legislators voted down an endorsement of the meat boycott, but

FIG. 5.1 Women at meat boycott headquarters at 58 W. 25th St, New York City, April 3, 1973. Courtesy of Getty Images.

in Maine, the House of Representatives officially endorsed the action and urged all state employees to "join in the boycott." At the New Jersey State House, legislators, employees, and administrators ate fish, eggs, and cheese during the boycott with the governor's approval. Similarly, members of the Los Angeles Board of Supervisors voted unanimously to support the boycott, but they refused to ask their colleagues not to consume meat at their own dinner tables. Supervisor Kenneth Kahn "balked" at the prospect of elected officials upholding the boycott. Los Angeles city councilman and mayoral candidate Tom Bradley expressed "outrage" at the high cost of meat, and he promised that he and his wife would abstain from meat during the one-week boycott and not buy meat on Tuesdays and Thursdays after the boycott ended until prices dropped. Bradley also called on the city's Bureau of Consumer Affairs to "enlist volunteers to monitor" meat prices and publish the comparisons, a move reminiscent of the actions of the wartime Office of Price Administration. In Cleveland, Ohio, a city council resolution called for a "Boycott Meat Month," as opposed to the one-week April Fool's boycott.[6]

While local, state, and federal politicians debated the merits of the meat boycott, families across the country began to turn to alternate forms of protein to supplement their diets. Housewives in Portland, Oregon, replaced expensive beef with cheaper horsemeat. One store sold 3,600 pounds of horsemeat in six hours. With a price difference of $2.00 a pound, horsemeat grew in appeal, and customers lined up through the night. In Hellerton, Pennsylvania, one woman resorted to dog food as she picketed with other housewives outside a local A&P Supermarket. Wearing a placard calling for the boycott of meat, Mona Guth downed a spoonful of wet dog food to demonstrate that the dog was eating better than its human companions. In New York City, Dorothea Hoskins reached for neck bones instead of sirloin steaks in her grocery store. She noted, however, that the neck bones would take longer to cook, causing higher gas bills. Some women participating in the boycott, such as Janet Muchnik of Park Forest, Illinois, grew concerned after reading in *Consumer Reports* that "hot dogs have a large percentage of water, and peanut butter is filthy." Another Chicago area consumer bristled at Nixon's suggestion that housewives buy offal—such as brains and intestines—rather than standard cuts of meat. "I wonder how often those cuts show up on his plate," the consumer asked.[7] Rejecting meat altogether, a Kansas City taco stand substituted cheese for meat, with little comment by customers, while a fast food chain in Omaha, Nebraska—home of the Omaha Steak—introduced the soybean burger.[8]

Vegetarian menus popped up everywhere. To encourage housewives to stick with the boycott, rally organizers offered alternative menus for women to use at home. The Housewives of Azusa for Lower Priced Meat (HALPM) organized a parade through downtown Azusa, a suburb of Los Angeles in the San Gabriel Mountain foothills. Patricia Greenwalt, an organizer of the group, saw the parade as another opportunity for housewives to "exchange ideas for meatless meals."[9] The *Washington Post* published two weekly menus provided by the Virginia Citizens Consumer Council (VCCC), an organization promoting the boycott, and the Maryland Seafood Marketing Authority, who saw the high prices of red meat and chicken as an opportunity to encourage women to buy fish. The VCCC board urged all consumers to switch to eggs, cheese, beans, and other high-protein items, stating that they were "outraged by the recent climb in prices." On Capitol Hill, Representative Cotter published a "meatless menu" in the *Congressional Record*, suggesting that congressmen eat vegetarian meals for the boycott week.[10]

Housewives in suburban Los Angeles organized "Baloney Rallies" and adopted slogans like "Let Them Eat Cheese" as the federal government failed to close the widening gap between wages and the cost of living. At a Santa

Monica playgroup, a group of young mothers joined the protest after one explained the call for a weeklong boycott. At the urging of one mother who had previously worked with the media, the women organized picket lines that had "as many press as people." Other women joined in the boycott, and the momentum grew as pickets were set up weekly. The rest of the country also pressured the meat industry to lower process and the federal government to curb the rising cost of living.

Within a couple of months, many of the Santa Monica housewives had stopped their pickets and protests, but the experience proved transformative for one Santa Monica housewife. Ruth Yannatta Goldway was a young mother who had recently relocated to the Los Angeles area.[11] On hiatus from graduate school to raise her young son, she saw the meat boycott as an exciting entree into consumer politics. Goldway was not entirely new to political activism. Her parents were Jewish intellectuals who had been involved in left-wing politics in New York, and Goldway was familiar with the UFW grape boycott and the Civil Rights Movement.[12] Until the meat protests, however, Goldway did not see herself as a political activist. She was deeply influenced by Frances Moore Lappé's *Diet for a Small Plant*, a 1971 manifesto against industrial agriculture, and the rampant practice of redlining in California communities. Rather than "going back to [her] regular life," Goldway decided to channel her anger into organizing, and she took over Fight Inflation Together (FIT), a local consumer organization.[13]

FIT quickly became a front-line organization for food issues. Much as Schakowsky's organization had done in Chicago, Goldway's group focused on better pricing and food labeling. With some grant money, FIT was able to expand its programs and make connections across the state. This shift from local neighborhood pickets to a "real organization that worked on food" helped to institutionalize the work. FIT joined with other California groups—such as the UAW and the Consumer Federation of California—to fight the "war on high prices." Goldway and others took the momentum from the price boycotts to address larger issues in the food industry. As Goldway built more networks, Governor Brown's administration hired her to serve as the assistant to the director in the Department of Consumer Affairs. "Yes, I'm now a government bureaucrat!" she declared in a letter to friends. Maintaining her base in Los Angeles, Goldway reported that her "first and major goal is to make this L.A. office a focal point for consumer activity." As she recalls, "In building this movement, I . . . naturally became more political."[14] Indeed, Goldway's position in the Brown administration marked the beginning of a long political career for her.

National Consumer Congress

The momentum of the 1973 boycott was contagious. Unlike earlier meat boycotts, the consumer movement had gained enough energy and influence that many consumer activists believed it could be turned into a nationally coordinated grassroots organization much like the Consumer Clearing House (CCH) in the 1940s. Alberta Slavin, a housewife from suburban St. Louis, was dogged in her efforts to bring a national organization to fruition. Born and raised in South Dakota, Slavin's upbringing was not unlike that of Eleanor Fowler and Caroline Ware. She earned both a bachelor's and master's degree in music and continued playing the violin with the St. Louis String Ensemble even after marrying Raymond G. Slavin, a physician. They raised their four children in Clayton, a small largely white middle-class suburb just west of St. Louis, where Slavin was deeply committed to social issues.[15] She pushed aside concerns from veteran consumer organizers about the impossibility "launching a significant national consumer organization." In correspondence with Roy Kiesling, a consumer activist in California and founding member of the Consumer Alliance, Slavin want to know if he had even a "shred of interest left" in forming a national organization as "an outgrowth of the meat boycott and urged him to support her effort to establish the National Consumer Congress (NCC)."[16] At the founding convention in Chicago, Ellen Zawel, "a busy wife and mother who . . . got . . . fed up with rising prices" and who had been active in the 1973 meat boycott in New York, was elected the organization's president, and Sandra DeMent, a staffer from Ralph Nader's Citizen's Action Group, was elected treasurer. The 150 delegates pledged a commitment that the NCC, rather than becoming another national organization, would focus on local organizations. The objective was "to build a strong grassroots consumer movement that can mobilize nationally when appropriate."[17]

In the words of the members, "NCC is primarily an action organization, born out of action in the meat boycott. Action is also the key to organizing the movement." The NCC's vision was threefold: first, sharing local resources among local organizations; second, engaging in nationally coordinated efforts such as the Berkeley Co-op's study of breakfast cereals; and third, responding and mobilizing in response to a consumer issue that was quickly growing such as the 1973 meat boycott.[18] NCC's organizational structure was not that different from that of the CCH. However, by the 1970s, there was far more organizational support for the NCC than there was for the CCH in the 1940s. The NCC was financially backed by a start-up grant from the Consumers' Union, membership dues from over 500 individuals, and "substantial in-kind contributions from Ralph Nader." Interestingly, the NCC also received a grant from Grand Union, a large East Coast grocery store chain, to assist with travel expenses and to distribute NCC materials in their stores.

Support by grocery stores for consumer activism was not all that unusual. At the time, Esther Peterson had left public service to work in the private sector as the consumer advocate at Giant Foods, based on a close relationship she had developed during her tenure in the White House with the president of the grocery chain. While many in public service as well as her friends questioned Peterson's decision to move into the private sector, her choice seemed to have been driven by her desire to work directly with consumers and to enact practical changes on their behalf. This is something that she was not able to do from her post–White House position in the Department of Labor.

However, the NCC leadership decided at their first board meeting that "no further assistance would be accepted from corporations unless and until a way could be found to take this kind of money without comprising either the flexibility or credibility of NCC."[19] While the NCC was not flush with funds, their balance sheet reflected a budget that allowed them to focus on their three areas of interest, whereas the CCH's lack of funds and institutional support meant that their impact did not move to far beyond the Washington, DC Beltway.

The NCC's vision marked a moment when key issues of the economy, employment, consumer issues, and the environment were interwoven. Within a year, the NCC was credited with a series of achievements on behalf of consumers. Members of the NCC lobbied for the Consumer Protection Agency Bill and against special interest anti-trust exemptions; they also understood the importance of banking and credit reform legislation to working families. They pressured Secretary of Agriculture Earl Butz to establish a monthly question-and-answer meeting of the top USDA staff members with consumers and the press, and sought from him a commitment to clarify USDA policies that impacted consumers. This interaction was in stark contrast to the behavior of then-Secretary of Agriculture Henry Wallace who "beat a hasty retreat" when 1935 meat boycott leader Mary Zuk and her sister protesters arrived in Washington, DC, to lobby on behalf of consumers.[20] NCC's "teams of citizen monitors" focused on food issues broadly defined. Looking forward, the NCC was committed to "increas[ing] the voice of the consumer within government" as well as focusing on the importance and relevance of "full-employment" and agricultural policies that supported local farming rather than a food industry dominated by "agribusiness corporations."[21]

In 1947, the CCH had explored the possibility of launching localized organizing campaigns around consumer issues. There was widespread local interest,
but the funding for such activities did not exist. By 1975, the NCC decided to
establish "a pilot project in a movement towards building grassroots consumer
organizing." A year later, the NCC hired two professional organizers with backgrounds in grassroots neighborhood organizing. They targeted Westchester
County in New York because of its history of consumer organizing and their
findings that 25 percent of the county's families lived below the poverty line and
another 53 percent were in a moderate-income bracket. After an initial meeting with representatives of consumer, senior citizen, open government, tenant,
and homeowner organizations, the Westchester Action Council (WAC) was
formed. The group chose to build a campaign against "the illegal collection of
sales taxes on tax exempt items at county supermarkets." According to their initial research, the campaign would mean "a savings of over one and a half million
dollars a year" for Westchester County shoppers.[22] Using a mix of protests, sur-
veys, meetings, and a call for the district attorney investigate consumer fraud at
local grocery stores, WAC was able to get a commitment from the county's legislative committee for regulation and inclusion at future meetings on the issue.
The NCC believed that this grassroots training program with WAC helped
launch an organization that is "capable of expanding its boundaries not simply
in terms of membership, but also in terms of the goals of the group."[23]

Technological advances at supermarkets created new challenges for the
fight for consumer transparency. The introduction of the Universal Price
Code (UPC) allowed supermarkets to stop pricing individual goods and
instead use computerized barcodes on each product. After the Codebreakers
had finally helped to abolish the secret coding system for expiration dates,
consumers now faced a new setback as grocery stores could display the price
of goods only on the shelf rather than on individual products. When shoppers
loaded their carts with goods and went to check out, the food prices remained
fixed to the shelf. "With actual prices appearing only on the shelf, consumers
will have no safeguards against arbitrary and unknown price changes between
the shelf and the computer," predicted Catherine Johnson, a spokeswoman
for San Francisco Consumer Action (SFCA), a consumer activist organization in the Bay Area. The elimination of item pricing meant that consumers
would have increased difficulty in comparison shopping, little protection
against getting overcharged, and small probability of seeing any savings from
a speedier checkout. Furthermore, Johnson noted, "In an age when computerized information banks are more and more threatening individual privacy,

consumers are 50 percent of every food transaction and no longer should they tolerate the corporate arrogance that denies them a voice in the marketplace proportionate to their role."[24]

The backlash to UPC coding reflected a general frustration with corporate influence in the domestic sphere. By the mid-1970s, large grocery stores were the norm. The relationship between the consumer and the vendor was nearly two generations removed. Yet many consumers still believed—as Johnson noted—that they deserved a voice in the marketplace. Consumer activists took a legislative approach and began proposing local ordinances and state bills. In California, they urged the Assembly members in Sacramento to pass a pricing bill to regulate the use of UPC codes. According to the SFCA, testimony by "consumer representatives" was silenced when the conservative Democrat and chair of the Assembly's Committee on Banking and Finance Alister McAlister "limited the amount of time devoted to a hearing about the bill and hearing from its supporters." Kay Pachtner, executive director of SFCA, attempted to take the floor "to protest the Chairman's affrontry," but she was silenced. A student activist and housewife eager to join the consumer movement, Pachtner founded San Francisco Consumer Affairs in 1971. By 1975, she was running the organization with a small staff. As Pachtner's and other activists' efforts to testify were denied, SFCA reported that McAlister opened the floor to an industry representative, who testified for twenty minutes on the benefits of UPC pricing.[25]

California consumers were not the only ones frustrated by the UPC pricing trend. In Evanston, Illinois, the Codebreakers regrouped and allied themselves with the local League of Women Voters (LWV) to pass an item pricing ordinance that required prices be marked on all goods. By the mid-1970s, Jan Schakowsky and Jackie Kendall had moved to Evanston, a progressive college town along the shores of Lake Michigan. Bonnie Wilson moved to Evanston less than a month before her second child was due. Already an active member of the LWV, she soon joined the Codebreakers and began organizing around consumer issues.[26]

Schakowsky and Wilson pitched the idea of an item pricing study to the Evanston LWV. They were concerned about item pricing for two reasons. First, like Californians, Illinois consumers were facing a lack of price transparency. Having prices listed only on the shelves made price comparison shopping very difficult. Also, by the time a consumer got to the register, it was impossible to remember the original price of the goods. If the scanner rang up a higher price, the shopper was either oblivious or had to challenge the cashier and hold up the line while a clerk ran to the aisle to check the price. As Wilson recalls, "People . . . would go around with markers and mark the items so that when it went through the scanner, you could see if it was correct."[27] The second concern for the Codebreakers was job loss for grocery store employees. "We were getting political," Kendall noted. "This is going to cost jobs."[28] The use of the UPC scanners potentially made many grocery clerks unnecessary. Six months were required for the study to be conducted and the participants to reach consensus. With the study complete, the Evanston LWV presented their findings to the city council and asked them to pass an ordinance protecting item pricing. Although it passed, the victory was short-lived. As other grocery stores wanted to enter the Evanston market, they demanded that the city council rescind the ordinance. The city council agreed. Wilson worked with the city council on compromise language that required stores with UPC code scanners to post a notice on each register that the store would charge the shelf price if the item rang up higher when it was scanned.

By the time of the Ford administration, the Codebreakers were seasoned street theater activists. Their piece de la resistance was a mock "Baloney and Crumbs Luncheon" at Northwestern University meant to illustrate the reality of food costs for the average consumer. The protest, which coincided with the visit of Secretary of Agriculture Butz and special assistant to the president for Consumer Affairs Virginia Knauer, was a reaction to President Ford's introduction of the Whip Inflation Now (WIN) program in 1974. Evoking the New Deal days of President Roosevelt, Ford called on Americans to "make a list of 10 ways to fight inflation and save energy." Rather than implementing an executive order or asking Congress to pass specific legislation, Ford hoped to foment a grassroots reaction similar to that of World War II when consumers planted victory gardens and managed their homes on austerity budgets. Ford asked consumers, "rich or poor . . . to share everything you can and a little bit more. And it will strengthen our spirits as well as our economy."[29] Hoping for "an all-out nationwide volunteer mobilization," Ford took the WIN program on a national tour. The first stop was Illinois where they were set to have a large press conference at Norris Hall on the Northwestern University campus. The Codebreakers were ready.

By 1974, the Codebreakers were legendary among consumer activists. Kendall and Schakowsky were the public faces of their consumer work. As part of Ford's effort toward a national volunteer effort, it was not surprising that Kendall and Schakowsky were invited to dine with Butz and Knauer the night before the press conference. While the other Codebreakers organized the action, Kendall and Schakowsky headed to downtown Chicago to dine at the elegant Drake Hotel.[30] The next morning, activists who naturally blended into the campus atmosphere, handed out leaflets inviting attendees and students to a "baloney and crumbs luncheon" on the steps of Norris Hall as the press conference was taking place. The leaflets read, "Today's luncheon has been organized to reflect the content of the hearing and proposed regulations, there will be a great deal of baloney and not many crumbs for consumers."[31] Meanwhile, inside Room 1B of Norris Hall, microphones were arranged to allow for community and press questions. Little did the press conference coordinators know that the Codebreakers had lined up behind each set of microphones with questions on hand. The room was filled to capacity, with an overflow room set up that included closed circuit television. Once the floor was opened for questions and comments, the Codebreakers bombarded the officials with criticisms of the WIN program and the Ford administration's lack of action on inflation. As one microphone shut down, another set of Codebreakers launched into questions at a different microphone. In the end, the press conference was a failure.

The Codebreakers called the hearings "nothing more than a political smokescreen aimed at shielding the President while he kills serious consumer legislation." In their view, Ford's proposed regulations did nothing more than "give consumers stale crumbs of worthless rhetoric, while the President denies us the whole loaf of a serious Consumer Protection Agency."[32] The WIN program was the perfect fodder for consumer activists looking to challenge the ineffective response to inflation of the Ford administration. The "catchy slogan" designed for a different moment in time "ended up a political battering ram against the administration," as one historian put it.[33] And the Codebreakers scored a victory as they ended Butz and Knauer's national tour before it ever got off the ground.

The Carter Years

With the election of Jimmy Carter, consumer activists hoped that they would find a receptive voice in the White House. President Carter was quick to reappoint Esther Peterson, offering a renewed connection to the Oval Office that promised to be more transparent than in the Johnson administration. By 1977, the NCC merged with the National Consumers' League.[34] The shuttering of NCC was not a surprise. As with many coalitions, the effort to keep a small group of committed activists spread across the country engaged in both their local work and functioning as a national organization is both expensive and logistically demanding. Even in the early days of NCC, it was difficult to get responses from the organization's executive board. In one example, only four people responded to a need to vote on an issue before the executive board.[35] While their creative efforts such as the training program in Westchester County were innovative, their financial and membership base was too weak to sustain a long-term organization. Just as the CCH marked a generational shift that helped further establish the influence of domestic politics in the public sphere, the NCC was the next generation of that movement. Yet the simultaneous influence of the women's movement meant that domestic politics was fading, despite the seeming growth of consumer activism. With a Democrat back in the White House, a broad base of organizations representing many constituencies came together to address the financial challenges for consumers brought on by stagflation. The Consumers Opposed to Inflation in the Necessities (COIN) Campaign was the brainchild of two men in their early thirties: Roger Hickey who worked at the National Center for Economic Alternatives, the predecessor of the well-regarded Economic Policy Institute, and Mark Green who worked at Public Citizen, the Washington, DC-based consumer watchdog group. Crafting a campaign centered on basic necessities for a broad constituency base, Hickey and Green mobilized over sixty organizations addressing the needs of consumers, senior citizens, the environment, and energy supply, as well as gaining broad support from organized labor.[36]

The Carter administration was facing double-digit inflation, with an annual rate increase of 10 percent.[37] COIN's mission was to urge the Carter administration to avoid a macro-economic approach that would include austerity measures and the Federal Reserve's "cracking down," leading to inflation. Instead, COIN wanted Carter to take an "activist strategy" and focus on four key areas of inflation—energy, food, housing, and healthcare.[38] By focusing on these four discrete areas, COIN created a diverse coalition of partners that were each invested in driving down inflation, which had led to families spending "nearly three out of every four dollars . . . for these necessities."[39]

COIN's early efforts culminated in a meeting with President Carter, an event that was largely coordinated by Peterson. Unlike her days in the Johnson administration—when access to the president was so guarded she could not even coordinate a photo opportunity with him—Peterson now worked closely with the Oval Office to maintain a consistent flow of communication. Carter said, "You have spoken up for consumers through this nation effectively. I want COIN to be a partner of this Administration in our common efforts to control inflation."[40] Coming out of the meeting, Carter's "top inflation fighter" Alfred Kahn began setting up working groups for the White House to study each of the sectors. After the meeting, Hickey and Green both seemed pleased. "We got the point across," Hickey told the *Washington Post*. "They agreed with us that if we don't get control over these areas, then we have lost the inflation war." Green added that the meeting was "a good wind up, but we'll be looking for the follow-up. This is a small, but necessary first step down a very long road towards solving the structural problems if inflation."[41]

In the year after their meeting with President Carter, COIN was tasked with helping the White House monitor price hikes. While not as extensive and bureaucratic as the wartime OPA program that enlisted tens of thousands of housewives as price monitors, the AFL-CIO and COIN worked with Alfred Kahn, chairman of the White House Council on Wage and Price Stability. In public, Kahn announced that he was hopeful that the two groups would be able to "provide the 'missing link' for his office."[42] However, the AFL-CIO and COIN believed that simply monitoring was inadequate. Using the data from their price watching, the AFL-CIO drafted reports that would help to "channel all the bitterness and frustration that people feel about prices toward getting a workable, fair anti-inflation program."[43]

In June 1979, COIN organized a daylong anti-inflation teach-in that drew more than 2,000 people. Keynote speakers included union presidents such as the UAW's Douglas Fraser and the International Association of Machinists' William Winpisinger. Alfred Kahn told the audience that their demands for a sectoral approach to inflation to bring down the costs of necessities was rooted in "faulty economic analysis."[44] Gar Alperovitz, a founder of COIN and a well-regarded Washington, DC, economist, challenged Kahn's claims. Alperovitz reiterated COIN's economic argument that an aggressive sectoral approach would drive down prices of food, housing, and heating oil, which would have a direct benefit to consumers. "There is no way to control inflation," he said, "unless the price of basic necessities is brought under control."[45] This debate between the implementation of an austerity program versus a sector-by-sector approach illustrates the growing power of neo-liberal economic influences and the dismantling of economic regulations set in place during the New Deal.

The Personal Is Political

The consumer activism during the 1970s was a turning point for many housewives creating political inroads that reached beyond their communities. The personal became truly political. In communities across the country,

housewives were following in the footsteps of Mary Zuk. Several housewives active in local consumer activism chose to run for political office. In
California, two women launched political campaigns after their involvement in Fight Inflation Together (FIT) during the 1973 meat boycott. In San
Fernando Valley, Arline Mathews ran against incumbent Barry Goldwater Jr.
for the twentieth congressional district. Embracing her role as a "consumer
advocate," she used this to craft a political identity that would connect with
"the American housewife and her worker husband." Mathews's campaign
focused on grassroots support for making "the American system work, [to]
take back the Federal Reserve Board and give it to the people."[46] In a fundraising letter sent to consumer activists, Mathews touted her skills as a "bat-
tler." She wrote, "The timing is right. It's the year for the consumer advocate.
It's a winning year for challengers to replace politicians—especially ones
like Goldwater who . . . [have] been indifferent to the 'pocketbook' issues
of inflation, unemployment and shortages."[47] In the end, Mathews won the
Democratic primary but lost in the general election to Goldwater. Mathews,
with the support of her husband, who was once quoted as saying he "enjoys
having an intelligent wife," continued to run for political office.[48] She eventually won a seat as a commissioner in Los Angeles County from which she
focused on issues such as the environment and gay, lesbian, bisexual, transgen-
der, and queer (GLBTQ) rights.[49]

In Missouri, Alberta Slavin was following a similar path. Slavin found her
political voice in reaction the economic crisis of the 1970s. Like housewives
elsewhere, she began a grassroots campaign to thwart inflation. She was the
founding member of Housewives Elect Lower Prices (HELP) in which she
coordinated a volunteer effort to survey food prices in the St. Louis area
over a five-year period. In addition, Slavin organized the Utility Consumers'
Council of Missouri to intervene on the issue of skyrocketing residential utility bills. She tied this work to the importance of preserving the environment
and worked with Missouri's Committee for Environmental Information.

In 1976 Slavin was president of the Utility Consumers' Council of
Missouri when she decided to run for lieutenant governor of Missouri on
the Democratic ticket. Her appeal was broad. As a consumer activist, she was
invited to speak to organizations as diverse as labor unions such as the UAW
and Amalgamated Clothing Workers of America, the Knights of Columbus,
the Grace Hill Settlement House, the St. Louis County Young Republicans,
the American Farm Bureau Federation, and the Woman's Club of Belleville
(Illinois).[50] By the mid-1970s, Slavin was a national figure in the consumer
movement. She was vice-president of the NCC and ran her campaign as

an "outgrowth of her efforts to have the public represented in energy decisions." In one promotional statement, Slavin said, "As Lt. Governor, I hope
to represent . . . [the consumer] interest, in planning for energy without profiteering."[51] Slavin ran her campaign like a true grassroots organizing effort,
collecting a penny per voter for political donations and training people to
canvass the state on behalf of her campaign. Her messaging was consistent
with her consumer activism and, in the midst of the energy crisis, it likely
rang true not only to urban consumers but also to Missouri farmers who faced
high energy costs to run their farms. In the end, Slavin lost the election to the
better-known speaker of the Missouri House Richard Rabbit. However, she
was appointed to the Missouri Public Service Commission in 1977 after a
protracted battle for Senate confirmation.[52]

Harnessing the momentum from her consumer activism, Ruth Goldway
also sought political office. She first ran for a seat on the state assembly and
earned widespread support among the Los Angeles entertainment elite.

FIG. 5.2 Alberta Slavin, Democrat for Lieutenant Govenor, promotional flyer from her
unsuccessful bid in 1974.

Courtesy Alberta Slavin Papers, State Historical Society of Missouri—St. Louis.

Goldway used her experience as a consumer activist to craft her political image. After losing the state assembly race, she ran for the Santa Monica City Council focusing on her identity as a "consumer advocate," who would fight inflation, speak out for crime control, improve family life, and get "the Politicians to work for us."[53] Goldway's political image was dependent on her identity as a mother, housewife, and consumer activist. In 1981, she was elected on a progressive slate to the Santa Monica City Council, which later appointed her mayor. Her tenure as mayor focused on consumer issues, such as access to healthy foods (they established a farmers' market) and the introduction of rent control. In the 1970s and early 1980s, Santa Monica was a sleepy town, filled with aging renters rather than movie stars. Focusing on rent control, Goldway's slate mobilized more residents to vote than ever before.[54] This "urban populism" is reminiscent of the populism of the early twentieth century, which made its mark on the industrial triangle of Cleveland, Toledo, and Detroit.[55] With these "building blocks" of progressivism, the local leaders of Santa Monica were able to counter growing pressures from Reaganism and the New Right.[56] Goldway's political career moved beyond California, when Goldway left Santa Monica for Norway, after President Clinton appointed her husband ambassador of that country. Upon her return to the United States, Goldway was appointed chairman of the Postal Regulatory Commission by the Clinton administration, a post she held for decades.

Across town from Goldway's office at the Postal Regulatory Commission was the office of US Representative Jan Schakowsky. After the National Consumers United (NCU) campaigns, Schakowsky worked for Illinois Public Action and the Illinois State Council of Senior Citizens. She found herself excited about the possibility of a political career, and more than fifteen years after her first consumer campaign, she ran for the Cook County Board. She lost, but in the process Schakowsky discovered that she loved electoral politics. "I loved to campaign! I just loved it. . . . I put a thousand miles a week on the car just driving around the county. . . . It was the women that were just amazing."[57] Eventually, Schakowsky won a seat on the Cook County Board and then in the Illinois State Assembly, where she served for eight years. She was elected to the United States House of Representatives in 1998 and represents Illinois's Ninth District. Schakowsky's political identity is inextricably linked to her work a consumer advocate.

The ability of these women to make such choices reflects a marriage of domestic politics and the 1970s women's movement, which created an environment in which women were seen as more than housewives. The flip side of this progress, however, was the end of an era of the citizen housewife and collective action on behalf of domestic politics. This was particularly true as a wave of conservatism swept through the country giving way to a reframing of the housewife as an ambassador of conservativism and traditional family values. Most notably, Phyllis Schlafly and her Eagle Forum began to promote a conservative "pro-family" agenda including opposition to the recent Supreme Court decision on *Roe v. Wade*, legalizing abortion.[58]

Within the labor movement, there was also a decline of domestic politics as the AFL-CIO National Auxiliary had become an increasingly irrelevant organization. During the 1973 meat boycott, the AFL-CIO National Auxiliaries met in Miami in conjunction with the AFL-CIO's national convention.[59] Not once did Novella Porter, the National Auxiliaries' Executive Director, or any other auxiliary member, raise the issue of the meat boycott. In his opening remarks at the auxiliary convention, however, Wes Reedy, a representative from the AFL-CIO, focused on the high cost of living and President Nixon's failed price controls. However, he never appealed to the auxiliary members to engage as housewives in the boycotts. In fact, his only reference to housewives was in the third person: "Every housewife knows that the price of meat is the fastest climbing item in the consumer price index."[60] Unlike a generation earlier, when union leaders called on housewives to use their roles to become politically active, Reedy called on the auxiliary members to "fight for a law to reform political campaign financing so that 1974 and 1976 elections will be decided by public issues and not secret dollars."[61]

Between the momentum of the women's movement and the numbers of women continuing to enter the workforce, organized labor put its resources toward the passage of the Equal Rights Amendment (ERA) and the establishment of women's organizations, such as the National Organization of Women (NOW) and the Coalition of Labor Union Women (CLUW). Established in 1974, CLUW was born of the success of the women's movement and the lack of women's leadership despite their growing union membership. Unlike the contentious debates over the impact of the ERA on women in the labor force, the 1970s marked the dawn of a new era in the relationship between working women and feminism.[62] Under pressure from union women's committees, many women union leaders eventually came out in support of the ERA.[63] In the 1940s, the Congress of Women's Auxiliaries set the agenda for women in the labor movement; now, CLUW was pioneering a new platform for women, emphasizing the rights of women workers as both trade unionists and women.[64]

Housewives no longer comprised a political interest group. In fact, "housewife" had become a "dirty word." Politicians no longer addressed the "concerns of housewives" as they had done in the past, nor did they seek the "expertise" of housewives on domestic issues. Mainstream media outlets stopped referring to women as housewives. This shift took place for two reasons. First, the influence of the women's movement created an environment in which the heterosexual nuclear family was seen as an agent of oppression. As influential as Betty Friedan's *The Feminine Mystique* was in the 1960s, Kate Millet's 1970 *Sexual Politics* proclaimed that the nuclear family was "a force frustrating revolutionary change."[65] For many feminists, the family became the place where the oppression of women was most overt.[66] Furthermore, the effect of growing conservativism on the women's liberation debate drove home the belief that the terms "housewife" and "feminist" were antithetical to one another.[67]

The 1973 meat boycott has not been remembered in the year that witnessed Nixon's resignation, the passage of *Roe v. Wade*, American troops being pulled out of Vietnam, and the sky-rocketing prices of oil imposed by OPEC. However, when placed in the context of a larger consumer movement that spanned two generations, from 1935 to the 1970s, the 1973 boycott complicates the declentionist narrative of the 1970s. This was the decade during which the political identity of the housewife and domestic politics was up for grabs. While it is clear that the New Deal–style citizen housewife was a diminishing public figure, the growth of the women's movement throughout the 1970s meant that individual women who found their voices in consumer activism were able to pursue careers beyond the home. Mary Zuk faded into obscurity, but others did not. The momentum of the 1973 meat boycott and the founding of the National Consumer Congress (NCC) demonstrates the urgency of domestic politics—the ability of the American household to meet their most basic needs. However, just as business leaders and conservative politicians waited until war's end to end shutter agencies such as the Office of Price Administration, stop funding federally subsidized childcare, and pass restrictive legislation such as the Taft-Hartley Act, the next generation of conservative leaders built a political network that would promote individual needs over collective needs by harnessing fear. Working-class white workers feared the loss of their ability to support their families as inflation dragged on, and they felt what they saw as the loss of the idealism of their communities as schools were integrated.[68] The women's movement categorized all housewives as the "enemy," missing a critical opportunity to work in partnership with consumer activists. And organized labor dismissed the potential of their auxiliary movements in focusing on community organizing as a critical tool to engage families in labor struggles. In short, the lead up to and election of Ronald Reagan in 1980 marked a moment when many Americans chose to abandon their belief that government should play a role in the well-being of the American public.[69] In doing so, they made a political agenda rooted in domestic politics obsolete—dismissed as merely "politics of the pantry."[70]

Epilogue

"WHAT WE WANT IS FOOD": FOOD POLICY AND PROTESTS IN THE TWENTY-FIRST CENTURY

WITH THE ELECTION of Ronald Reagan in 1980, domestic politics was reframed as "kitchen table politics."[1] Rallying against abortion rights and the Equal Rights Amendment, a growing cadre of socially conservative housewives did not see themselves reflected back when they watched the growing women's movement of the 1970s. They gained momentum by setting an agenda focused on conservative social issues that matched the shifting neo-liberal economic ideology that was taking root. As the women's movement floundered in its desire to incorporate housewives into their movement, going so far as to allow Robin Morgan to frame them as the "enemy," conservative Republicans saw an opportunity to appeal to the growing population of discontented white housewives. Not unlike Mary Zuk and others, conservative housewives crafted an identity that pitted them as "simple homemakers and mothers facing elite, politically connected feminists who disavowed what they and other women were pleased to have found."[2] Domestic politics was no longer the legacy of a New Deal vision of state intervention to protect the American standard of living. Domestic politics 1980s style would be defined by individual over collective needs. So what happened to the food fights?

In 1998, Jan Schakowsky represented Evanston in the Illinois State Assembly. She was such a persistent legislator that one of her legislative colleagues described her as "a dog with a bone." When the Ninth Congressional District's Sidney Yates retired, Schakowsky decided to take her persistence all the way to Washington. Framed by the media as "a consumer-oriented state representative with a feminist pitch," Schakowsky was running against two men—Howard Carroll, a state senator and ward committeeman, and J.B. Pritzker, a businessman and "scion of one of Chicago's wealthiest families." It was a tight race and Schakowsky put her years of consumer organizing into action. "My goal is to meet 200 people a day. . . . I go to a lot of bingos . . . where there are women who wouldn't identify themselves as feminists. They will lower their voices and say, 'This is what we need—more women running for office.'"[3] In her many years as a congresswoman, Schakowsky has never shied away from her early days as an activist housewife. It shaped her political identity.

Despite their different path, the same can be said for most of the women featured in this book. Ruth Goldway went on to work on California's food security issues before her appointment by President Clinton as chair of the Postal Regulatory Commission. Mickey DeLorenzo opted to stay out of electoral politics but committed her life to social work. Jackie Kendall spent decades teaching others how to organize at the Midwest Academy. Bonnie Wilson remains active in Evanston politics. Eleanor Fowler returned to political work with the Women's International League of Peace and Freedom after a hiatus on a Pennsylvania farm raising her children. Catherine Gelles retired from the UAW after spending almost four decades with the union. And the stories go on. But domestic politics faded.

The fight for affordable food has not faded; it has been moved to the shadows of impoverished neighborhoods and overseas to countries that struggle to feed their citizens under the weight of lopsided trade deals and structural adjustment programs mandated by the International Monetary Fund and other global economic giants. While many families have cut their food bills by 35 percent since 1973, the accessibility of high-quality, healthy food has significantly diminished.[4] In 2009, "50.2 million Americans did not know where their next meal was coming from. At the same time there [are] more diet-related diseases like diabetes, and more food, in the US than ever before."[5] The capacity to earn a living wage has been sharply diminished along with union density. The federal minimum wage, which peaked in 1968, was once enough to help a family keep a roof over their heads and basic food on the table, but it is now so low that many full-time workers earning the minimum wage need to work multiple jobs and may rely on public assistance to make ends meet.[6]

The ability to afford food is one issue. The other is food deserts, or areas of inaccessibility to healthy, affordable food. The US Department of Agriculture defines food deserts as "parts of the country vapid of fresh fruit, vegetables, and other healthful whole foods, usually found in impoverished areas."[7] Poor communities in the United States are likely to have four times fewer

supermarkets in their neighborhoods than are found in wealthy neighborhoods. Food is also three times more likely to be sold in places that sell alcohol. Full-service supermarkets are replaced by corner stores or quickie marts
that sell alcohol along with an array of high-sugar, high-fat convenience foods,
often at inflated prices. Fast-food restaurants are also disproportionately more
concentrated in poor communities and communities of color.[8] The growing
concern over food deserts has increased significantly over the past decade as
scholars, journalists, and community activists have drawn attention to uneven
development in urban and suburban areas.

Let's go back to where our story began—Detroit. According to a public
health study of the Motor City, "over half a million Detroit residents live in
areas that have an imbalance of healthy food options. They are statistically
more likely to suffer or die prematurely from a diet-related disease, holding
other key factors constant."[9] The number of full-service supermarkets in the
city has long been declining, with the last major grocery chain leaving the city
in 2007. Detroiters now must travel to the suburbs to shop at a grocery store,
and this is a problem for the one-fifth of the population without access to a
car for transportation.[10] A city built on the manufacturing of cars, Detroit is
notorious for its poor public transportation system. In response to this epi-
demic, Detroiters organized.

The Detroit Black Community Food Security Network (DBCFSN) is a
non-profit grassroots community organization founded in 2006. Spearheaded
by Malik Yani, a longtime black liberation activist, bookstore owner, and
school administrator, he reached out to the community to "grasp larger control over the food system."[11] Similar to the women of the Adams-Morgan
community in Washington, DC, the DBCFSN has worked with the community and the local government to create a comprehensive food security
policy that includes the U-Ujamma Food Buying Co-Op, the D-Town Farm,
and the Detroit Food Policy Council. A critical component of the food security movement in Detroit is questioning the role of government in controlling access to food. According to the 2000 US Census, Detroit is 82 percent
African American, and almost 20 percent of its residents live below the poverty line. In fact, many see the government as the problem. In response, the
D-Town Farm launched a comprehensive program of self-sufficiency within
the city to both grow their own food and educate the community on healthy
eating. As one historian noted, "D-Town activists challenge the White priv-
ilege embedded in the food security movement."[12] The connections between
race, class, and food insecurity give little incentive for the community to turn
to the government to solve the problem.

The passage of the Commodities Futures Modernization Act of 2000 (CFMA) was not met with the same street protests as the Agricultural Adjustment Act (AAA) was in 1935. Outside the United States, however, is the place where protesters are hitting the streets. The global food crisis results in large part from US neo-liberal economic policy such as the CFMA. To put it very simply, the CFMA allows financial traders to make bets on the price of food. And, to add fuel to the fire, the development of the agrofuel industry set the price of food on an inflationary spike. Like the 1933 AAA, crops are not grown to be eaten, but, unlike the AAA, they are grown to create ethanol. In 2008, President George Bush attributed a 15 percent food price inflation to agrofuels while the World Bank placed the blame closer to 75 percent. Food security scholars and policy analysts put it somewhere between 15 and 75 percent.[13]

The inflation of food prices paired with global trade agreements such as the structural adjustment programs promoted by the IMF that encourage the export of staple food items to reduce state-owned debt has led to protests across the globe. The Arab Spring followed steep agricultural price inflation. In 2007 and 2008, there were protests related to the high cost of food in more than thirty countries. In import-dependent countries such as Ghana and Pakistan, some people are spending upward of 70 percent of their income on food.[14] In Mozambique, the 30 percent increase in the cost of bread was defeated when citizens protested the government policy.[15] In Venezuela, an oil-rich country, protesters blocked the streets of Caracas shouting "We want food!" A mother of three lined up at a local supermarket in hopes of buying a chicken and some rice, "I haven't been able to buy chicken in more than a month, so I was there early at about 4 am." The food shortages have lasted almost three years as the country's economy flounders. The political climate is complex in Venezuela, but as one woman who runs a newsstand commented, "We don't care who's in Miraflores [the presidential palace]. What we want is food."[16] And this is really the bottom line. We must move away from policies that use food as a political puppet subject to the whims of elected leaders and industry lobbyists.

Notes

INTRODUCTION

1. "Elbow Macaroni Drafted in War on Meat Prices," *New York Times,* April 2, 1973; Henry Scarupa, "The Beef Stew: Costs Rise, Housewives Rebel," *Sun*, April 8, 1973; "GW Thoughts on Consumers," *Washington Post*, April 28, 1965.

2. Meg Jacobs, William J. Novak, and Julian E. Zelizer, eds., *The Democratic Experience: New Directions in American Political History* (Princeton, NJ: Princeton University Press, 2003), 1.

3. This book is largely influenced by the work of the following: Dorothy Sue Cobble, *The Other Women's Movement: Workplace Justice and Social Rights in Modern America* (Princeton, NJ: Princeton University Press, 2004); Tracey Deutsch, *Building a Housewives' Paradise: Gender, Politics, and American Grocery Stores in the Twentieth Century* (Chapel Hill: University of North Carolina Press, 2010); Lawrence Glickman, *Buying Power: A History of Consumer Activism in America* (Chicago: University of Chicago Press, 2009); Meg Jacobs, *Pocketbook Politics: Economic Citizenship in Twentieth Century America* (Princeton, NJ: Princeton University Press, 2005); Joanne Meyerowitz, *Not June Cleaver: Women and Gender in Postwar America, 1945–1960* (Philadelphia: Temple University Press, 1994).

4. Michelle M. Nickerson, *Mothers of Conservatism: Women and the Postwar Right* (Princeton, NJ: Princeton University Press, 2012); Ronnee Schreiber, *Righting Feminism: Conservative Women and American Politics* (New York: Oxford University Press, 2008); Donald T. Critchlow, *Phyllis Schlafly and Grassroots Conservatism: A Woman's Crusade* (Princeton, NJ: Princeton University Press, 2005).

5. T. H. Breen, *The Marketplace of Revolution: How Consumer Politics Shaped American Independence* (New York: Oxford University Press, 2004); Victoria De Grazia and Ellen Furlough, *The Sex of Things: Gender and Consumption in Historical Perspective* (Berkeley: University of California Press, 1996); Lawrence B. Glickman, *A Living Wage: American Workers and the Making of Consumer Society* (Ithaca, NY: Cornell

University Press, 1997); Glickman, *Buying Power*; Roger Horowitz and Arwen Mohun, *His and Hers: Gender, Consumption, and Technology* (Charlottesville: University Press of Virginia, 1998); Jacobs, *Pocketbook Politics*; Jennifer Scanlon, *Inarticulate Longings: The Ladies' Home Journal, Gender, and the Promises of Consumer Culture* (New York: Routledge, 1995); Robert E. Weems Jr., *Desegregating the Dollar: African American Cosumerism in the Twentieth Century* (New York: New York University Press, 1998).

6. There has been a recent surge in work on motherhood in the twentieth century that is excellent. Jodi Vandenberg-Daves, *Modern Motherhood: An American History* (New Brunswick, NJ: Rutgers University Press, 2014); Rebecca Jo Plant, *Mom: The Transformation of Motherhood in Modern America* (Chicago: University of Chicago Press, 2010); and, of course, the classic Adrienne Rich, *Of Woman Born: Motherhood as Experience and Institution* (New York: W.W. Norton, 1995).

7. Ann Folino White, *Plowed Under: Food Policy Protests and Performance in New Deal America* (Bloomington: Indiana University Press, 2015), 125.

8. Carolyn M. Goldstein, *Creating Consumers: Home Economists in Twentieth Century America* (Chapel Hill: University of North Carolina Press, 2012).

9. See chapter 7 in Glenna Matthews, *"Just a Housewife": The Rise and Fall of Domesticity in America* (New York: Oxford University Press, 1987), and Lizbeth Cohen, *A Consumers' Republic: The Politics of Mass Consumption in Postwar America* (New York: Alfred Knopf, 2003).

10. Paula E. Hyman, "Immigrant Women and Consumer Protest: The New York City Kosher Meat Boycott of 1902," *American Jewish History* 70, no.1 (September 1980): 91–105; Annelise Orleck, *Common Sense & a Little Fire: Women and Working-Class Politics in the United States, 1900–1965* (Chapel Hill: University of North Carolina Press, 1995); Folino, *Plowed Under.*

11. While Dana Frank's excellent article ("Housewives, Socialists, and the Politics of Food: The 1917 New York Cost-of-Living Protests," *Feminist Studies* 11, no. 2 [1985]: 255–285) notes that Jewish housewives turned their attention to New York's mayor in the 1917 meat boycotts, the women focused their attention at the city level with little to no critique of national public policy.

12. Jackie Kendall, interview by Emily E. LB. Twarog, October 14, 2014, Grayslake, Illinois.

13. Mary Heaton Vorse, *Labor's New Millions* (New York: Modern Age Books, 1938), 234.

14. Elizabeth Faue, *Community of Suffering and Struggle: Women, Men and the Labor Movement in Minneapolis, 1915–1945* (Chapel Hill: University of North Carolina Press, 1991), 9.

15. Faue, *Community of Suffering and Struggle,* 10.

16. Temma Kaplan, "Female Consciousness and Collective Action: The Case of Barcelona, 1910–1918," *Signs: Journal of Women in Culture and Society* 7, no. 3 (1982): 547.

17. Recent studies on the connection between consumption and citizenship include Breen, *The Marketplace of Revolution*; Cohen, *A Consumers' Republic*; Tracey Deutsch, *Building a Housewife's Paradise: Gender, Politics, and American Grocery Stores in the Twentieth Century* (Chapel Hill: University of North Carolina Press, 2010); Kathleen G. Donohue, *Freedom from Want: American Liberalism and the Idea of the Consumer* (Baltimore, MD: Johns Hopkins University Press, 2003); Glickman, *Buying Power*; Charles McGovern, "Consumption and Citizenship in the United States, 1900–1940," in Susan Strasser, Charles McGovern, and Matthias Judt, eds., *Getting and Spending: European and American Consumer Societies in the Twentieth Century* (Cambridge: Cambridge University Press, 1998); Charles McGovern, *Sold American: Consumption and Citizenship, 1890–1945* (Chapel Hill, NC: University of North Carolina Press, 2006); Jacobs, *Pocketbook Politics*; Linda Kerber, *No Constitutional Right to Be Ladies: Women and the Obligations of Citizenship* (New York: Hill and Wang, 1998); Theda Skocpol, *Protecting Soldiers and Mothers: The Political Origins of Social Policy in the United States* (Cambridge, MA: Belknap Press of Harvard University Press, 1992); Emilie Stoltzfus, *Citizen, Mother, Worker: Debating Public Responsibility for Child Care after the Second World War* (Chapel Hill: University of North Carolina Press, 2003).

18. My theoretical framework is largely influenced by the work of feminist theorist Nancy Fraser, specifically her use of the terms "androcentric" and "state-managed capitalism," in Nancy Fraser, *Fortunes of Feminism: From State-Managed Capitalism to Neoliberal Crisis* (London: Verso Press, 2013).

19. Robert E. Weems Jr., *Desegregating the Dollar: African American Consumerism in the Twentieth Century* (New York: New York University Press, 1998); Devin Fergus, *Liberalism, Black Power, and the Making of American Politics, 1965–1980* (Athens: University of Georgia Press, 2009); Lauren Araiza, *To March for Others: The Black Freedom Struggle and the United Farm Workers* (Philadelphia: University of Pennsylvania Press, 2014).

20. Darlene Clark Hine, *Hine Sight: Black Women and the Reconstruction of American History* (Bloomington: Indiana University Press, 1997); Melinda Chateauvert, *Marching Together: Women of the Brotherhood of Sleeping Car Porters* (Urbana: University of Illinois Press, 1998); Jeffrey Helgeson, *Crucibles of Black Empowerment: Chicago's Neighborhood Politics from the New Deal to Harold Washington* (Chicago: University of Chicago Press, 2014).

21. White, *Plowed Under*, 112–151.

22. Howard Zinn, Dana Frank, and Robin D. G. Kelley, *Three Strikes: Miners, Musicians, Salesgirls, and the Fighting Spirit of Labor's Last Century* (Boston: Beacon Press, 2001); Sidney Fine, *The General Motors Strike of 1936–37* (Ann Arbor: University of Michigan Press, 1969).

23. Katherine Archibald, *Wartime Shipyard: A Study in Social Disunity* (Urbana: University of Illinois Press, 2006).

24. Stephanie Coontz, *A Strange Stirring: The Feminine Mystique and American Women at the Dawn of the 1960s* (New York: Basic Books, 2011).

25. Joseph A. McCartin, *Collision Course: Ronald Reagan, the Air Traffic Controllers, and the Strike that Changed America* (New York: Oxford University Press, 2011).

26. Rebecca Traister, "Feminists Killed Home Ec.: Now They Should Bring It Back—for Boys and Girls," *New Republic*, May 28, 2014.

27. Esther Peterson, "The Reminiscences of Oral History, Columbia University," Papers of Esther Peterson, Schlesinger Library, Radcliffe Institute for Advanced Study, Harvard University (hereafter—EP/SL-RI), pp. 287–289.

28. Meg Jacobs, William J. Novak, and Julian E. Zelizer, eds., *The Democratic Experience: New Directions in American Political History* (Princeton, NJ: Princeton University Press, 2003).

29. Pauli Murray, "Letter to Esther Peterson, August 10, 1968," Box 7, Folder Correspondence—Murray, Pauli, EP/SL-RI.

CHAPTER 1

1. "Loga ludowa omawia sprawy obywatelstwa Hamtramickiego." *Głos Ludu,* April 1936. Translation provided by Michal Wilczewski.

2. "Loga ludowa omawia sprawy obywatelstwa Hamtramickiego."

3. Greg Kowalski, *Wicked Hamtramck: Lust, Liquor and Lead* (Charleston, SC: History Press, 2011). See Chapter 4 for more details on Zuk's election.

4. "Apel do Obywatelstwa w Hamtramck," *Głos Ludu*, Spring 1936. Translation provided by Michal Wilczewski.

5. Paula E. Hyman, "Immigrant Women and Consumer Protest: The New York City Kosher Meat Boycott of 1902," *American Jewish History* 70, no. 1 (September 1980): 91–105; Dana Frank, "Housewives, Socialists, and the Politics of Food: The 1917 New York Cost-of-Living Protests," *Feminist Studies* 11, no. 2 (1985): 355–385; T. H. Breen, *The Marketplace of the Revolution: How Consumer Politics Shaped American Independence* (New York: Oxford University Press, 2004).

6. US Congress, "19th Amendment," May 19, 1919, http://www.archives.gov/historical-docs/document.html?doc=13, June 20, 2016. Leila J. Rupp and Verta Taylor, *Survival in the Doldrums: The American Women's Rights Movement, 1945 to the 1960s* (New York: Oxford University Press, 1987); Nancy A. Hewitt, ed., *No Permanent Waves: Recasting Histories of U.S. Feminism* (New Brunswick, NJ: Rutgers University Press, 2010).

7. Theda Skocpol, *Protecting Soldiers and Mothers: The Political Origins of Social Policy in the United States* (Cambridge, MA: Belknap Press of Harvard University Press, 1992), 37.

8. Sonya O. Rose, "Class Formation and the Quintessential Worker," in John R. Hall, ed., *Reworking Class* (Ithaca, NY: Cornell University Press, 1997).

9. There has been recent attention paid to the 1935 meat boycott and the role of house-wives in consumer action. See Anne Folino White, *Plowed Under: Food Policy Protests and Performance in New Deal America* (Bloomington: Indiana University Press, 2014), 112–151; Angela D. Dillard, *Faith in the City: Preaching Radical Social Change in Detroit* (Ann Arbor: University of Michigan Press, 2007), 70–74; Greg Kowalski, *Wicked Hamtramck: Lust, Liquor and Lead* (Charleston, SC: History Press, 2010).

10. Michael B. Katz, *The Price of Citizenship: Redefining the American Welfare State* (New York: Metropolitan Books, 2001), 2.

11. Seth Koven and Sonya Michel, *Mothers of a New World: Maternalist Politics and the Origins of Welfare States* (New York: Routledge, 1993).

12. Belinda Davis, *Home Fires Burning: Food, Politics, and Everyday Life in World War I Berlin* (Chapel Hill: University of North Carolina Press, 2000); Julie Guard, "A Mighty Power against the Cost of Living: Canadian Housewives Organize in the 1930s," *International Labor and Working Class History* 77, no. 1 (Spring 2010); Ruth Frager, "Politicized Housewives in the Jewish Communist Movement of Toronto, 1923–1933," in Kinda Kealey and Joan Sangster, eds., *Beyond the Vote: Canadian Women and Politics* (Toronto: University of Toronto Press, 1989); Joanne Hollows, "'We Won't Pay': Price Rises and Socialist Feminist Consumer Activism in the 1970s." Unpublished; in the author's possession.

13. For more on the theater of protests, see White, *Plowed Under.*

14. David Montgomery, *Workers' Control in America: Studies in the History of Work, Technology, and Labor Struggles* (New York: Cambridge University Press, 1979), 4.

15. From 1936 to 1937, work stoppages doubled, from 2,172 in 1936 to 4,740 in 1937, with close to 2 million workers participating in work stoppages that averaged twenty days in duration. At General Motors alone, workers organized 435 unauthorized work stoppages between mid-1937 and mid-1939. See Robert Asher, Ronald Edsforth, and Stephen Merlino, *Autowork* (Albany: State University of New York Press, 1995), 103.

16. Mary Zuk, as quoted in "Detroit Meat Strike Spreads over Country," *Daily Worker,* August 7, 1935.

17. The use of labor tactics was common during the 1969 meat boycott in Levittown, Long Island. In fact, Mickey DeLorenzo, the local leader of the boycott, looked to her father-in-law, a UAW organizer, for training and advice throughout the boycott. According to an interview with DeLorenzo, his "dos and don'ts" for the picket line were critical, and she carried the number of his lawyer in her back pocket at all times.

18. The number of striking housewives is up for debate. According to the Communist Party's *Party Organizer,* 75 percent of the city's population engaged in the strike. However, the *Detroit Free Press* set the number much lower at 200. The number certainly exceeded 200, as all sources report that at least 200 butcher shops closed;

that would have required the muscle of far more than 200 housewives. Regardless of the precise number, the strike impacted the community in a way that would have made it hard for the town's approximately 50,000 residents to ignore. See Section Organizer, "How the Meat Strike Started in Hamtramck," *Party Organizer* 8, no. 9, Box 2, Folder Mary Zuk, Don Binkowski Papers, Walter P. Reuther Library, Archive of Labor and Urban Affairs, Wayne State University (hereafter WRL-ALUA).

19. Hasia R. Diner, *Hungering for America: Italian, Irish, and Jewish Foodways in the Age of Migration* (Cambridge, MA.: Harvard University Press, 2001), 180.

20. For a detailed narrative of the relationship between food and migration, see Diner, *Hungering for America.*

21. Nick Fiddes, *Meat, a Natural Symbol* (New York: Routledge, 1991).

22. Meg Jacobs, *Pocketbook Politics: Economic Citizenship in Twentieth-Century America* (Princeton, NJ: Princeton University Press, 2005), 44.

23. While there are some exceptions to the exclusion of consumer protest from labor history narratives, the majority of labor histories focus on organizational histories or the experiences of workers on the shop floor. For examples of consumer protests as part of labor history, see Melinda Chateauvert, *Marching Together: Women of the Brotherhood of Sleeping Car Porters* (Urbana: University of Illinois Press, 1998); Erik S. McDuffie, *Sojourning for Freedom: Black Women, American Communism, and the Making of Black Left Feminism* (Durham, NC: Duke University Press, 2011); Frank, "Housewives, Socialists, and the Politics of Food."

24. Elizabeth Ewen, *Immigrant Women in the Land of Dollars: Life and Culture on the Lower East Side, 1890–1925* (New York: Monthly Review Press, 1985).

25. John Bodnar, "Immigration, Kinship, and the Rise of Working-Class Realism in Industrial America," *Journal of Social History* 14, no. 1 (1980); Ewen, *Immigrant Women in the Land of Dollars*; John E. Bodnar, *The Transplanted: A History of Immigrants in Urban America* (Bloomington: Indiana University Press, 1985); Nicholas Lemann, *The Promised Land: The Great Black Migration and How It Changed America* (New York: Vintage Books, 1992); Joe William Trotter, *The Great Migration in Historical Perspective: New Dimensions of Race, Class, and Gender* (Bloomington: Indiana University Press, 1991); James N. Gregory, *The Southern Diaspora: How the Great Migrations of Black and White Southerners Transformed America* (Chapel Hill: University of North Carolina Press, 2005).

26. For more on the role of the family manager, see Martha May, "The 'Good Managers': Married Working Class Women and Family Budget Studies, 1895–1915," *Labor History* 25, no. 3 (1984); Louise Tilly and Joan Wallach Scott, *Women, Work, and Family* (New York: Methuen, 1987).

27. Eve Stone, "'A Year Has Gone By' in Union Auxiliary Women Advance, January 1938," Box 1, Folder 17—Union Auxiliary Women Advance, Lillian Sherwood Papers, WRL-ALUA.

28. Alice Kessler-Harris, *In Pursuit of Equity: Women, Men, and the Quest for Economic Citizenship in 20th Century America* (New York: Oxford University Press, 2001), 6.

29. Thomas A. Stapleford, *The Cost of Living in America: A Political History of Economic Statistics, 1880–2000* (Cambridge: Cambridge University Press, 2009), 135.

30. Stapleford, *The Cost of Living in America*.

31. E. P. Thompson, "The Moral Economy of the English Crowd in the Eighteenth Century," *Past & Present* 50 (February 1971): 79.

32. Henry Demarest, *The Safety of the Future Lies in Organized Labor* (Washington, DC: A.F.L., 1893). My understanding of the origins of the living wage is largely informed by Glickman's detailed discussion in *A Living Wage*, 61–77.

33. American Federation of Labor, *Some Reasons for Chinese Exclusion. Meat vs. Rice. American Manhood against Asiatic Coolieism, Which Shall Survive?* (Washington, DC: US Government Printing Office, 1902).

34. Roger Horowitz takes an important look at the history of American meat consumption, but it is also a broader study of the evolution of the technology of meat production and how it impacted American eating. Richard Horowitz, *Putting Meat on the American Table: Taste, Technology, Transformation* (Baltimore, MD: Johns Hopkins University Press, 2005)

35. Horowitz, *Putting Meat on the Table*, 24–25.

36. As Robert Bruno recalls in his book *Steelworker Alley*, his neighborhood butcher would often look out for his mother when autoworkers in Youngstown, Ohio, went on strike, despite the fact that his mother was unable to afford their usual cuts of meat while managing the family budget on strike pay. Robert Bruno, *Steelworker Alley: How Class Works in Youngstown* (Ithaca, NY: Cornell University Press, 1999).

37. Horowitz, *Putting Meat on the American Table*, 18.

38. Jack London, "A Piece of Steak," http://www.classicshorts.com/stories/steak.html (accessed July 6, 2014).

39. London, "A Piece of Steak."

40. James A. Cain, *Mildred Pierce* (New York: Vintage Crime/Black Lizard, 2010).

41. "Quiet Prevails in Meat Strike," *Detroit Free Press*, August 8, 1935.

42. Belmont County Probate Court, Ohio, "Certified Copy of Birth Record of Mary Stanzeus, 1905," Box 2, Folder Zuk, Don Binkowski Papers, WRL-ALUA.

43. Kowalski, *Wicked Hamtramck*. Neffs, Ohio was dominated by the M. A. Hanna Company. Zuk's father most likely died in the March 30, 1915, Hanna Coal Company disaster, which took the lives of twenty-three miners. In 1940, the Hanna Coal Company was again in the news, after seventy-two men died in the Willow Grove mine disaster.

44. Beth Tompkins Bates, *The Making of Black Detroit in the Age of Henry Ford* (Chapel Hill: University of North Carolina Press, 2012), 144–171.

45. According to historian Thaddeus Radzilowski, Poles were the poorest and least skilled ethnic group in Detroit. And by 1930, joblessness and poverty were rampant in the Polish community. Not since the severe depression of 1893 had Detroit's Polish population suffered such economic hardships. Thaddeus Radzialowski and Donald Binkowski, "Polish Americans in Detroit Politics," in Angela T. Pienkos,

ed., *Ethnic Politics in Urban America: The Polish Experience in Urban America* (Chicago, IL: Polish American Historical Association, 1978), 54.

46. Radzialowski and Binkowski, "Polish Americans in Detroit Politics," 48.

47. Section Organizer, "How the Meat Strike Started in Hamtramck."

48. In 1935, Hamtramck's population was approximately 50,000 people. See Greg Kowalski, *Hamtramck: The Driven City* (Charleston, SC: Arcadia).

49. Section Organizer, "How the Meat Strike Started in Hamtramck."

50. Section Organizer, "How the Meat Strike Started in Hamtramck."

51. Elizabeth Faue, *Community of Suffering and Struggle: Women, Men, and the Labor Movement in Minneapolis, 1915–1945* (Chapel Hill: University of North Carolina Press, 1991); Georg Schrode, "Mary Zuk and the Detroit Meat Strike of 1935," *Polish American Studies* 43, no. 2 (1986): 9.

52. There are many inconsistencies in the name of the Hamtramck meat boycott organization. According to independent historian Don Binkowski, who was responsible for accessing and depositing Mary Zuk's personal papers at Wayne State University's Archive for Labor and Urban Affairs, the Hamtramck organization was called the Committee for Action against the High Cost of Living. Meanwhile, the *Detroit Free Press* referred to Zuk's organization as the Women's Committee for Action against the High Cost of Living, whereas historian Georg Schrode called the Hamtramck organization the Action Committee against the High Cost of Living. For the purposes of this book, I am following Binkowski's lead and referring to the Hamtramck group as the Committee for Action against the High Cost of Living. For the remainder of the chapter, I will refer to Zuk's group as the Committee.

53. Section Organizer, "How the Meat Strike Started in Hamtramck."

54. "Joseph Campau Avenue and the Shopping Districts of the City of Hamtramck," http://wayne.migenweb.net/shopping.htm (accessed on January 27, 2017).

55. Federal Writers Project, Michigan: A Guide to the Wolverine State (New York: Oxford University Press, 1946).

56. "Women Close Meat Markets in Hamtramck," *Detroit Free Press,* July 28, 1935.

57. H. C. Garrison, "Hamtramck Councilwoman a Fiery Friend of Worker," *Detroit News*, April 9, 1936.

58. "Six Are Arrested in Meat Boycott," *New York Times*, May 31, 1935.

59. "Chicago Food Shops Hit by Meat Strike," *New York Times*, September 19, 1935.

60. Darlene Clark Hine, *Hine Sight: Black Women and the Re-Construction of American History* (Bloomington: Indiana University Press, 1994), 59–60.

61. Hine, *Hine Sight*, 60.

62. Committee for Action against the High Cost of Living, "Statement of the Delegation"; "Meat Strike Group to Send Delegation to Washington," *Detroit Free Press*, August 14, 1935.

63. "How the Meat Strike Started in Hamtramck," *Party Organizer* 8, no. 9 (September 1935), Box 2, Folder Zuk, Mary, Don Binkowski Papers, WRL-ALUA.

64. "Crowd Storms Police Station; Wives Freed," *Detroit Free Press*, August 3, 1935.

65. "Crowd Storms Police Station; Wives Freed," *Chicago Daily Tribune*, August 3, 1935. Interestingly, Patrona Jakstys, a Polish housewife, was fined $35, which she paid. Since, in present day dollars, the amount was equivalent to $556, that was a curious decision. There is no way to confirm who actually paid the fine. But given the involvement of the Communist Party, many labor unions, and the local Federation, Jakstys possibly received some financial support. During Zuk's successful run for Hamtramck City Council, she was able to raise $547.90 (approximately $9,726 in 2017) through donations from a variety of ethnic organizations, labor unions, fundraising activities, and individual donations. Perhaps fundraising of this kind was used to offset legal fees incurred from the protests.

66. Committee for Action against the High Cost of Living, "Statement of the Delegation."

67. "Facts for Speakers," Box 2, Folder Zuk, Mary, Don Binkowski Papers, WRL-ALUA.

68. "Facts for Speakers."

69. Angela D. Dillard, *Faith in the City*.

70. This was not the first delegation to head to Washington, DC. In June 1935, a group of Chicago activists, led by Rose Saffern and accompanied by Rose Nelson of New York, the Secretary of the United Council of Working Class Women, traveled to Washington, DC, to demand a reduction in meat prices. Both of these women were actively involved in the Communist Party's attempts to grow support for a nationwide meat boycott. "Wallace Beats Hasty Retreat before Irate Detroit Women," *Detroit Free Press*, August 20, 1935.

71. "Wallace Beats Hasty Retreat Before Irate Detroit Women."

72. Henry Wallace, "Pigs and Pig Iron Speech—November 12, 1935," in Russell Lord, ed., *Democracy Reborn* (New York: Reynal & Hitchcock, 1944), 103.

73. Committee for Action against the High Cost of Living, "Statement of the Delegation."

74. Otis B. Johnson, "Letter to Mary Zuk, September 5, 1935," Box 2, Folder Zuk Coorespondence, Don Binkowski Papers, WRL-ALUA.

75. "Facts for Speakers."

76. "Four Day Meat Boycott Launched in Minneapolis in Fight on Prices," *Atlanta Constitution*, October 19, 1935.

77. "Boycott Called by Restaurants against AAA," *New York Herald Tribune*, October 12, 1935.

78. *United States v. Butler*, 297 U.S. 1 (1936); Wayne D. Rasmussen, Gladys L. Baker, and James S. Ward, "A Short History of Agricultural Adjustment, 1933–75." Economic Research Service, United States Department of Agriculture, Agriculture Information Bulletin No. 391 (March 1976), 4.

79. Both Kosciusko and Pulaski were Polish American Revolutionary War heroes who have been held in high esteem throughout Polonia. In Illinois, public school

students are given the day off from school for Pulaski Day, and many local government agencies and libraries close for the day. "Facts for Speakers."

80. "Facts for Speakers."

81. Eric Leif Davin, "Defeat of the Labor Party Idea," in Staughton Lynd, ed., *"We Are All Leaders": The Alternative Unionism of the 1930s* (Urbana: University of Illinois Press, 1996), 139–141.

82. Offering a transnational focus of municipal politics, Stromquist argues that historians have by and large failed to "take seriously the realm of municipal politics" and have bypassed the framing of the city as a political space. Shelton Stromquist, "Claiming Political Space: Workers, Municipal Socialism, and the Reconstruction of Local Democracy in Transnational Perspective," in Leon Fink, ed., *Workers across the Americas: The Transnational Turn in Labor History* (New York: Oxford University Press, 2011), 320–321.

83. Stromquist, "Claiming Political Space"; Melvin G. Holli, *Reform in Detroit: Hazen S. Pingree and Urban Politics* (Westport, CT: Greenwood Press, 1981).

84. Margaret Collingwood Nowak, *Two Who Were There: A Biography of Stanley Nowak* (Detroit: Wayne State University Press, 1989).

85. "Beaten Weekly," *Detroit News* (May 23, 1937); "Spouse Failed to Support Her, She Testifies," *Citizen* (September 17, 1937).

86. "Spouse Failed to Support Her She Testifies."

87. US Department of Labor, *Hours and Earnings in the United States, 1932–1940* (Washington, DC: US Government Printing Office, 1942), 2–3.

88. "Councilwoman Gets Alimony," *Detroit News*, May 23, 1937.

89. "Reds Blamed for Housewives' Meat Boycott," *Chicago Daily Tribune*, August 9, 1935.

90. "Spread the Meat Strike," *Working Woman* (July 1935). The *Working Woman* was published between 1929 and 1935 by the Communist Party's Women's Commission, at which point they changed the name of the magazine to *Woman Today* (1935–1937). See Constance Coiner, *Better Red: The Writing and Resistance of Tillie Olsen and Meridel Le Sueur* (New York: Oxford University Press, 1995), 41.

91. Annelise Orleck, *Common Sense & a Little Fire: Women and Working-Class Politics in the United States, 1900–1965* (Chapel Hill: University of North Carolina Press, 1995); Mark Naison, *Communists in Harlem during the Depression*, (Urbana: University of Illinois Press, 2005); Randi Storch, *Red Chicago: American Communism at Its Grassroots, 1928–35* (Urbana: University of Illinois Press, 2007); Fraser M. Ottanelli, *The Communist Party of the United States: From the Depression to World War II* (New Brunswick, NJ: Rutgers University Press, 1991); Nelson Lichtenstein, *Walter Reuther: The Most Dangerous Man in Detroit* (Urbana: University of Illinois Press, 1995); Michael Denning, *The Cultural Front: The Laboring of American Culture in the Twentieth Century* (New York: Verso, 1998).

92. "Meat Prices Boosted Again, Despite Housewives' Strike," *Detroit Free Press*, August 9, 1935.

93. "Zuk Demands Recount; $5 Alimony, Says Judge," *Detroit News*, May 23, 1937.

94. *The Value of a Dollar, 1860–1999* (Millerton, NY: Grey House), s.v. "Selected Income, 1935–1939."

95. "Spouse Failed to Support Her, She Testifies," *Citizen*, September 17, 1937.

96. Lou Tendler, "Voters Rebel at a 'High Hat,'" *Detroit News,* n.d.

97. Tendler, "Voters Rebel at a 'High Hat.'"

98. Tendler, "Voters Rebel at a 'High Hat.'"

99. Victor S. Navasky, *Naming Names* (New York: Hill and Wang, 2003); Special Committee on Un-American Activities, *Investigation of Un-American Propaganda Activities in the United States,* 1940.

CHAPTER 2

1. Pittsburgh District Labor Meeting, "Meeting Minutes, September 24, 1943," Box 19, Folder Consumer Materials, Consumer Clearinghouse, 1943, Caroline Ware Papers, Franklin Delano Roosevelt Presidential Library (hereafter—FDRL); C. A. Blanchett, "Letter to Reuther, June 2, 1946," Box 378, Folder 10, Walter P. Reuther Papers, WPR-ALUA.

2. J. Paul Leonard, "Memo, May 19, 1943," Box D-8, Folder Community Prices—Plan for Housewives, RG 188, National Archives at College Park, College Park, MD (hereafter NACP)

3. J. Paul Leonard, "Memo, May 19, 1943."

4. J. Paul Leonard, "Memo, May 19, 1943."

5. Ina Zweiniger-Bergielowska, *Austerity in Britain: Rationing, Controls, and Consumption, 1939–1955* (Oxford: Oxford University Press, 2002), 102–127; Caitríona Beaumont, "What *Do* Women Want? Housewives' Associations, Activism, and Changing Representations of Women in the 1950s," *Women's History Review* 26, no. 1, February 2016): 1–16.

6. Donna B. Knaff, *Beyond Rosie the Riveter: Women of World War II in American Popular Graphic Art* (Lawrence: University Press of Kansas, 2013), 48–80.

7. Hester LaDuke, "'What Price Milk?' 1938," Box 1, Folder 17, Lillian Sherwood Collection, WRL-ALUA.

8. CIO auxiliaries were vastly different in both agenda and organization compared to the more established AFL auxiliaries, which focused much of their attention on "Buy Union" campaigns and were largely led by male union leaders. For more on the history of AFL auxiliaries, see Emily E. LaBarbera-Twarog, "Women's Auxiliaries" in *Encyclopedia of U.S. Labor and Working-Class History*, Vol. I, ed. Eric Arnesen (New York: Routledge Press, 2006).

9. For more on this topic, see Chapter 1. Meg Jacobs, "'How about Some Meat?' The Office of Price Administration, Consumption Politics, and State Building from the Bottom Up, 1941–1946," *Journal of American History* 84, no. 3 (1997): 910–941; Elizabeth Cohen, *A Consumers' Republic: The Politics*

of Mass Consumption in Postwar America (New York: Alfred Knopf, 2003); T. H. Breen, *The Marketplace of Revolution: How Consumer Politics Shaped American Independence* (New York: Oxford University Press, 2004); Meg Jacobs, *Pocketbook Politics: Economic Citizenship in Twentieth-Century America* (Princeton, NJ: Princeton University Press, 2005); Lawrence Glickman, *Buying Power: A History of Consumer Activism in America* (Chicago: University of Chicago Press, 2009); Landon Storrs, "Left-Feminism, the Consumer Movement, and Red Scare Politics in the United States, 1935–1960," *Journal of Women's History* 18, no. 3, Fall 2006, 40–67.

10. J. W. Skeels, "Catherine Gelles—July 7, 1961," Oral History Collection, Folder—Catherine Gelles, WPR-ALUA.

11. For more on Walter Reuther, see Nelson Lichtenstein, *Walter Reuther: The Most Dangerous Man in Detroit* (Urbana: University of Illinois Press, 1995).

12. Skeels, "Catherine Gelles."

13. Skeels, "Catherine Gelles."

14. Skeels, "Catherine Gelles."

15. Catherine Gelles, Vertical File—Gelles, WPR-ALUA; Dorothy Sue Cobble, *The Other Women's Movement: Workplace Justice and Social Rights in Modern America* (Princeton, NJ: Princeton University Press, 2004).

16. Carleton Jackson, *Child of the Sit-Downs: The Revolutionary Life of Genora Dollinger* (Kent, OH: Kent State University Press, 2008); Nancy Gabin, *Feminism in the Labor Movement: Women and the United Auto Workers, 1935–1975* (Ithaca, NY: Cornell University Press, 1990; August Meier and Elliott M. Rudwick, *Black Detroit and the Rise of the UAW* (Ann Arbor: University of Michigan Press, 2007).

17. Jackson, *Child of the Sit-Downs.* Genora eventually divorced Kermit and married Sol Dollinger, a man with whom she organized in New York City. For more on Sol and Genora Dollinger, see Sol Dollinger and Genora Johnson Dollinger, *Not Automatic: Women and the Left in the Forging of the Auto Workers' Union* (New York: Monthly Review Press, 2000)

18. Genora D. Johnson, *Striking Flint: Genora (Johnson) Dollinger Remembers the 1936–37 General Motors Sit-Down Strike* (Chicago: L.J. Page, 1996).

19. Jackson, *Child of the Sit-Downs.*

20. Skeels, "Catherine Gelles."

21. Johnson, *Striking Flint.*

22. "Women's Brigade Uses Heavy Clubs," *New York Times,* February 2, 1937; "Striker's Wife Tells Goal of 'Amazon' Corps," *Chicago Daily Tribune,* February 2, 1937.

23. Sidney Fine, *Sit-down: The General Motors Strike of 1936–1937* (Ann Arbor: University of Michigan Press, 1969).

24. For more on Dollinger's perspective, see *With Babies and Banners: Story of the Women's Emergency Brigade.* Directed by Lorraine Gray. Harriman, NY, New Day Films (1979).

25. "UAW Faye Stephenson, Chairman, International Coordinating Committee," Vertical Files, Biography, A-Z: Stephenson, Faye, WPR-ALUA.

26. UAW Women's International Coordinating Committee, "Fifth Annual Officers Report Auxiliary, 1943," Box 1-3, Folder—Buffalo, New York, UAW Women's Auxiliaries Papers, WPR-ALUA.

27. I have chosen to retain the original organizational language of the auxiliaries rather than convert "chairman" into a more contemporary gender neutral term of "chair" or "chairperson." Faye Stephenson, "A Year of Progress, 1939–1940, March 1940," in *Women's Auxiliary News,*" Box 3N-D-7(6), Folder 1940 v. 1, Women's Department—Women's Auxiliaries, WPR-ALUA.

28. Stephenson, "A Year of Progress."

29. Stephenson, "A Year of Progress."

30. Catherine Gelles, untitled, n.d., Box 1, Folder 2, Catherine Gelles Papers, WPR-ALUA; UAW Women's Auxiliaries, "Some of Our Gripes," n.d., Box 1, Folder 2, Catherine Gelles Papers, WPR-ALUA.

31. " 'Women Oppose Rent Increases'—*Women's Auxiliary News,* January 1941," Box 3N-D-7(6), Folder 1941 v. 2, UAW Women's Department—Women's Auxiliary News, WPR-ALUA.

32. Jessamyn Neuhaus, *Manly Meals and Mom's Home Cooking: Cookbooks and Gender in Modern America* (Baltimore, MD: Johns Hopkins University Press, 2003); Jacobs, *Pocketbook Politics*; Cohen, *A Consumers' Republic.*

33. Congress of Women's Auxiliaries, "Let's Get Organized!" Box 41, Folder—Women's Auxiliaries, RG 188, NACP.

34. Eleanor Fowler, "Some Must Reading for a Lot of Men," *CIO News,* January 24, 1944.

35. "*Women's Auxiliary News*, 1942," Box 3N-D-7(6), Folder 1942, v. 3, UAW Women's Department, Women's Auxiliary News, WPR-ALUA.

36. Timothy W. Vanderburg, *Cannon Mills and Kannapolis: Persistent Paternalism in a Textile Town* (Knoxville: University of Tennessee Press, 2013), 123–142; Robert Rodgers Korstad, *Civil Rights Unionism: Tobacco Workers and the Struggle for Democracy in the Mid-Twentieth Century South* (Chapel Hill: University of North Carolina Press, 2003).

37. Kathryn Kish Sklar, *Florence Kelley and the Nation's Work: The Rise of Women's Political Culture, 1830–1900* (New Haven, CT: Yale University Press, 1995).

38. The *CIO News* was edited by Len De Caux, a labor journalist, a member of the Communist Party of America, and one of the more radical voices in the CIO. De Caux's wife, Caroline Abrams De Caux, was also a leader in the CWA. During the 1940s, Fowler and De Caux shared responsibility for building partnerships with other organizations. They were also good friends with the Fowlers. Len De Caux, *Labor Radical: From the Wobblies to CIO* (Boston: Beacon Press, 1970).

39. For more on these issues, see Andrew Edmund Kersten, *Race, Jobs, and the War: The FEPC in the Midwest, 1941–46* (Urbana: University of Illinois Press, 2000); Susan Levine, *School Lunch Politics: The Surprising History of America's Favorite Welfare Program*, (Princeton, NJ: Princeton University Press, 2008); Emilie Stoltzfus, *Citizen, Mother, Worker: Debating Public Responsibility for Child Care after the Second World War* (Chapel Hill: University of North Carolina Press, 2003); James Wolfinger, *Philadelphia Divided: Race & Politics in the City of Brotherly Love* (Chapel Hill: University of North Carolina Press, 2007).

40. Eleanor Fowler, "Women's 'Rights' Line Slick and Dangerous," *CIO News*, February 2, 1944.

41. Congress of Women's Auxiliaries, "Financial Statement, November 20, 1941—October 31, 1942," Box 41, Folder—Women's Auxiliary Conference CIO, RG 188, NACP.

42. Jane Morse, email message to author, June 8, 2011.

43. Eleanor Fowler, "Letter to Mary Anderson, Director, Women's Bureau, December 29, 1943," Box 50, Folder CIO, Women's Bureau Papers, NACP.

44. Ann Folino White, *Plowed Under: Food Policy Protests and Performance in New Deal America* (Bloomington: Indiana University Press, 2015).

45. Congress of Women's Auxiliaries, "Officers' Report to the Second Annual Conference of the Congress of Women's Auxiliaries-CIO, 1942," Box 41, Folder—Women's Auxiliary Conference CIO, RG 188, NACP.

46. Mark H. Leff, "The Politics of Sacrifice on the American Home Front in World War II," *Journal of American History* 77, no. 4 (1991): 1296–1318.

47. Franklin Delano Roosevelt, "Fireside Chat #21—On Sacrifice, April 28, 1942," http://millercenter.org/president/fdroosevelt/speeches/speech-3327 (accessed on January 13, 2016),

48. Katherine Leonard Turner, *How the Other Half Ate: A History of Working-Class Meals in the Twentieth Century* (Berkeley: University of California Press, 2014).

49. Jacobs, *Pocketbook Politics*.

50. *"Women's Auxiliary News*, 1942," Box 3N-D-7(6), Folder 1942, v. 3, UAW Women's Department Papers, WPR-ALUA.

51. Lyrics from Louis Jordan and His Tympany Five, "Ration Blues," http://www.metrolyrics.com/ration-blues-lyrics-louis-jordan.html (accessed on January 13, 2016).

52. Consumer Clearing House, "Meeting Minutes, January 2, 1947," Folder—Consumer Materials, Consumer Clearinghouse, 1947, Caroline F. Ware Papers, FDRL.

53. Anne Firor Scott, ed., *Pauli Murray and Caroline Ware: Forty Years of Letters in Black and White* (Chapel Hill: University of North Carolina Press, 2006).

54. The CCH was a coalition made up of a diverse group of labor, women's, community, and racial and ethnic organizations.

55. A study of CCH meeting minutes shows a diverse coalition of organizations that united over the issue of cost of living. Between 1943 and 1945, the minutes reflect monthly meetings with about a quarter of the thirty-five member organizations attending. By 1947, attendance had significantly declined. Many of the meeting minutes are housed at the FDR Library in the Caroline Ware papers. For an example of some of the meeting minutes, see Consumer Clearing House, "Meeting Minutes, 1943," Box 19, Folder—Consumer Materials, Consumer Clearinghouse, 1943, Caroline F. Ware Papers, FDRL; Consumer Clearing House, "Meeting Minutes, February 12, 1945," Box 19, Folder—Consumer Materials, Consumer Clearinghouse, 1945, Caroline F. Ware Papers, FDRL; Consumer Clearing House, "Consumer Clearing House Constitution, May 21, 1943," Box 19, Folder—Consumer Materials, Consumer Clearinghouse, 1945, Caroline F. Ware Papers, FDRL.

56. Consumer Clearing House, "Consumer Clearing House Constitution, May 21, 1943," Box 19, Folder—Consumer Materials, Consumer Clearinghouse, 1945, Caroline F. Ware Papers, FDRL.

57. Consumer Clearing House, "Meeting Minutes, December 18, 1944," Box 19, Folder—Consumer Materials, Consumer Clearinghouse, 1945, Caroline F. Ware Papers, FDRL.

58. Consumer Clearing House, "Meeting Minutes, April 9, 1943," Box 19, Folder—Consumer Materials, Consumer Clearinghouse Minutes, February 19-June 22, 1943, Caroline F. Ware Papers, FDRL.

59. Pittsburgh OPA Labor Advisory Committee, "Meeting Minutes, November 1943," Box 78, Folder—Pittsburgh LAC, RG 188, NACP.

60. For more on housewives' views on the development of grocery stores, see Tracey Deutsch, *Building a Housewives' Paradise: Gender, Politics, and American Grocery Stories in the Twentieth Century* (Chapel Hill: University of North Carolina Press, 2010).

61. Consumer Clearing House, "Meeting Minutes, February 12, 1945," Box 19, Folder—Consumer Materials, Consumer Clearinghouse, 1945, Caroline F. Ware Papers, FDRL.

62. Consumer Clearing House, "Meeting Minutes, February 12, 1945."

63. Franklin Delano Roosevelt, "Executive Order 8802—Prohibition of Employment Discrimination in the Defense Industry—June 25, 1941," 2016, http://docs.fdrlibrary.marist.edu/odex8802.html (accessed on November 28, 2016). For more on the history of African American consumers, see Robert E. Weems Jr., *Desegregating the Dollar: African American Consumerism in the Twentieth Century* (New York: New York University Press, 1998), 31–32.

64. Weems, *Desegregating the Dollar*, 37.

65. J. Katz, "Memorandum on Participation of Housewives in the Enforcement of Price Ceilings and Rationing Regulations, July 1942," Box D-6 (Women),

Folder Correspondence of Flora Y. Hatcher, July 1941–December 1942, RG188 (OPA), NACP.

66. Robert H. Zieger, *The CIO, 1935–1955* (Chapel Hill: University of North Carolina Press, 1995).

67. In her memo to Dr. Leonard, Hatcher shared that she was unsure of the usefulness of American Federation of Women's Auxiliaries of Labor (AFWAL), the AFL's auxiliary organization. And while AFWAL's militancy and organizational skills paled in comparison to those of the CWA, its leadership did encourage members to focus on consumer issues. The membership sometimes also attended consumer coalition conferences, such as the Consumer Clearing House meetings.

68. F. Y. Hatcher, "Memorandum to Dr. J. Paul Leonard, November 5, 1942," Box D-6 (Women), Folder Correspondence of Flora Y. Hatcher, July 1941–December 1942, RG188 (OPA), NACP.

69. Office of Price Administration, "Report of Meeting with Labor Delegation, April 26, 1943," Box 78, Folder Philadelphia LAC (2)—Correspondence with OPA Office, RG188 (OPA), NACP.

70. C. W. Fowler, "Your Eating Habits at Stake," *CIO News*, March 20, 1944.

71. Through the 1930s, the Communist Party worked to mobilize neighborhoods to fight the high cost of living. So the party's presence at the table was not particularly surprising. Chapter 1 provides more details. By the end of the war, however, the Communist Party was no longer an active participant in coalitional efforts like the CCH.

72. Keene, D., "Do Your Part, March 1943," Box 3N-D-7(6), Folder 1943, v.4, UAW Women's Department—Women's Auxiliary News, WPR-ALUA.

73. "'STOP!!!' Auxiliaries Mobilize to Fight High Prices, *Women's Auxiliary News,* May 1943," Box 3N-D-7(6), Folder 1943, v.4, UAW Women's Department—Women's Auxiliary News, WPR-ALUA.

74. "Women's Place in Labor's Fight Discussed by Auxiliaries," *CIO News,* November 24, 1941; Congess of Women's Auxiliaries, "Proceedings: First Annual Conference of the Congress of Women's Auxiliaries of the CIO, November 17–21, 1941, Box 32, Folder—Consumer Materials, National Defense Advisory Commission, Consumer Advisory Committee Consumer Movement: Printed Materials," Caroline F. Ware Papers, FDRL.

75. "Women's Place in Labor's Fight Discussed by Auxiliaries," *CIO News.*

76. "CIO Women Map Program to Aid Defense," *CIO News*, December 1, 1941.

77. Consumers Clearing House, "Press Release, November 15, 1943," Box 19, Folder—Consumer Materials, Consumer Clearinghouse Current, Caroline Ware Papers, FDRL.

78. "Hamburger Hits the Headlines, July 1943," Women's Auxiliary News, Box 3N-D-7(6), Folder 1943, v. 4, UAW Women's Department, WPR-ALUA.

79. Susan Strasser, *Waste and Want: A Social History of Trash* (New York: Holt, 2014), 254–255; Adee Braun, "Turning Bacon into Bombs: The American Fat Salvage Committee," *Atlantic*, April 18, 2014.

80. Greater New York Council of CIO Women's Auxiliaries, "The Auxiliary Woman, September 1942," Box 41, Folder—Women's Auxiliaries, RG 188 (OPA), NACP.

81. F. Y. Hatcher, "Memorandum to Miss. Ruth Ayers, June 6, 1942," Box D-6 (Women), Folder—Correspondence of Flora Y. Hatcher, July 1941–December 1942, RG 188 (OPA), NACP.

82. Jacobs, *Pocketbook Politics.*

83. Katharine Armatage, "Letter to League of Women Shoppers membership, January 31, 1944," Box 19, Folder Consumer Materials, Caroline Ware Papers, FDRL.

84. Jacobs, *Pocketbook Politics.*

85. "Price Control Fight Unites People," *CIO News,* May 29, 1944.

86. E. Fowler, "Why Steelworkers Need a Wage Hike," *CIO News,* May 1, 1944.

87. Fowler, "Why Steelworkers Need a Wage Hike."

88. "Memo to BLS—Paste Statistics in Your Hat," *CIO News,* June 5, 1944. For more on the Rochdale principles and the proliferation of cooperative markets such as the Rochdale Stores, see Joseph A. Pierce, *Negro Business and Business Education: Their Present and Prospective Development* (New York: Plenum Press, 1994); Steve Leikin, "The Citizen Producer: The Rise and Fall of Working-Class Cooperatives in the United States," in Ellen Furlough and Carl Strikwerda, eds., *Consumers against Capitalism?: Consumer Cooperation in Europe, North America, and Japan, 1840–1990* (Lanham, MD: Rowman & Littlefield, 1999); Deutsch, *Building a Housewife's Paradise.*

89. "Memo to BLS—Paste Statistics in Your Hat," *CIO News.*

90. Chateauvert, *Marching Together*; Darlene Clark Hine, *Hine Sight: Black Women and the Re-Construction of American History* (Bloomington: Indiana University Press, 1994).

91. Andrew Edmund Kersten, *Race, Jobs, and the War*, 105–107; Dominic J. Capeci Jr. and Martha Wilkerson, *Layered Violence: The Detroit Rioters of 1943* (Jackson: University Press of Mississippi, 2009).

92. Frances H. Williams, "Letter to J. Paul Leonard, July 14, 1943," Box D-7, Folder Frances Williams and Sunie Steele Reports, RG 188, NACP.

93. Letter from Charles P. Browning, "Letter to Alfred Standford, March 22, 1945," Box D-8, Folder Chicago Defender Forum, RG 188, NACP.

94. C. W. Fowler, "Brother, Can You Spare $1.74 for $1's Worth of Groceries," *CIO News,* January 31, 1944.

95. C. W. Fowler spent his life as a labor journalist. He wrote for the *CIO News* and was on staff with the UE. He was married to Eleanor Fowler, the secretary-treasurer of the CWA, and he was also a frequent writer for the *CIO News.* During the 1940s, Eleanor Fowler based much of her work in Washington, DC, and she functioned as the voice and representative of the CWA, with coalition partners and on Capitol Hill. For more biographical details, see Chapter 3.

96. Fowler, "Can You Spare $1.74 for $1's Worth of Groceries?"; Thomas A. Stapleford, "Housewife vs. Economist: Gender, Class, and Domestic Economic Knowledge in Twentieth-Century America," *Labor: Studies in Working-Class History of the*

Americas 1, no. 2 (Summer 2004): 89–112; Thomas A. Stapleford, *The Cost of Living in America: A Political History of Economic Statistics, 1880–2000* (Cambridge: Cambridge University Press, 2009).

97. As quoted in Meg Jacobs, *Pocketbook Politics*; George Meany and R. J. Thomas, *Cost of Living: Recommended Report for the Presidential Committee on the Cost of Living* (Washington, DC: Congress of Industrial Organizations, 1944).

98. Jacobs, *Pocketbook Politics*.

99. National League of Women Voters, "Statement to Senate Committee on Banking and Currency, March 8, 1945," Box 477, File—Consumer Interests, misc., League of Women Voters, Series II, Library of Congress (hereafter—LOC)

100. Eleanor Fowler, "Greedy Meat Packers Scream for More Profits," *CIO News,* April 16, 1945.

101. Martha Sawyer, "Letter to Oliver Peterson, April 6, 1945," Box D-7, Folder—League of Women Shoppers, RG 188, NACP.

102. Fowler, "Greedy Meat Packers Scream for More Profits."

103. "Keep Your Eye on Congress," *CIO News,* May 28, 1945.

104. Florence Richardson Wycoff, "Fifty Years of Grassroots Social Activism," transcript of an oral history conducted by Randall Jarrell, Regional Oral History Collection, UC Santa Cruz Library, University of California, Santa Cruz, 1987–1990.

105. Wycoff, "Fifty Years of Grassroots Social Activism."

106. Senator Robert A. Taft, "*Inflation Control Programs of OPA, Hearing,*" Senate Commitee on Banking and Currency, 79th Cong., 1st sess., October 23–25, 1945.

107. Meg Jacobs, "The Uncertain Future of American Politics, 1940–1973," in Eric Foner and Lisa McGirr, eds., *American History Now* (Philadelphia: Temple University Press, 2011), 151–174; Nelson Lichtenstein and Elizabeth Tandy Shermer, *The Right and Labor in America: Politics, Ideology, and Imagination* (Philadelphia: University of Pennsylvania Press, 2012); Charles J. Morris, "How the National Labor Relations Act Was Stolen and How It Can Be Recovered: Taft-Hartley Revisionism and the National Labor Relations Board's Appointment Process," *Berkeley Journal of Employment and Labor Law* 33, no. 1 (2012): 1–71.

108. For a detailed account of childcare during and after World War II, see Natalie M. Fousekis, *Demanding Child Care: Women's Activism and the Politics of Welfare, 1940–1971* (Urbana: University of Illinois Press, 2011), 39.

109. Labor historians' inattention to the attack on price controls reflects what Ava Baron calls the "ghettoization" of women's history—the narrow focus on the workplace misses the broader historical narrative that includes the home and community as well. Ava Baron, "Gender and Labor History: Learning from the Past, Looking to the Future," in Ava Baron, ed., *Work Engendered: Toward a New History of American Labor* (Ithaca, NY: Cornell University Press, 1991).

110. *Women's Auxiliary News*, untitled, Box 3N-D-7(6), Folder 1946 v. 7, UAW Women's Department, WPR-ALUA.

111. *Women's Auxiliary News*, untitled.

112. Jacobs, *Pocketbook Politics*.

113. "Something to Get Excited About—Prices Skyrockets, September 1947," Women's Auxiliary News, Box 3N-D-7(6), Folder 1947 v. 5, UAW Women's Department, WPR- ALUA.

114. Steven K. Ashby, "Shattered Dreams: The American Working Class and the Origins of the Cold War, 1945–1949," Ph.D. diss., Chicago, University of Chicago, 1993.

115. Jacobs, *Pocketbook Politics*.

116. Orleck, *Common Sense and a Little Fire*, 216–217. For a more complete history of Shavelson's life see, 215–249.

117. Annie Stein, "Post-War Consumer Boycotts," *Radical America* 9, no. 4 (July–August 1975): 4–5, 159.

118. *UAW Women's Auxiliary*, August 1946. ALUA, UAW Women's Department, *Women's Auxiliary News*, Box 3N-D-7(6), Folder 1946 v. 7.

119. Stein, "Post-War Consumer Boycotts."

120. Stein, "Post-War Consumer Boycotts," 160.

121. Ashby, *Shattered Dreams*, 273.

122. Jacobs, *Pocketbook Politics*.

123. Consumer Clearing House, "Meeting Minutes, January 2, 1947," Box 19, Folder—Consumer Materials, Consumer Clearinghouse, 1947, Caroline F. Ware Papers, FDRL.

124. C. W. Bradley, "Letter to Mrs. Edith L. Christenson, December 15, 1945," Box 40, Folder Labor Office, Women's Advisers File, 1944–1946, RG 188 (OPA), NACP. For more on the racism and segregation of railroad unions, see Eric Arnesen, "Railroad Brotherhoods," in Eric Arnesen, ed., *Encyclopedia of U.S. Labor and Working-Class History*, Vol. 1 (New York: Routledge, 2007); Eric Arnesen, "'Like Banquo's Ghost, It Will Not Down': The Race Question and the American Railroad Brotherhoods, 1880–1920," *American Historical Review* 99 (December 1994): 1601–1633.

125. V. E. Bell, "Letter to Chester Bowles, November 24, 1945," Box 40, Folder Labor Office, Women's Advisers File, 1944–1946, RG 188 (OPA), NACP.

126. C. Gelles, "UAW-CIO Women's Auxiliaries, ICC Minutes, Quarterly Report of Secretary-Treasurer's Activities, November 1946–February 1947," Box 1, Folder 1-7, ICC Minutes, 1942-49, UAW Women's Auxiliaries, WPR- ALUA.

127. Ruth Roemer, "Women Naturally OPA Rooters," *CIO News,* June 17, 1946.

CHAPTER 3

1. Ronald L. Filippelli and Mark McColloch, *Cold War in the Working Class: The Rise and Decline of the United Electrical Workers* (Albany: State University of New York Press, 1995); Robert W. Cherny, Willian Issel, and Kieran Walsh Taylor,

American Labor and the Cold War: Grassroots Politics and Postwar Political Culture (New Brunswick, NJ: Rutgers University Press, 2004).

2. Dorothy Keene, "Opening Remarks: Proceedings of the 8th Annual Conference of the International Women's Auxiliaries, UAW-CIO, 1947," Box 3, Folder 1, UAW Women's Collection, Series I, WPR-ALUA.

3. Keene, "Opening Remarks."

4. Keene, "Opening Remarks."

5. Elizabeth Cohen, *A Consumers' Republic: The Politics of Mass Consumption in Postwar America* (New York: Alfred Knopf, 2003), 109.

6. UAW-CIO, "President's Report—Women's Auxiliaries," *Proceedings of the 10th Constitutional Convention/International Union, United Automobile, Aerospace, and Agricultural Implement Workers* (Detroit, MI: UAW-CIO, 1946).

7. UAW-CIO, *Proceedings: Constitutional Convention/International Union, United Automobile, Aerospace, and Agricultural Implement Workers, 1949* (Detroit, MI: UAW-CIO, 1949).

8. UAW-CIO, *Proceedings: Constitutional Convention/International Union.*

9. UAW-CIO, *Proceedings of the Thirteenth Constitutional Convention, UAW-CIO* (Detroit, MI: UAW-CIO, 1951).

10. Emil Mazey, "Letter to Catherine Gelles, 1951," Box 7, Folder 21, UAW Women's Auxiliaries, WPR-ALUA.

11. Catherine Gelles, "Letter to Ruth M. Gladow, August 20, 1956," Box 7, Folder 21, UAW Women's Auxiliaries, WPR- ALUA.

12. Gelles, "Letter to Ruth M. Gladow."

13. Catherine Gelles, "Memo, 1955," Box 7, Folder 21, UAW Women's Auxiliaries, WPR- ALUA.

14. Gelles, "Memo, 1955."

15. Gelles, "Memo, 1955."

16. Mrs. Anna P. Kelsey, "Letter, March 9, 1952," Box 4, Folder 52, RG 52-001, Series I, George Meany Memorial AFL-CIO Archive, University of Maryland, College Park (hereafter GMMA-UMCP).

17. Lillian Sherwood, "Letter to All Michigan AFL-CIO Auxiliaries, August 13, 1958," GMMA, RG52-001, Series 1, Box 4, Folder 69.

18. Sherwood, "Letter to All Michigan AFL-CIO Auxiliaries, August 13, 1958." Emphasis in original.

19. Elda Luebbert, "Letter to Donald Walter, Secretary, Grand Traverse Area CLC-AFL-CIO, April 27, 1962," Box 4, Folder 84, RD-52-001, GMMA-UMCP.

20. Catherine Gelles, "Letter to Venus E. Swyers, Auxiliary #357, UAW, January 15, 1963," Box 6, Folder 27, RG52, GMMA-UMCP.

21. Keene, "Opening Remarks."

22. Jeffery Helgeson, *Crucibles of Black Empowerment: Chicago's Neighborhood Politics from the New Deal to Harold Washington* (Chicago: University of Chicago Press, 2014), 163–164.

23. Erik S. McDuffie, *Sojourning for Freedom: Black Women, American Communism, and the Making of Black Left Feminism* (Durham: Duke University Press, 2011), 161.

24. See McDuffie, *Sojourning for Freedom*, 160–192, for more on the Sojourners.

25. "Housewives Protest Proposed Rent Hikes," *New York Amsterdam News*, February 3, 1951, 2.

26. George Barner, "Angry Tenants on Rent Strike," *New York Amsterdam News*, July 4, 1959, 1. For more on consumer activism in the African American community in the post–World War II period, see Robert E. Weems Jr., *Desegregating the Dollar: African American Consumerism in the Twentieth Century* (New York: New York University Press, 1998).

27. Andrew Wiese, *Places of Their Own: African American Suburbanization in the Twentieth Century* (Chicago: University of Chicago Press, 2004), 104–106.

28. Jessica Weiss, "'Fraud of Femininity': Domesticity, Selflessness, and Individualism in Response to Betty Friedan," in Kathleen G. Donohue, ed., *Liberty and Justice for All? Rethinking Politics in Cold War America* (Amherst: University of Massachusetts Press, 2012), 125.

29. Jennifer Klein, "The Politics of Economic Security after World War II," in Kathleen G. Donohue, ed., *Liberty and Justice for All? Rethinking Politics in Cold War America* (Amherst: University of Massachusetts Press, 2012), 347.

30. Kate Weigand, *Red Feminism: American Communism and the Making of Women's Liberation* (Baltimore, MD: Johns Hopkins University Press, 2001), 115.

31. Storrs, *The Second Red Scare and the Making of the New Deal Left*, 229.

32. For more on this subject, see Landon R.Y. Storrs, *The Second Red Scare and the Unmaking of the New Deal Left* (Princeton, N.J: Princeton University Press, 2015).

33. Susan Kastner, "Angry Housewives Keep Up the Boycott," *New York Post*, October 28, 1966, Box 66, Folder 1276, Papers of Esther Peterson, Schlesinger Library, Radcliffe Institute for Advanced Study, Harvard University (hereafter—EP/SL-RI).

34. Esther Peterson, "The Reminiscences of Esther Peterson," Columbia University: Oral History Research Office, SL-RI.

35. Peterson, "The Reminiscences of Esther Peterson."

36. Anne O'Hagan, "An Adventure in Education: The Summer School for Women Workers at Bryn Mawr," in *The Woman Citizen* (New York: The Women's Citizen Corporation, August 13, 1921), 9–10, http://bit.ly/1QQZX50 (accessed on March 13, 2016).

37. Peterson, "The Reminiscences of Esther Peterson."

38. Dorothy Sue Cobble and Julia Bowes, "Esther Peterson," www.anb.org/articles/15/15-01361.html (accessed on March 20, 2016).

39. Storrs, *The Second Red Scare and the Unmaking of the New Deal Left,* 231.

40. Dorothy Sue Cobble, *The Other Women's Movement: Workplace Justice and Social Rights in Modern America* (Princeton, NJ: Princeton University Press, 2004), 155.

41. Colston E. Warne, "Letter to Esther Peterson, August 23, 1961," Box 25, Folder 461, EP/SL-RI.

42. Pauli Murray, "Letter to Esther Peterson, August 10, 1969," Box 7, Folder: Correspondence Murray, Pauli, EP/SL-RI.

43. John F. Kennedy, "Special Message to Congress on Protecting Consumer Interest, March 15, 1962," http://www.jfklibrary.org/Asset-Viewer/Archives/JFKPOF-037-028.aspx/ (accessed on March 21, 2016).

44. Betty Friedan, *The Feminine Mystique* (New York: W.W. Norton, 2013), xi.

45. Friedan, *The Feminine Mystique*, xi.

46. "*New York Times*, January 11, 1964," Box 66, Folder 1270, EP/SL-RI.

47. David Swankin, phone interview by Emily E. LB. Twarog, Cambridge, MA, April 22, 2013.

48. Esther Peterson, "Untitled, 1965," Box 4, Folder 68, EP/SL-RI.

49. Moss, "Tribute to Esther Peterson, Congressional Record—Senate, January 29, 1969," Box 4, Folder 55, EP/SL-RI.

50. Swankin, phone interview. April 22, 2013.

51. "Excerpts from Consumer Letters, n.d.," Box 69, Folder 1335, EP/SL-RI.

52. Esther Peterson, "Press Release, 2/28/64," Box 64, Folder 1235, EP/SL-RI.

53. Esther Peterson, "Report, 1965," Box 4, Folder 68, EP/SL-RI.

54. Esther Peterson, "Address, National Auxiliaries of AFL-CIO, December 10, 1965," Box 64, Folder 1237, EP/SL-RI.

55. Peterson, "Address, National Auxiliaries of AFL-CIO, December 10, 1965."

56. Esther Peterson, "Statement: Annual Meeting of the Consumers Association of Canada, June 8, 1965," Box 4, Folder 68, EP/SL-RI.

57. Esther Peterson, "Memo to Jack Valenti," Box 67, Folder 1298, EP/SL-RI.

58. Peterson, "Memo to Jack Valenti."

59. Klein, "The Politics of Economic Security," 354.

60. "FBI Report on Esther Peterson, p. 180" Box 4, Folder 70, EP/SL-RI.

61. Storrs, "Left-Feminism," 46.

62. "FBI Report on Esther Peterson, p. 180," Box 4, Folder 70, EP/SL-RI.

63. Swankin, phone interview, April 22, 2013.

64. Esther Peterson, "Memo: A Working and Living Conditions Program, April 1966," Box 67, Folder 1298, EP/SL-RI.

65. Peterson, "Memo: A Working and Living Conditions Program, April 1966," 2–3.

66. Peterson, "Memo: A Working and Living Conditions Program, April 1966," 7–9. Klein, "The Politics of Economic Security after World War II."

67. Esther Peterson, "Testimony, Senate Commerce Committee, April 28, 1965."

68. Esther Peterson, "Telegram, April 1, 1966," Box 64, Folder 1238, EP/SL-RI.

69. Esther Peterson, "Press Release, April 16, 1966," Box 64, Folder 1238, EP/SL-RI.

70. Mauritz Erkkila, "Memo to Esther Peterson, November 22, 1966," Box 66, Folder 1274, EP/SL-RI.

71. Cohen, *Consumers' Republic*, 369.

72. Monroe Friedman, "The 1966 Consumer Protest as Seen by Its Leader," *Journal of Consumer Affairs* 5 (1968): 1–23.

73. Paula E. Hyman, "Immigrant Women and Consumer Protest: The New York City Kosher Meat Boycott of 1902," *American Jewish History* 70, no. 1 (September 1980): 91–105.

74. *Washington Post*, October 28, 1966, Box 66, Folder 1275, EP/SL-RI.

75. "Blame Government, Chain Head Says," Box 66, Folder 1276, EP/SL-RI.

76. Jean R. Hailey, "Consumers Outline Food Store Boycott, *Washington Post,* 10/26/66"; "Housewives Picket Food Stores, *Washington Daily News*, 10/27/66," Box 66, Folder 1276, EP/SL-RI.

77. David R. Jones, "U.S. Studies Price Impact on Food Stores Promotions, *New York Times*, 10/29/66," Box 66, Folder 1276, EP/SL-RI.

78. "Editorial: Prices, Gimmicks and the FTC," *Washington Daily News*, October 31, 1966, Box 66, Folder 1276, EP/SL-RI.

79. "Food Executives Hear Transportation Ads, 10/27/66," Box 66, Folder 1276, EP/SL-RI.

80. Nicholas von Hoffman, "Chain Store Pickets Play 'Boycott Bingo,'" *Washington Post*, October 31, 1966, Box 66, Folder 1276, EP/SL-RI.

81. Topper Carew, phone interview with Emily E. LB. Twarog, Providence, Rhode Island, April 8, 2016. To be clear, there was a practice in the Civil Rights Movement to push women into the background. However, based on the phone interview with Mr. Carew, it seems unlikely that this was the case during the protest in Adams-Morgan. For more on gender and the civil rights movement, see Barbara Ransby, *Ella Baker and the Black Freedom Movement: A Radical Democratic Vision* (Chapel Hill: University of North Carolina Press, 2003).

82. "Blame Government, Chain Head Says," Box 66, Folder 1276, EP/SL-RI.

83. "Markets Offer Women Food Price Peace Parley, 10/26/66," Box 66, Folder 1276, EP/SL-RI.

84. Hilmi Toros, "Food Store Executives Meet in Miami as Housewives Threaten New Action," *Cape Girardeau Southeast Missourian*, October 25, 1966, 7.

85. Hyman, "Immigrant Women and Consumer Protest"; Breen, *The Marketplace of the Revolution.*

86. Toros, "Food Store Executives Meet in Miami as Housewives Threaten New Action."

87. "Charge by Goldwater, *New York Times*, 10/27/66;" Joan Hanauer, "'Girlcott' Picket Lines Hit Stores, *World Journal Tribune*, 10/28/66," Box 66, Folder 1276, EP/SL-RI.

88. Susan Kastner, "Angry Housewives Keep Up the Boycott, *New York Post*, 10/28/66," Box 66, Folder 1276, EP/SL-RI.

89. Kastner, "Angry Housewives Keep Up the Boycott."

90. Kastner, "Angry Housewives Keep Up the Boycott."

91. David R. Jones, "G.O.P. Fears Food Boycott Weakens Its Inflation Issue, *New York Times,* 11/2/66," Box 66, Folder 1276, EP/SL-RI.

92. Swankin, phone interview, April 22, 2013.

93. Esther Peterson, "Notes for Talk with Moyers, n.d.," Box 4, File 55, EP/SL-RI.

94. Peterson, "Notes for Talk with Moyers, n.d."

95. Esther Peterson, "Notes for LBJ, n.d." Box 4, File 55, EP/SL-RI.

96. Peterson, "Notes for Talk with Moyers, n.d."

97. Housewife from Boulder, "Letter to Esther Peterson, March 8, 1967," Box 69, Folder 1344, EP/SL-RI.

98. Housewife from Boulder, "Letter to Esther Peterson, March 8, 1967."

99. Paul Scott Forbes, "Letter to Esther Peterson, March 8, 1967," Box 69, Folder 1344, EP/SL-RI.

100. "Editorial Less Concern Now for Consumers? *Louisville Times*," Box 69, Folder 1344, EP/SL-RI.

101. Peterson, "The Reminiscences of Esther Peterson," 268.

CHAPTER 4

1. A surge in historical literature challenges the arguments that the suburbs were homogenous places devoid of political activism and grassroots organizing. This chapter builds on that literature. Sylvie Murray, *The Progressive Housewife: Community Activism in Suburban Queens, 1945–1965* (Philadelphia: University of Pennsylvania Press, 2003); Dorothy Sue Cobble, *The Other Women's Movement: Workplace Justice and Social Rights in Modern America* (Princeton, NJ: Princeton University Press, 2004); Stephanie Coontz, *A Strange Stirring: The Feminine Mystique and American Women at the Dawn of the 1960s* (New York: Basic Books, 2011); Michael Schudson, *The Rise of the Right to Know: Politics and Culture of Transparency, 1945–1976* (Cambridge, MA: Belknap Press of Harvard University Press, 2015).

2. Betty Friedan, *The Feminine Mystique*, 20th ed. (New York: Dell, 1984).

3. Tracey Deutsch, *Building a Housewives' Paradise: Gender, Politics, and American Grocery Stores in the Twentieth Century* (Chapel Hill: University of North Carolina Press, 2010).

4. Esther Peterson, "Press Release, April 13, 1964," Box 64, Folder 1235, Esther Peterson Papers, Schlesinger Library, Radcliffe Institute, Harvard University (hereafter referred to as EP/SL-RI).

5. Peterson, "Press Release, April 13, 1964."

6. *Architectural Forum*, March 1949, 114.

7. Deutsch, *Building a Housewife's Paradise*, 199.

8. US Representative Jan Schakowsky, interview by Emily E. LB. Twarog, February 8, 2011, Evanston, IL.

9. Deutsch, *Building a Housewife's Paradise*, 184

10. Deutsch, *Building a Housewife's Paradise*,184.

11. Deutsch, *Building a Housewife's Paradise*,184.

12. Mickey DeLorenzo, phone interview with Emily E. LB. Twarog, Chicago, January 6, 2011.

13. Lizabeth Cohen, *A Consumers' Republic: The Politics of Mass Consumption in Postwar America* (New York: Knopf, 2003), 369; Glickman, *Buying Power*.

14. See chapter 4 in Andrew Wiese, *Places of Their Own: African American Suburbanization in the Twentieth Century* (Chicago: University of Chicago Press, 2004).

15. For more on Levittown, see Barbara M. Kelly, *Expanding the American Dream: Building and Rebuilding Levittown* (Albany: State University of New York Press, 1993). For more on the evolution of the suburbs, see Rosalyn Fraad Baxandall and Elizabeth Ewen, *Picture Windows: How the Suburbs Happened* (New York: Basic Books, 2000).

16. Jefferson Cowie, *Stayin' Alive: The 1970s and the Last Days of the Working Class* (New York: New Press, 2010), 28.

17. Shane Hamilton, *Trucking Country: The Road to America's Wal-Mart Economy* (Princeton, NJ: Princeton University Press, 2008), 152.

18. James R. Dorsey, "Soaring Meat Prices," *Long Island Press*, July 27, 1969, 37.

19. Mrs. Ross DeLorenzo, "Federal Responsibility for Retail Price Increases for Beef," in *Subcommittee of the Committee on Government Operations*, House of Representatives (Washington, DC: US Government Printing Office, October 7, 1969), 8.

20. "Plan Boycott over High Meat Prices," *Long Island Press*, August 10, 1969, 23.

21. DeLorenzo, interview, January 6, 2011.

22. For more on the Freeport, Long Island, integration movement, see Baxandall and Ewen, *Picture Windows*, 191–209.

23. "L.I. Housewives Stage Boycott on Meat Sales," *New York Times*, August 12, 1969; Anthony Panzarella, "Housewives Lead a March on Meat," *Long Island Press*, August 12, 1969.

24. DeLorenzo, interview, January 6, 2011.

25. "An Angry Wife Warns of High Meat Costs," *Chicago Tribune*, October 8, 1969; "More Store Boycotts?," *Long Island Press*, August 18, 1969, 8.

26. "Meat Boycott Leader Criticizes House Panel," *Los Angeles Times*, October 8, 1969; "An Angry Wife Warns of High Meat Costs," *Chicago Tribune*.

27. "Housewives Fight Prices," *Washington Post*, September 25, 1969.

28. DeLorenzo, interview, January 6, 2011.

29. "L.I. Meat Boycott Draws a Real Beef," *New York Times*, September 8, 1969.

30. DeLorenzo, interview, January 6, 2011; "L.I. Meat Boycott Draws a Real Beef," *New York Times*, September 8, 1969; Barry Bishin, "LI Cowpokes Get Their Beef," *Long Island Press*, September 8, 1969.

31. "Women Bombard Cattlemen with Requests for Calves," *Long Island Press*, September 3, 1969, 11; "Nickerson Supports Upcoming Women's Meat Counter

Boycott," *Long Island Press*, August 8, 1969; "Pickets Cut Meat Sales," *Long Island Press*, August 15, 1969, 18.

32. DeLorenzo, interview, January 6, 2011.

33. DeLorenzo, interview, January 6, 2011.

34. DeLorenzo, interview, January 6, 2011.

35. For a complete list of legislative activity in the 1960s and 1970s, see Cohen, *A Consumer's Republic,* 360; Glickman, *Buying Power.*

36. http://www.poorpeoplescampaignppc.org/King-s-Last--March.html (accessed January 4, 2015).

37. Recent scholarship has begun to challenge the historical narrative that the Poor People's Campaign was a universal flop. See Gordon K. Mantler, *Power to the Poor: Black-Brown Coalition and the Fight for Economic Justice, 1960–1974* (Chapel Hill: University of North Carolina Press, 2013).

38. Jackie Kendall, interview by Emily E. LB. Twarog, October 14, 2014, Grayslake, Illinois; George Tagge, "Political Lookout," *Chicago Tribune*, November 1, 1969.

39. Kendall, Interview, October 14, 2014.

40. US Department of Labor, "The Employment Situation: March 1967," April 11, 1967; for a detailed narrative of grassroots organizing among African American women, see Annelise Orleck, *Storming Caesars Palace: How Black Mothers Fought Their Own War on Poverty* (Boston: Beacon Press, 2005).

41. This chapter is influenced significantly by the work of Sylvie Murray, whose study of Queens reveals that housewives were politically active within their suburban spaces after World War II. Friedan's claim of isolation was overblown, especially given Friedan's own background in the labor movement and suburban organizing in Queens. It also builds on Roselyn Baxandall and Elizabeth Ewen's study of suburbia, which challenges the notion of homogenization in suburbia, especially on Long Island. See Sylvie Murray, *The Progressive Housewife*; Baxandall and Ewen, *Picture Windows.*

42. Lynne Heidt, interview by Emily E. LB. Twarog, Evanston, Illiniois, January 13, 2011.

43. "Union Tours Local Chain Store," *The Daily Herald*, October 14, 1969.

44. The group was initially named National Consumers' Union, until they realized that the name was already taken by the Consumers' Union. Lynn Taylor, "Suburban Housewives Declare Consumer Independence Day," *Chicago Tribune*, December 18, 1969; Schakowsky, interview, February 8, 2011; Heidt, interview, January 13, 2011.

45. Interestingly, the media never recognized the name change and continued to refer to them as the National Consumers Union. They never heard from Peterson again.

46. Schakowsky, interview, February 8, 2011.

47. Helena Znaniecka Lopata, *Occupation: Housewife* (New York: Oxford University Press, 1971), 23.

48. The 2010 amount is based on the nominal GDP per capita. The nominal GDP per capita is the average personal output of the economy in the prices of the current year.

49. Lopata, *Occupation: Housewife,* 23.

50. Unfortunately Kendall, Schakowsky, and Heidt lost contact with Marian Skinner, and I have been unable to locate her for an interview. But each woman distinctly recalled her leadership in consumer organizing.

51. Schakowsky, interview, February 8, 2011.

52. Taylor, "Suburban Housewives Declare Consumer Independence Day."

53. Schakowsky, interview, February 8, 2011.

54. Kendall, interview, October 14, 2014.

55. Heidt, interview, January 13, 2011. The National Tea Company should not be confused with the Great Atlantic and Pacific Tea Company, established in 1859, and now known as A&P.

56. "Norman Stepelton, National Tea Vice Chairman, Dies at 57," *Chicago Tribune,* August 8, 1970; Heidt, interview, January 13, 2011.

57. J. J. Asongu, *Strategic Corporate Social Responsibility in Practice* (Lawrenceville, GA: Greenview, 2007), 36–37. The Interfaith Center for Corporate Responsibility (ICCR) has pioneered shareholder activism as a strategy to hold corporations accountable to civic society. Founded in 1971, this group of Protestant denominations challenged the role of banks in Apartheid South Africa. "Interfaith Center on Corporate Responsibilty," http://www.iccr.org/about/ (accessed February 25, 2011).

58. Mike Royko, *Boss: Richard J. Daley of Chicago* (New York: Dutton, 1971).

59. Schakowsky, interview, February 8, 2011; Stepelton, "National Tea Vice Chairman, Dies at 57."

60. Heidt, interview, January 13, 2011; Schakowsky, interview, February 8, 2011.

61. Carrie Pitzulo, *Bachelors and Bunnies: The Sexual Politics of Playboy* (Chicago: University of Chicago Press, 2011), 165.

62. Schudson, *The Rise of the Right to Know,* 67.

63. DeLorenzo, interview, January 6, 2011; Schakowsky, interview, February 8, 2011; Kendall, interview, October 14, 2014.

64. Jean Osgood Rainey, "Letter to Robin Morgan, July 16, 1971," Box SP1, Lectures and Readings, 1971–1974, Robin Morgan Papers, David M. Rubenstein Rare Book & Manuscript Library, Duke University.

65. Jacqui Michot Cebellos, "Letter to Robin Morgan, February 23, 1971," Box SP1, Lectures and Readings, 1971–1974 Robin Morgan Papers, David M. Rubenstein Rare Book & Manuscript Library, Duke University.

66. Robin Morgan, "What Robin Morgan Said at Denver," *Journal of Home Economics* 65 (January 1973), 13.

CHAPTER 5

1. "Around the Nation," *Washington Post*, March 23, 1973.

2. AFL-CIO National Auxiliaries, "Proceedings: The Ninth Constitutional Convention, 1973," Box 13, Folder 12, American Federation of Women's Auxiliaries of Labor, Records, 1935–1977, GMMA-UMCP; Deirdre Carmondy, "Even Onion Prices Are Bringing Tears," *New York Times*, March 24, 1973.

3. William A. Elsen, "Consumers Plan Rally on Ellipse," *Washington Post*, March 27, 1973.

4. Edward Cowan, "If Consumer Leagues Spring Up," *New York Times*, March 25, 1973; Paul and Donald Baker Hodge, "Meat Prices Drop in Face of Revolt," *Washington Post*, March 28, 1973; "Legislators Oppose Boycott," *New York Times*, March 28, 1973; "Supervisors Back Meat Boycott," *Los Angeles Times*, March 28, 1973.

5. A cartoon caricature of an American housewife and a Midwestern farmer going toe-to-toe graced the cover of *Time*, April 9, 1973.

6. The political support of this boycott is reminiscent of the 1910 meat boycott covered in Chapter 1. "Bradley and Wife Boycott Meat in Protest on Prices," *Los Angeles Times*, March 22, 1973; "Bradley to Join Meat Boycott," *Los Angeles Times*, March 22, 1973; "Endorse Meat Boycott," *Chicago Defender*, March 29, 1973; Joseph F. Sullivan, "Employes in Capitol to Get Meatless Meals," *New York Times*, March 29, 1973; Hodge, "Meat Prices Drop in Face of Revolt"; "Legislators Oppose Boycott"; "Supervisors Back Meat Boycott."

7. Christine Winter, "The Meat of the Matter: They Won't Bring Home the Bacon," *Chicago Tribune*, March 29, 1973.

8. Carmondy, "Even Onion Prices Are Bringing Tears"; Cowan, "If Consumer Leagues Spring Up"; Hodge, "Meat Prices Drop in Face of Revolt"; Grace Lichtenstein, "The Roast Beef Rebellion!" *New York Times*, March 25, 1973.

9. Carmondy, "Even Onion Prices Are Bringing Tears"; Cowan, "If Consumer Leagues Spring Up"; Hodge, "Meat Prices Drop in Face of Revolt"; Mike Ward, "Housewives' Parade to Protest Meat Prices," *Los Angeles Times*, March 21, 1973.

10. Richard Madden, "Congressmen Get Compaints on Mailes and Add Their Own," *New York Times*, March 24, 1973; "One-Week Meatless Menus," *Washington Post*, March 22, 1973.

11. During her activism and political work in Southern California, Goldway went by the name "Ruth Goldway Yannatta," although she frequently shortened it to "Ruth Yannatta." Because she currently holds an appointed government position under the name Ruth Goldway, I have opted to simplify my references and use only her present-day name.

12. "David Goldway, 83; Led Marxist Journal," *New York Times*, July 28, 1990.

13. Ruth Goldway, phone interview by the author, Chicago, February 1, 2011; Frances Moore Lappé, *Diet for a Small Planet*, 20th anniversary ed. (New York: Ballantine Books, 1991).

14. Goldway, interview by the author, February 1, 2011.

15. "But She Can't Swim!, *Galley Slave*, November 1972," Box 1, Folder 11, Alberta Slavin Papers (S0392), The State Historical Society of Missouri Manuscript Collection (hereafter, ASP/SHSM).

16. Alberta Slavin, "Letter to Roy Kiesling, May 17, 1973," Box 14, Folder 30, Roy Kiesling Paper, Richard L. D. and Marjorie J. Morse Department of Special Collections, Kansas State University Library (hereafter, RKP/MDSC-KSUL).

17. Roy Alper, "National Consumer Congress, Report on First Board Meeting, October 1–3, 1973," Box 13, Folder 9 RKP/MDSC-KSUL; "1974 Prospectus, National Consumers Congress and National Consumer Resource Center, January 1, 1974," Box 8, Folder 207, ASP/SHSM.

18. Alper, "National Consumer Congress, Report on First Board Meeting, October 1–3, 1973."

19. Alper, "National Consumer Congress, Report on First Board Meeting, October 1–3, 1973." Jackie Kendall, "Deciphering Food Codes: Milk and Dairy Products," *Chicago Free Press*, November 9, 1970. For more on Esther Peterson's tenure at Giant Foods, see Michael Schudson, *The Rise of the Right to Know: Politics and Culture of Transparency, 1945–1976* (Cambridge, MA: Belknap Press of Harvard University Press, 2015), 64–102.

20. "1974 Prospectus, National Consumers Congress and National Consumer Resource Center, January 1, 1974," Box 8, Folder 207, ASP/SHSM; "Wallace Beats Hasty Retreat before Irate Detroit Women," *Detroit Free Press*, August 20, 1935.

21. "1974 Prospectus, National Consumers Congress and National Consumer Resource Center, January 1, 1974," Box 8, Folder 207, ASP/SHSM.

22. National Consumers Congress, "Annual Report, 1975," Box 8, Folder 209, ASP/SHSM, p. 1–3.

23. National Consumers Congress, "Annual Report, 1975."

24. San Francisco Consumer Action, "SFCA Demands Item Pricing, *CA News*, January 1975," Box 4, Folder 5, RKP/MDSC-KSUL.

25. San Francisco Consumer Action, "SFCA Demands Item Pricing, *CA News*, February–March 1975," Box 4, Folder 5, RKP/MDSC-KSUL; "Veteran Legislator Alister McAlister Dies," *Sacramento Bee*, November 9, 2010.

26. Bonnie Wilson, interview by author, Evanston, Illinois, October 23, 2014.

27. Wilson, interview by author, October 23, 2014.

28. Kendall, interview, October 14, 2014.

29. Gerald Ford, "Whip Inflation Now" Speech, October 8, 1974, http://miller-center.org/president/speeches/speech-3283 (accessed on April 19, 2016). For more on Gerald Ford's response to inflation and the WIN campaign, see Yanek Mieczkowski, *Gerald Ford and the Challenges of the 1970s* (Lexington: University of Kentucky Press, 2005), 132–144.

30. Kendall, interview, October 14, 2014.

31. "The Consumer Coalition Cordially Invites You to Attend a Baloney and Crumbs Luncheon," original flyer, Bonnie Wilson, personal papers.

32. "The Consumer Coalition Cordially Invites You To Attend a Baloney and Crumbs Luncheon," original flyer, Bonnie Wilson, personal papers.

33. Mieczkowski, *Gerald Ford and the Challenges of the 1970s*, 143.

34. Sandy DeMent, "Letter to NCC Executive Board, April 4, 1977," Box 8, Folder 209, ASP/SHSM.

35. Aileen Gorman, "Letter, May 1974," Box 8, Folder 207, ASP/SHSM.

36. Roger Hickey, phone interview with Emily E. LB. Twarog, Evanston, Illinois, March 23, 2016; COIN Campaign, "People Attending White House Meeting, December 19, 1978," Box 93, Folder 1819, EP/SL-RI.

37. Robert A. Rosenblatt and Ellen Hume, "Inflation Can Be Slowed to 7% if Carter's Guidelines Are Followed, Bosworth Says," *Los Angeles Times*, December 20, 1978; Hickey, interview by the author, Evanston, Illinois, March 23, 2016.

38. Hickey, interview by the author, Evanston, Illinois, March 23, 2016.

39. "President's Statement Prepared for Release at COIN Meeting, December 19, 1978," Box 93, Folder 1819, EP/SL-RI.

40. "President's Statement Prepared for Release at COIN Meeting, December 19, 1978." Larry Kramer, "President Pledges Continued Support for Consumer Efforts," *Washington Post*, December 20, 1978.

41. Office of the White House Press Secretary, "Statement by the President, December 20, 1978," Box 93, Folder 1819, EP/SL-RI; Larry Kramer, "President Pledges Continued Support for Consumer Efforts."

42. Lucia Mouat, "Watchdogs May Torpedo Inflation Plan," *Christian Science Monitor*, May 22, 1979.

43. Mouat, "Watchdogs May Torpedo Inflation Plan."

44. Edward Cowan, "Carter's Measures on Prices Criticized," *New York Times*, June 28, 1979.

45. Cowan, "Carter's Measures on Prices Criticized."

46. "Arline Mathew to Run against Goldwater, Jr., *Los Angeles Times*, March 9, 1974," Box 1, Folder 14, Curren Shields Papers, MDSC-KSUL (hereafter CSP/MDSC-KSUL).

47. Arline Mathews, "Arline Mathews for Congress, March 1974," Box 1, Folder 14, CSP/MDSC-KSUL.

48. "Arline Mathew to Run against Goldwater, Jr., *Los Angeles Times*, March 9, 1974," Box 1, Folder 14, CSP/MDSC-KSUL.

49. Richard M. Mathews, "Richard M. Mathews for L.A. County Democratic Central Committee: Bio," http://www.voterichard.org/about.html (accessed on April 21, 2016).

50. See Box 1, Folder 11, ASP/SHSM for volumes of correspondence between Slavin and various local, regional, and national organizations.

51. "Alberta Slavin, Democrat for Lt. Governor, Press Release, June 27, 1976," Box 8, Folder 212, ASP/SHSM.

52. Mark Schklinkmann, "Consumer Advocate Alberta Slavin Dies," *St. Louis Post-Dispatch*, October 27, 2008.

53. "Ruth and Bill Will Work for You," Box 14, Folder 30, RKP/MDSC-KSUL.

54. James Ring Adams, "Santa Monica's Surburban Radicals," *Wall Street Journal,* July 1, 1981; Goldway, phone interview by the author, February 1, 2011; Derek Shearer, "How the Progressive Won in Santa Monica," *Social Policy*, Winter 1982.

55. Shelton Stromquist, "Claiming Political Space: Workers, Municipal Socialism, and the Reconstruction of Local Democracy in Transnational Perspective," in Leon Fink, ed., *Workers across the Americas: The Transnational Turn in Labor History* (New York: Oxford University Press, 2011).

56. Shearer, "How the Progressive Won in Santa Monica."

57. Schakowsky, interview, February 8, 2011.

58. See chapter 18 in Phyllis Schlafly, *A Choice Not an Echo* (Washington, DC: Regnery, 2014).

59. AFL-CIO National Auxiliaries, "AFL-CIO National Auxiliaries. Proceedings."

60. AFL-CIO National Auxiliaries, "AFL-CIO National Auxiliaries. Proceedings," 17.

61. AFL-CIO National Auxiliaries, "AFL-CIO National Auxiliaries. Proceedings," 25.

62. Diane Balser, *Sisterhood and Solidarity: Feminism and Labor in Modern Times* (Boston: South End Press, 1987), 151–153.

63. Of course, support for the ERA was not unanimous. See Cobble, *The Other Women's Movement.*

64. Balser, *Sisterhood and Solidarity*, 154.

65. Kate Millett, *Sexual Politics* (Garden City, NY: Doubleday, 1970).

66. Monica Dux and Zora Simic, *The Great Feminist Denial* (Carlton, Victoria: Melbourne University Press, 2008), 112–113. As Dux and Simic point out, not all feminist intellectuals of the time argued that motherhood was inherently "dirty." They point out that feminist Adrienne Rich's *Of Woman Born* suggested, "Women's biological capacities could revolutionize society." Adrienne Rich, *Of Woman Born: Motherhood as Experience and Institution* (New York: Norton, 1986).

67. Todd Gitlin, *The Twilight of Common Dream: Why America Is Wracked by Culture Wars* (New York: Metropolitan Books, 1995); Rick Perlstein, *Nixonland: The Rise of a President and the Fracturing of America* (New York: Scribner, 2008); Bruce J. Schulman, *The Seventies: The Great Shift in American Culture, Society, and Politics* (Cambridge: Da Capo Press, 2001); Judith Stein, *Pivotal Decade: How the United States Traded Factories for Finance in the Seventies* (New Haven, CT: Yale University Press, 2010).

68. Ronald P. Formisano, *Boston against Bussing: Race, Class, and Ethnicity in the 1960s and 1970s* (Chapel Hill: University of North Carolina Press, 2004); Katherine Turk, *Equality on Trial: Gender and Rights in the Modern American Workplace* (Philadelphia: University of Pennsylvania Press, 2016).

69. Meg Jacobs, *Panic at the Pump: The Energy Crisis and the Transformation of American Politics in the 1970s* (New York: Hill and Wang, 2016).

70. For a discussion of the decline of the working class, see Cowie, *Stayin' Alive*.

EPILOGUE

1. Lisa McGirr, *Suburban Warriors: The Origins of the New American Right* (Princeton, NJ: Princeton University Press, 2001); Stacie Taranto, *Kitchen Table Politics: Conservative Women and Family Values in New York* (Philadelphia: University of Pennsylvania Press, 2017).

2. Stacie Taranto, *Kitchen Table Politics,* 14.

3. Grant Pick, "Three of a Kind," *Reader*, January 29, 1998.

4. Edward Gresser, "American Families Have Cut Their Bills for Food and Home by Good 40 Percent since the 1970s," February 4, 2015, http://www.progressive-economy.org/ (accessed on February 28, 2017).

5. Raj Patel, *Stuffed and Starved: The Hidden Battle for the World Food System* (Brooklyn: Melville House, 2012), 10.

6. Drew Desilver, "5 Facts about the Minimum Wage," Pew Research Center, January 4, 2017.

7. "USDA Defines Food Deserts," http://americannutritionassociation.org/newsletter/usda-defines-food-deserts (accessed on March 27, 2017).

8. Patel, *Stuffed and Starved*, 273–274.

9. Mari Gallagher, "Examining the Impact of Food Deserts on Public Health in Detroit," Mari Gallagher Research and Consulting Group, 2007, http://www.mari-gallagher.com/site_media/dynamic/project_files/1_DetroitFoodDesertReport_Full.pdf (accessed on March 27, 2017).

10. Gallagher, "Examining the Impact of Food Deserts on Public Health in Detroit."

11. Monica White, "D-Town: African American Farmers, Food Security and Detroit," https://www.blackagendareport.com/content/d-town-african-american-farmers-food-security-and-detroit (accessed on March 27, 2017).

12. White, "D-Town: African American Farmers, Food Security and Detroit."

13. Patel, *Stuffed and Starved*, 2.

14. Ben Schiller, "Food Riots Are Coming: Here's Why," *Fast Company*, March 2, 2015.

15. Patel, *Stuffed and Starved*, 8

16. Sibylla Brodzinsky, "We Are like a Bomb': Food Riots Show Venezuela Crisis Has Gone Beyond Politics," *Guardian,* May 20, 2016.

Bibliography

ARCHIVES

BHC   Burton Historical Collection, Detroit Public Library, Detroit,
                Michigan
DMR/DU   David M. Rubenstein Rare Book & Manuscript Library, Duke
                University.
FDRL   Franklin D. Roosevelt Presidential Library and Museum, Hyde
                Park, New York
GMMA-UMCP   George Meany Memorial Archives, University of Maryland,
                College Park, Maryland
LOC   Library of Congress, Washington, DC
MDSC-KSUL   Richard L. D. and Marjorie J. Morse Department of Special
                Collections, Kansas State University Library, Manhattan, Kansas
NACP   National Archives and Research Administration, College Park,
                Maryland
SCUA-SDSU   Department of Special Collections and University Archives, San
                Diego State University, San Diego, California
SHSM   The State Historical Society of Missouri, St. Louis, Missouri
SLA   Southern Labor Archives, Pullen Library, Georgia State
                University, Atlanta, Georgia
SL-RI   Schlesinger Archives, Radcliffe Institute for Advanced Study,
                Harvard University, Cambridge, Massachusetts
SSC   Sophia Smith Collection, Smith College, Northampton, Massachusetts
WPR-ALUA   Archives of Labor and Urban Affairs, Walter P. Reuther Library,
                Wayne State University, Detroit, Michigan

PUBLICATIONS

Abramovitz, Mimi. *Regulating the Lives of Women: Social Welfare Policy from Colonial
    Times to the Present*. Rev. ed. Boston: South End Press, 1996.

American Federation of Labor. *Some Reasons for Chinese Exclusion. Meat vs. Rice. American Manhood against Asiatic Coolieism, Which Shall Survive?* Washington, DC: US Government Printing Office, 1902.

Anderson, Karen. *Wartime Women: Sex Roles, Family Relations, and the Status of Women during World War II*. Westport, CT: Greenwood Press, 1981.

Araiza, Lauren. *To March for Others: The Black Freedom Struggle and the United Farm Workers*. Philadelphia: University of Pennsylvania Press, 2014.

Archibald, Katherine. *Wartime Shipyard: A Study in Social Disunity*. Urbana: University of Illinois Press, 2006.

Arnesen, Eric. "'Like Banquo's Ghost, It Will Not Down': The Race Question and the American Railroad Brotherhoods, 1880–1920." *American Historical Review* 99 (December 1994): 1601–1633.

Arnesen, Eric. "Whiteness and the Historians' Imagination." *International Labor and Working-Class History* 60 (2001): 3–32.

Ashby, Steven K. "Shattered Dreams: The American Working Class and the Origins of the Cold War, 1945–1949." Ph.D. diss., Chicago, University of Chicago, 1993.

Asher, Robert, Ronald Edsforth, and Stephen Merlino. *Autowork*. Albany: State University of New York Press, 1995.

Asongu, J. J. *Strategic Corporate Social Responsibility in Practice*. Lawrenceville, GA: Greenview, 2007.

Babson, Steve. *Working Detroit: The Making of a Union Town*. Detroit: Wayne State University Press, 1986.

Baker, Ellen R. *On Strike and on Film: Mexican American Families and Blacklisted Filmmakers in Cold War America*. Chapel Hill: University of North Carolina Press, 2007.

Balser, Diane. *Sisterhood and Solidarity: Feminism and Labor in Modern Times*. Boston: South End Press, 1987.

Baron, Ava. "Gender and Labor History: Learning from the Past, Looking to the Future," in Ava Baron, ed., *Work Engendered: Toward a New History of American Labor*. Ithaca, NY: Cornell University Press, 1991.

Barrett, James R. *Work and Community in the Jungle: Chicago's Packinghouse Workers, 1894–1922*. Urbana: University of Illinois Press, 1987.

Barrett, James R. "Americanization from the Bottom Up: Immigration and the Remaking of the Working Class in the United States, 1880–1930." *Journal of American History* 79, no. 3 (1992): 996–1020.

Barrett, James R., and David Roediger. "Inbetween Peoples: Race, Nationality, and the 'New Immigrant' Working Class." *Journal of American Ethnic History* 16, no. 3 (1997): 3–44.

Bates, Beth Tompkins. *The Making of Black Detroit in the Age of Henry Ford*. Chapel Hill: University of North Carolina Press, 2012.

Baxandall, Rosalyn Fraad, and Elizabeth Ewen. *Picture Windows: How the Suburbs Happened*. New York: Basic Books, 2000.

Beaumont, Caitríona. "What *Do* Women Want? Housewives' Associations, Activism, and Changing Representations of Women in the 1950s." *Women's History Review* 16, no. 1 (February 2016): 1–16.

Becker, Susan D. *The Origins of the Equal Rights Amendment: American Feminism between the Wars.* Westport, CT: Greenwood Press, 1981.

Bender, Daniel E., and Richard A. Greenwald. *Sweatshop USA: The American Sweatshop in Historical and Global Perspective.* New York: Routledge, 2003.

Benson, Susan Porter. *Household Accounts: Working-Class Family Economies in the Interwar United States.* Ithaca, NY: Cornell University Press, 2007.

Bentley, Amy. *Eating for Victory: Food Rationing and the Politics of Domesticity.* Urbana: University of Illinois Press, 1998.

Bernard, John. *American Vanguard: The United Auto Workers during the Reuther Years, 1935–1970* Detroit, MI: Wayne State University, 2004.

Bernstein, Barton J. "The Truman Administration and Its Reconversion Wage Policy." *Labor History* 6 (1965): 214–231.

Bix, Amy Sue. "Equipped for Life: Gendered Technical Training and Consumerism in Home Economics, 1920–1980." *Technology and Culture* 43, no. 4 (2002): 728–754.

Bloch, Ruth H. "American Feminine Ideals in Transition: The Rise of the Moral Mother, 1785–1815." *Feminist Studies* 4, no. 2 (1978): 101–126.

Bodnar, John. "Immigration, Kinship, and the Rise of Working-Class Realism in Industrial America." *Journal of Social History* 14, no. 1 (1980): 45–66.

Bodnar, John E. *The Transplanted: A History of Immigrants in Urban America.* Bloomington: Indiana University Press. 1985.

Bohstedt, John. *Riots and Community Politics in England and Wales, 1790–1810.* Cambridge, MA: Harvard University Press, 1983.

Bohstedt, John. *The Politics of Provisions: Food Riots, Moral Economy, and Market Transition in England, C. 1550–1850.* Surrey, England: Ashgate, 2010.

Biondi, Martha. *To Stand and Fight: The Struggle for Civil Rights in Postwar New York City.* Cambridge, MA: Harvard University Press, 2003.

Borda, Jennifer L. *Women Labor Activists in the Movies: Nine Depictions of Workplace Organizers, 1954–2005.* Jefferson, NC: McFarland, 2010.

Boris, Eileen. "The Racialized Gendered State: Constructions of Citizenship in the United States." *Social Politics* 2 (1995): 160–180.

Bowden, Sue, and Avner Offer. "Household Appliances and the Use of Time: The United States and Britain since the 1920s." *Economic History Review* 47, no. 4 (1994): 725–748.

Boydston, Jeanne. *Home and Work: Housework, Wages, and the Ideology of Labor in the Early Republic.* New York: Oxford University Press, 1990.

Boyer, Richard Owen, and Herbert M. Morais. *Labor's Untold Story.* New York: United Electrical, Radio & Machine Workers of America, 1975.

Boylan, Anne M. *The Origins of Women's Activism: New York and Boston, 1797–1840.* Chapel Hill: University of North Carolina Press, 2002.

Boyle, Kevin. *The UAW and the Heyday of American Liberalism, 1945–1968*. Ithaca, NY: Cornell University Press, 1995.

Boyle, Kevin, and Victoria Getis. *Muddy Boots and Ragged Aprons: Images of Working-Class Detroit, 1900–1930*. Detroit, MI: Wayne State University Press, 1997.

Blackwell, Joyce. *No Peace without Freedom: Race and the Women's International League for Peace and Freedom, 1915–1975*. Carbondale: Southern Illinois University Press, 2004.

Blum, John Morton. *V Was for Victory: Politics and American Culture during World War II*. New York: Harcourt Brace Jovanovich, 1976.

Braun, Adee. "Turning Bacon into Bombs: The American Fat Salvage Committee." *Atlantic*, April 18, 2014.

Breen, T. H. *The Marketplace of Revolution: How Consumer Politics Shaped American Independence*. New York: Oxford University Press, 2004.

Brewer, Priscilla J. *From Fireplace to Cookstove: Technology and the Domestic Ideal in America*. Syracuse, NY: Syracuse University Press, 2000.

Brinkley, Alan. *The End of Reform: New Deal Liberalism in Recession and War*. New York: Alfred A. Knopf, 1995.

Brown, Elsa Barkley. "Womanist Consciousness: Maggie Lena Walker and the Independent Order of Saint Luke." *Signs: Journal of Women in Culture and Society* 14, no. 3 (1989): 610–633.

Bruno, Robert. *Steelworker Alley: How Class Works in Youngstown* (Cornell, NY: Cornell University Press, 1999.

Bukowczyk, John J. *And My Children Did Not Know Me: A History of the Polish-Americans*. Bloomington: Indiana University Press, 1987.

Bukowczyk, John J. *A History of the Polish Americans*. New Brunswick, NJ: Transaction, 2008.

Cain, James A. *Mildred Pierce*. New York: Vintage Crime/Black Lizard, 2010.

Caine, Barbara. *English Feminism, 1780–1980*. Oxford: Oxford University Press, 1997.

Capeci, Dominic J.Jr. , and Martha Wilkerson. *Layered Violence: The Detroit Rioters of 1943*. Jackson: University Press of Mississippi, 2009.

Carroll, Peter N. *It Seemed Like Nothing Happened: America in the 1970s*. New Brunswick, NJ: Rutgers University Press, 1990.

Chateauvert, Melinda. *Marching Together: Women of the Brotherhood of Sleeping Car Porters*. Urbana: University of Illinois Press, 1998.

Cherny, Robert W., Willian Issel, and Kieran Walsh Taylor. *American Labor and the Cold War: Grassroots Politics and Postwar Political Culture*. New Brunswick, NJ: Rutgers University Press, 2004.

Cobble, Dorothy Sue. "Rethinking Troubled Relations between Women and Unions: Craft Unionism and Female Activism." *Feminist Studies* 16, no. 3 (1990): 519–548.

Cobble, Dorothy Sue. *The Other Women's Movement: Workplace Justice and Social Rights in Modern America*. Princeton, NJ: Princeton University Press, 2004.

Cohen, Lizabeth. "Escaping Steigerwald's 'Plastic Cages': Consumers as Subjects and Objects in Modern Capitalism." *Journal of American History* 93 (September 2006): 409–413.

Cohen, Lizabeth. *Making a New Deal: Industrial Workers in Chicago, 1919–1939.* Cambridge: Cambridge University Press, 1990.

Cohen, Lizabeth. *A Consumers' Republic: The Politics of Mass Consumption in Postwar America.* New York: Knopf, 2003.

Coiner, Constance. *Better Red: The Writing and Resistance of Tillie Olsen and Meridel Le Sueur.* New York: Oxford University Press, 1995.

Coleman, Doriane Lambelet. *Fixing Columbine: The Challenge to American Liberalism.* Durham, NC: Carolina Academic Press, 2002.

Coles, Anthony James. "The Moral Economy of the Crowd: Some Twentieth-Century Food Riots." *Journal of British Studies* 18, no. 1 (Autumn 1978): 157–176.

Commons, John R. *Race and Immigrants in America.* New York: Augustus M. Kelley, 1967 (originally published in 1920).

Coontz, Stephanie. *A Strange Stirring: The Feminine Mystique and American Women at the Dawn of the 1960s.* New York: Basic Books, 2010.

Cott, Nancy F. *The Grounding of Modern Feminism.* New Haven, CT: Yale University Press, 1987.

Cott, Nancy F. "Comment on Karen Offen's 'Defining Feminism: A Comparative Historical Approach,'" *Signs* 15, no. 1 (1989): 203–205.

Cott, Nancy F. "What's in a Name? The Limits of 'Social Feminism;' or Expanding the Vocabulary of Women's History." *Journal of American History* 76, no. 3 (1989): 809–829.

Cowan, Ruth Schwartz. *More Work for Mother: The Ironies of Household Technology from the Open Hearth to the Microwave.* New York: Basic Books, 1983.

Cowan, Ruth Schwartz. *A Social History of American Technology.* New York: Oxford University Press, 1997.

Cowie, Jefferson. *Stayin' Alive: The 1970s and the Last Days of the Working Class.* New York: New Press, 2010.

Crane, Virginia Glenn. *The Oshkosh Woodworkers' Strike of 1898.* Oshkosh, WI: V. Crane, 1998.

Crane, Virginia Glenn. "'The Very Pictures of Anarchy': Women in the Oshkosh Woodworkers' Strike of 1898." *Wisconsin Magazine of History* 84, no. 3 (2001): 44–59.

Critchlow, Donald T. *Phyllis Schlafly and Grassroots Conservatism: A Woman's Crusade.* Princeton, NJ: Princeton University Press, 2005.

Crittenden, Ann. *The Price of Motherhood: Why the Most Important Job in the World Is Still the Least Valued.* New York: Metropolitan Books, 2001.

Cross, Jennifer. *The Supermarket Trap; the Consumer and the Food Industry.* Bloomington: Indiana University Press, 1970.

Cumming, Inez Parker. "The Edenton Ladies' Tea-Party." *Georgia Review* 8, no. 4 (Winter 1954): 389–395.

Currarino, Rosanne. *The Labor Question in America: Economic Democracy in the Gilded Age*. Urbana: University of Illinois Press, 2011.

Cutler, Jonathan. *Labor's Time: Shorter Hours, the UAW, and the Struggle for the American Unionism*. Philadelphia: Temple University Press, 2004.

Dallek, Robert. *Franklin D. Roosevelt and American Foreign Policy, 1932–1945: With a New Afterword*. New York: Oxford University Press, 1995.

Danese, Tracy E. *Claude Pepper and Ed Ball: Politics, Purpose, and Power*. Gainesville: University Press of Florida, 2000.

Davin, Eric Leif. "Defeat of the Labor Party Idea." In Staughton Lynd, ed., *"We Are All Leaders:" The Alternative Unionism of the 1930s*. Urbana: University of Illinois Press, 1996, 139–141.

Davis, Belinda Joy. *Home Fires Burning: Food, Politics, and Everyday Life in World War I Berlin*. Chapel Hill: University of North Carolina Press, 2000.

De Caux, Len. *Labor Radical: From the Wobblies to CIO*. Boston: Beacon Press, 1970.

De Grazia, Victoria, and Ellen Furlough. *The Sex of Things: Gender and Consumption in Historical Perspective*. Berkeley: University of California Press, 1996.

DeLorenzo, Mrs. Ross. "Federal Responsibility for Retail Price Increases for Beef." *Subcommittee of the Committee on Government Operations*, House of Representatives. Washington, DC: US Government Printing Office, October 7, 1969.

de Montigny, Stephanie May. "Building and Rebuilding Community Discourse, Public Memory, and the Grand Opera House of Oshkosh, Wisconsin." *Buildings and Landscapes: Journal of the Vernacular Architecture* 17, no. 2 (2010), 73–95.

Denning, Michael. *The Cultural Front: The Laboring of American Culture in the Twentieth Century*. New York: Verso, 1998.

Desilver, Drew. "5 Facts about the Minimum Wage." Pew Research Center, January 4, 2017.

Deslippe, Dennis A. *Rights, Not Roses: Unions and the Rise of Working-Class Feminism, 1945–80* Urbana: University of Illinois Press, 2000.

Deutsch, Tracey. *Building a Housewife's Paradise: Gender, Politics, and American Grocery Stores in the Twentieth Century*. Chapel Hill: University of North Carolina Press, 2010.

DeVault, Ileen A. *United Apart: Gender and the Rise of Craft Unionism*. Ithaca, NY: Cornell University Press, 2004.

Dillard, Angela D. *Faith in the City: Preaching Radical Social Change in Detroit*. Ann Arbor: University of Michigan Press, 2007.

Diner, Hasia R. *Hungering for America: Italian, Irish, and Jewish Foodways in the Age of Migration*. Cambridge, MA: Harvard University Press, 2001.

Dollinger, Sol and Genora Johnson Dollinger. *Not Automatic: Women and the Left in the Forging of the Auto Workers' Union*. New York: Monthly Review Press, 2000.

Donohue, Kathleen G. "What Gender Is the Consumer? The Role of Gender Connotations in Defining the Political." *Journal of American Studies* 33, no. 1 (1999): 19–44.

Donohue, Kathleen G. *Freedom from Want: American Liberalism and the Idea of the Consumer* Baltimore, MD: Johns Hopkins University Press, 2003.

Dublin, Thomas. *Women at Work: The Transformation of Work and Community in Lowell, Massachusetts, 1826–1860.* New York: Columbia University Press, 1979.

DuBois, Ellen Carol. "Comment on Karen Offen's 'Defining Feminism: A Comparative Historical Approach.'" *Signs* 15, no. 1 (1989): 195–197.

Dubois, Ellen, Mari Jo Buhle, Temma Kaplan, Gerda Lerner, and Carroll Smith-Rosenberg. "Politics and Culture in Women's History: A Symposium." *Feminist Studies* 6, no. 1 (1980): 26–64.

Dudziak, Mary L. *Cold War Civil Rights: Race and the Image of American Democracy.* Princeton, NJ: Princeton University Press, 2000.

Dux, Monica, and Zora Simic. *The Great Feminist Denial.* Carlton, Victoria: Melbourne University Press, 2008.

Edsall, Thomas Byrne, and Mary D. Edsall. *Chain Reaction: The Impact of Race, Rights, and Taxes on American Politics.* New York: W. W. Norton, 1991.

Engel, Barbara Alpern. "Not by Bread Alone: Subsistence Riots in Russia during World War I." *Journal of Modern History* 69, no. 4 (1997): 696–721.

Evans, Sara M. *Born for Liberty: A History of Women in America.* New York: Free Press, 1989.

Ewen, Elizabeth. *Immigrant Women in the Land of Dollars: Life and Culture on the Lower East Side, 1890–1925.* New York: Monthly Review Press, 1985.

Farber, David R., and Jeff Roche. *The Conservative Sixties.* New York: P. Lang, 2003.

Faue, Elizabeth. *Community of Suffering and Struggle: Women, Men and the Labor Movement in Minneapolis, 1915–1945.* Chapel Hill: University of North Carolina Press, 1991.

Federal Writers Project. *Michigan: A Guide to the Wolverine State.* New York: Oxford University Press, 1946.

Feldstein, Ruth. *Motherhood in Black and White: Race and Sex in American Liberalism, 1930–1965.* Ithaca, NY: Cornell University Press, 2000.

Fergus, Devin. *Liberalism, Black Power, and the Making of American Politics, 1965–1980.* Athens: University of Georgia Press, 2009.

Feurer, Rosemary. *Radical Unionism in the Midwest, 1900–1950.* Urbana: University of Illinois Press, 2006.

Fiddes, Nick. *Meat, a Natural Symbol.* London: Routledge, 1991.

Filippelli, Ronald L., and Mark McColloch. *Cold War in the Working Class: The Rise and Decline of the United Electrical Workers.* Albany: State University of New York Press, 1995.

Fine, Sidney. *Sit-Down: The General Motors Strike of 1936–1937.* Ann Arbor: University of Michigan Press, 1969.

Fink, Leon, and Alvis E. Dunn. *The Maya of Morganton: Work and Community in the Nuevo New South.* Chapel Hill: University of North Carolina Press, 2003.

Fink, Leon. *Workers across the Americas: The Transnational Turn in Labor History.* Oxford: Oxford University Press, 2011.

Folbre, Nancy. "Cleaning House: New Perspectives on Households and Economic Development." *Journal of Development Economics* 22 (1986): 5–40.

Foner, Philip Sheldon. *The Factory Girls: A Collection of Writings on Life and Struggles in the New England Factories of the 1840's.* Urbana: University of Illinois Press 1977.

Foner, Philip S. *Women and the American Labor Movement.* 2 vols. New York: Free Press, 1979.

Fones-Wolf, Elizabeth A. *Selling Free Enterprise: The Business Assault on Labor and Liberalism, 1945–60.* Urbana: University of Illinois Press, 1994.

Fones-Wolf, Elizabeth A. *Waves of Opposition: Labor and the Struggle for Democratic Radio.* Urbana: University of Illinois Press, 2006.

Formisano, Ronald P. *Boston against Bussing: Race, Class, and Ethnicity in the 1960s and 1970s.* Chapel Hill: University of North Carolina Press, 2004.

Foster, Carrie A. *The Women and the Warriors: The U.S. Section of the Women's International League for Peace and Freedom, 1915–1946.* Syracuse, NY: Syracuse University Press, 1995.

Fousekis, Natalie M. *Demanding Child Care: Women's Activism and the Politics of Welfare, 1940–1971.* Urbana: University of Illinois Press, 2011.

Frader, Laura L. "Dissent over Discourse: Labor History, Gender, and the Linguistic Turn." *History and Theory* 34, no. 3 (1995): 213–230.

Frager, Ruth "Politicized Housewives in the Jewish Communist Movement of Toronto, 1923–1933." In Kinda Kealey and Joan Sangster, eds., *Beyond the Vote: Canadian Women and Politics.* Toronto: University of Toronto Press, 1989.

Francois, Marie Eileen. "The Products of Consumption: Housework in Latin American Political Economies and Cultures." *History Compass* 6, no. 1 (2008): 207–242.

Frank, Dana. "Housewives, Socialists, and the Politics of Food: The 1917 New York Cost-of-Living Protests." *Feminist Studies* 11, no. 2 (1985): 255–285.

Frank, Dana. *Buy American: The Untold Story of Economic Nationalism.* Boston: Beacon Press, 1999.

Frank, Dana. *Purchasing Power: Consumer Organizing, Gender, and the Seattle Labor Movement, 1919–1929.* Cambridge: Cambridge University Press, 1994.

Fraser, Nancy. *Fortunes of Feminism: From State-Managed Capitalism to Neoliberal Crisis.* London: Verso Press, 2013.

Fraser, Steve, and Gary Gerstle, eds. *The Rise and Fall of the New Deal Order, 1930–1980.* Princeton, NJ: Princeton University Press, 1989.

Freedman, Estelle. "Separatism as a Strategy: Female Institution Building and American Feminism, 1870–1920." *Feminist Studies* 5, no. 3 (1979): 512–529.

Freeman, Joshua. "Delivering the Goods: Industrial Unionism during World War II." *Labor History* 19, no. 4 (1978): 574–591.

Freeman, Joshua Benjamin. *In Transit: The Transport Workers Union in New York City, 1933–1966.* Philadelphia: Temple University Press, 2001.

Freiburger, William. "War, Prosperity, and Hunger: The New York Food Riots of 1917." *Labor History* 25 (Spring 1984): 217–239.

Fried, Richard M. *Nightmare in Red: The Mccarthy Era in Perspective.* New York: Oxford University Press, 1990.

Friedan, Betty. *The Feminine Mystique.* New York: Dell, 1984.

Friedman, Monroe. "The 1966 Consumer Protest as Seen by Its Leader." *Journal of Consumer Affairs* 5 (1968): 1–23.

Furlough, Ellen, and Carl Strikwerda. *Consumers against Capitalism? Consumer Cooperation in Europe, North America, and Japan, 1840–1990.* Lanham, MD: Rowman & Littlefield, 1999.

Gabin, Nancy. "'They Have Placed a Penalty on Womanhood': The Protest Actions of Women Auto Workers in Detroit-Area UAW Locals, 1945–1947." *Feminist Studies* 8, no. 2 (1982): 373–398.

Gabin, Nancy. "Women Workers and the UAW in the Post–World War II Period: 1945–1954." *Labor History* 21, no. 1 (1979-80): 5–30.

Gabin, Nancy. *Feminism in the Labor Movement: Women and the United Auto Workers, 1935–1975.* Ithaca, NY: Cornell University Press, 1990.

Gilbert, Neil. *A Mother's Work: How Feminism, the Market, and Policy Shape Family Life.* New Haven, CT: Yale University Press, 2008.

Gilmore, Stephanie. *Feminist Coalitions: Historical Perspectives on Second-Wave Feminism in the United States.* Urbana: University of Illinois Press, 2008.

Gitlin, Todd. *The Twilight of Common Dreams: Why America Is Wracked by Culture Wars.* New York: Metropolitan Books, 1995.

Glenn, Susan A. *Daughters of the Shtetl: Life and Labor in the Immigrant Generation.* Ithaca, NY: Cornell University Press, 1990.

Glickman, Lawrence B. *A Living Wage: American Workers and the Making of Consumer Society.* Ithaca, NY: Cornell University Press, 1997.

Glickman, Lawrence B. *Consumer Society in American History: A Reader.* Ithaca, NY: Cornell University Press, 1999.

Glickman, Lawrence B. *Buying Power: A History of Consumer Activism in America.* Chicago: University of Chicago Press, 2009.

Göbel, Thomas. "Becoming American: Ethnic Workers and the Rise of the CIO." *Labor History* 29 (Spring 1988): 173–198.

Goldstein, Carolyn M. *Creating Consumers: Home Economists in Twentieth Century America.* Chapel Hill: University of North Carolina Press, 2012.

Gordon, Linda. *Pitied but Not Entitled: Single Mothers and the History of Welfare, 1890–1935.* New York: Free Press, 1994.

Gordon, Sarah A. "'Boundless Possibilities': Home Sewing and the Meanings of Women's Domestic Work in the United States, 1890–1930." *Journal of Women's History* 16, no. 2 (2004): 68–89.

Gray, Lorraine. *With Babies and Banners: Story of the Women's Emergency Brigade.* Harriman, NY: New Day Films, 1979.

Greenwald, Maurine Weiner. "Working-Class Feminism and the Family Wage Ideal: The Seattle Debate on Married Women's Right to Work, 1914–1920." *Journal of American History* 76, no. 1 (1989): 118–149.

Gregory, James N. *The Southern Diaspora: How the Great Migrations of Black and White Southerners Transformed America.* Chapel Hill: University of North Carolina Press, 2005.

Guard, Julie "A Mighty Power against the Cost of Living: Canadian Housewives Organize in the 1930s." *International Labor and Working Class History* 77, no. 1 (Spring 2010), 27–47.

Guglielmo, Jennifer. *Living the Revolution: Italian Women's Resistance and Radicalism in New York City, 1880–1945.* Chapel Hill: University of North Carolina Press, 2010.

Gutman, Herbert George, and Ira Berlin. *Power & Culture: Essays on the American Working Class.* New York: Pantheon Books, 1987.

Gutman, Herbert George. *Work, Culture, and Society in Industrializing America: Essays in American Working-Class and Social History.* New York: Knopf, distributed by Random House, 1976.

Hall, Jacquelyn Dowd. "Disorderly Women: Gender and Labor Militancy in the Appalachian South." *Journal of American History* 73, no. 2 (1986): 354–382.

Halpern, Martin. *UAW Politics in the Cold War Era.* SUNY Series in American Labor History. Albany: State University of New York Press, 1988.

Hamilton, Shane. *Trucking Country: The Road to America's Wal-Mart Economy.* Princeton, NJ: Princeton University Press, 2008.

Harrison, Cynthia. *On Account of Sex: The Politics of Women's Issues, 1945–1968.* Berkeley: University of California Press, 1988.

Hartmann, Heidi I. "The Family as the Locus of Gender, Class, and Political Struggle: The Example of Housework." *Signs: Journal of Women in Culture and Society* 6, no. 31 (1981): 366–394.

Hawes, Elizabeth. *Hurry Up, Please, Its Time.* New York: Reynal & Hitchcock, 1946.

Hepler, Allison L. "'And We Want Steel Toes Like the Men': Gender and Occupational Health during World War II." *Bulletin of the History of Medicine* 72, no. 4 (1998): 689–713.

Helgeson, Jeffery. *Crucibles of Black Empowerment: Chicago's Neighborhood Politics from the New Deal to Harold Washington.* Chicago: University of Chicago Press, 2014.

Hewitt, Nancy A. "Beyond the Search for Sisterhood: American Women's History in the 1980s." *Social History* 10, no. 3 (1985): 299–321.

Hewitt, Nancy A., ed., *No Permanent Waves: Recasting Histories of U.S. Feminism.* New Brunswick, NJ: Rutgers University Press, 2010.

Higonnet, Margaret R. *Behind the Lines: Gender and the Two World Wars.* New Haven, CT: Yale University Press, 1987.

Hine, Darlene Clark. *Hine Sight: Black Women and the Re-Construction of American History*. Bloomington: Indiana University Press, 1994.

Hofstadter, Richard. *The American Political Tradition and the Men Who Made It*. New York: A. A. Knopf, 1948.

Holli, Melvin G. *Reform in Detroit: Hazen S. Pingree and Urban Politics*. Westport, CT: Greenwood Press, 1981.

Hollows, Joanne. "'We Won't Pay': Price Rises and Socialist Feminist Consumer Activism in the 1970s." Unpublished, in the author's possession.

Horowitz, Daniel. "Rethinking Betty Friedan and *The Feminine Mystique*: Labor Union Radicalism and Feminism in Cold War America." *American Quarterly* 48, no. 1 (1996): 1–42.

Horowitz, Daniel. *Betty Friedan and the Making of the Feminine Mystique: The American Left, the Cold War, and Modern Feminism*. Amherst: University of Massachusetts Press, 1998.

Horowitz, Daniel. *The Anxieties of Affluence: Critiques of American Consumer Culture, 1939–1979*. Amherst: University of Massachusetts Press, 2004.

Horowitz, Richard. *Putting Meat on the American Table: Taste, Technology, Transformation*. Baltimore, MD: Johns Hopkins University Press, 2005.

Horowitz, Roger, and Arwen Mohun. *His and Hers: Gender, Consumption, and Technology*. Charlottesville: University Press of Virginia, 1998.

Hufton, Olwen H. "Women in Revolution 1789–1796." *Past and Present* 53 (November 1971): 90–108.

Hufton, Olwen H. *Women and the Limits of Citizenship in the French Revolution*. Toronto: University of Toronto Press, 1999.

Hyman, Paula E. "Immigrant Women and Consumer Protest: The New York City Kosher Meat Boycott of 1902." *American Jewish History* 70, no. 1 (September 1980): 91–105

Ingalls, Robert P. *Herbert H. Lehman and New York's Little New Deal*. New York: New York University Press, 1975.

Jackson, Carlton. *Child of the Sit-Downs: The Revolutionary Life of Genora Dollinger*. Kent, OH: Kent State University Press, 2008.

Jacobs, Meg. "'How About Some Meat?': The Office of Price Administration, Consumption Politics, and State Building from the Bottom Up, 1941–1946." *Journal of American History* 84, no. 3 (1997): 910–941.

Jacobs, Meg. *Pocketbook Politics: Economic Citizenship in Twentieth-Century America*. Princeton, NJ: Princeton University Press, 2005.

Jacobs, Meg. "The Uncertain Future of American Politics, 1940–1973." In Eric Foner and Lisa McGirr, eds., *American History Now*. Philadelphia: Temple University Press, 2011, 151–174.

Jacobs, Meg. *Panic at the Pump: The Energy Crisis and the Transformation of American Politics in the 1970s*. New York: Hill and Wang, 2016.

Jacobs, Meg, William J. Novak, and Julian E. Zelizer, eds. *The Democratic Experience: New Directions in American Political History*. Princeton, NJ: Princeton University Press, 2003.

Jenkins, Philip. *Decade of Nightmares: The End of the Sixties and the Making of Eighties America*. New York: Oxford University Press, 2006.

Jensen, Joan M., and Joy Parr. "Modern Kitchen, Good Home, Strong Nation." *Technology and Culture* 43, no. 4 (2002): 657–667.

Jensen, Joan M. *Loosening the Bonds: Mid-Atlantic Farm Women, 1750–1850*. New Haven, CT: Yale University Press, 1986.

Johnson, Genora D. *Striking Flint: Genora (Johnson) Dollinger Remembers the 1936–37 General Motors Sit-Down Strike*. Chicago: L. J. Page, 1996.

Kaplan, Amy. "Manifest Domesticity." *American Literature* 70, no. 3 (1998): 581–606.

Kaplan, Temma. "Female Consciousness and Collective Action: The Case of Barcelona, 1910–1918." *Signs: Journal of Women in Culture and Society* 7 (1982): 545–566.

Katz, Donald R. *Home Fires: An Intimate Portrait of One Middle-Class Family in Postwar America*. New York: Aaron Asher Books, 1992.

Katz, Michael B. *The Price of Citizenship: Redefining the American Welfare State*. New York: Metropolitan Books, 2001.

Katzman, David M. *Before the Ghetto; Black Detroit in the Nineteenth Century*. Urbana: University of Illinois Press, 1973.

Keeran, Roger. *The Communist Party and the Auto Workers Unions*. Bloomington: Indiana University Press, 1980.

Kelly, Barbara M. *Expanding the American Dream: Building and Rebuilding Levittown*. Albany: State University of New York Press, 1993.

Kennedy, David M. *Freedom from Fear: The American People in Depression and War, 1929–1945*. New York: Oxford University Press, 1999.

Kerber, Linda K. *Women of the Republic: Intellect and Ideology in Revolutionary America*. Chapel Hill: University of North Carolina Press, 1980.

Kerber, Linda K. "Separate Spheres, Female Worlds, Woman's Place: The Rhetoric of Women's History." *Journal of American History* 75, no. 1 (1988): 9–39.

Kerber, Linda K. *No Constitutional Right to Be Ladies: Women and the Obligations of Citizenship*. New York: Hill and Wang, 1998.

Kersten, Andrew Edmund. *Race, Jobs, and the War: The FEPC in the Midwest, 1941–46*. Urbana: University of Illinois Press, 2000.

Kersten, Andrew Edmund. *Labor's Home Front: The American Federation of Labor during World War II*. New York: New York University Press, 2006.

Kessler-Harris, Alice. "'Where Are the Organized Women Workers?'" *Feminist Studies* 3, no. 1/2 (1975): 92–110.

Kessler-Harris, Alice. *Out to Work: A History of Wage-Earning Women in the United States*. New York: Oxford University Press, 1982.

Kessler-Harris, Alice. *In Pursuit of Equity: Women, Men, and the Quest for Economic Citizenship in 20th Century America*. New York: Oxford University Press, 2001.

Kessler-Harris, Alice. "The Wages of Patriarchy: Some Thoughts about the Continuing Relevance of Class and Gender." *Labor: Studies in Working-Class History of the Americas* 3, no. 3 (2006): 7–21.

Kessler-Harris, Alice. *Gendering Labor History*. Urbana: University of Illinois Press, 2007.

Kessler-Harris, Alice. "In the Nation's Image: The Gendered Limits of Social Citizenship in the Depression Era." *Journal of American History* 86, no. 3 (December 1999): 1251–1279.

Keyssar, Alexander. *The Right to Vote: The Contested History of Democracy in the United States*. New York: Basic Books, 2000.

Killen, Andreas. *1973 Nervous Breakdown: Watergate, Warhol, and the Birth of Post-Sixties America*. New York: Bloomsbury, distributed by Holtzbrinck, 2006.

Klein, Jennifer. "The Politics of Economic Security after World War II." In Kathleen G. Donohue, ed., *Liberty and Justice for All? Rethinking Politics in Cold War America*. Amherst: University of Massachusetts Press, 2012.

Klinkner, Philip A., and Rogers M. Smith. *The Unsteady March: The Rise and Decline of Racial Equality in America*. Chicago: University of Chicago Press, 1999.

Knaff, Donna B. *Beyond Rosie the Riveter: Women of World War II in American Popular Graphic Art*. Lawrence: University Press of Kansas, 2013.

Komarovsky, Mirra. *Blue-Collar Marriage*. New York: Vintage Books, 1967 (originally published in 1962).

Kornbluh, Felicia. "A Human Right to Welfare? Social Protest among Women Welfare Recipients after World War II" in Linda K. Kerber and Jane Sherron De Hart, eds. *Women's America: Refocusing the Past*. New York: Oxford University Press, 2004.

Korstad, Robert Rodgers. *Civil Rights Unionism: Tobacco Workers and the Struggle for Democracy in the Mid-Twentieth Century South*. Chapel Hill: University of North Carolina Press, 2003.

Koven, Seth, and Sonya Michel. "Womanly Duties: Maternalist Politics and the Origins of the Welfare States in France, Germany, Great Britain, and the United States, 1880–1920." *American Historical Review* 95, no. 4 (1990): 1076–1108. .

Koven, Seth, and Sonya Michel. *Mothers of a New World: Maternalist Politics and the Origins of Welfare States*. New York: Routledge, 1999.

Kowalski, Greg. *Hamtramck: The Driven City*. Charleston, SC: Arcadia, 2002.

Kowalski, Greg. *Wicked Hamtramck: Lust, Liquor and Lead* (Charleston, SC: History Press, 2011.

Kraus, Henry. *The Many and the Few: A Chronicle of the Dynamic Auto Workers*. 2nd ed. Urbana: University of Illinois Press, 1985.

Kraus, Henry. *Heroes of Unwritten Story: The UAW, 1934–39*. Urbana: University of Illinois Press, 1993.

Kusmer, Kenneth L., and Joe William Trotter. *African American Urban History since World War II*. Chicago: University of Chicago Press, 2009.

LaBarbera-Twarog, Emily. "Women's Auxiliaries" in *Encyclopedia of U.S. Labor and Working-Class History*, Vol. I. Eric Arnesen, ed. New York: Routledge Press, 2006.

Lappé, Frances Moore. *Diet for a Small Planet*. 20th anniversary ed. New York: Ballantine Books, 1991.

Laughlin, Kathleen A. *Women's Work and Public Policy: A History of the Women's Bureau, U.S. Department of Labor, 1945–1970*. Boston: Northeastern University Press, 2000.

Leach, William. *Land of Desire: Merchants, Power, and the Rise of a New American Culture*. New York: Pantheon Books, 1993.

Leeds, John B. *The Household Budget: With a Special Inquiry into the Amount and Value of Household Work*. New York: Columbia University, 1917.

Leff, Mark H. "The Politics of Sacrifice on the American Home Front in World War II." *Journal of American History* 77, no. 4 (1991): 1296–1318.

Leffler, Melvyn P., and Eric Foner. *The Specter of Communism: The United States and the Origins of the Cold War, 1917–1953*. New York: Hill and Wang, 1994.

Leikin, Steve. "The Citizen Producer: The Rise and Fall of Working-Class Cooperatives in the United States," in Ellen Furlough and Carl Strikwerda, eds., *Consumers against Capitalism?: Consumer Cooperation in Europe, North America, and Japan, 1840–1990*. Lanham, MD: Rowman & Littlefield, 1999.

Lemann, Nicholas. *The Promised Land: The Great Black Migration and How It Changed America*. New York: Vintage Books, 1992.

Lerman, Nina E., Arwen Palmer Mohun, and Ruth Oldenziel. "Versatile Tools: Gender Analysis and the History of Technology." *Technology and Culture* 38, no. 1 (1997): 1–8.

Lerman, Nina E., Ruth Oldenziel, and Arwen Mohun. *Gender & Technology: A Reader*. Baltimore, MD: Johns Hopkins University Press, 2003.

Lerner, Sharon. *The War on Moms: On Life in a Family-Unfriendly Nation*. Hoboken, NJ: John Wiley, 2010.

Leuchtenburg, William Edward. *The Perils of Prosperity, 1914–32*. Chicago: University of Chicago Press, 1958.

Leuchtenburg, William Edward. *Franklin D. Roosevelt and the New Deal, 1932–1940*. New York: Harper & Row, 1963.

Levenstein, Harvey A. *Revolution at the Table: The Transformation of the American Diet*. Berkeley: University of California Press, 2003.

Levenstein, Harvey A. *Paradox of Plenty: A Social History of Eating in Modern America*. Berkeley: University of California Press, 2003.

Levine, Susan. "Workers' Wives: Gender, Class and Consumerism in the 1920s United States." *Gender and History* 3, no. 1 (1991): 45–64.

Levine, Susan. "Co-Opted Consumers." *Labor: Studies in Working-Class History of the Americas* 8, no. 1 (2011): 17–20.

Levine, Susan. *School Lunch Politics: The Surprising History of America's Favorite Welfare Program*. Princeton, NJ: Princeton University Press, 2008.

Lewis-Colman, David M. *Race against Liberalism: Black Workers and the UAW in Detroit*. Urbana: University of Illinois Press, 2008.

Lichtenstein, Nelson. "Auto Worker Militancy and the Structure of Factory Life, 1937–1955." *Journal of American History* 67, no. 2 (1980): 335–353.

Lichtenstein, Nelson. *Labor's War at Home: The CIO in World War II*. Cambridge: Cambridge University Press, 1982.

Lichtenstein, Nelson. *Walter Reuther: The Most Dangerous Man in Detroit*. Urbana: University of Illinois Press, 1995.

Lichtenstein, Nelson. *State of the Union: A Century of American Labor*. Princeton, NJ: Princeton University Press, 2002.

Lichtenstein, Nelson, and Stephen Meyer. *On the Line: Essays in the History of Auto Work*. Urbana: University of Illinois Press, 1989.

Lichtenstein, Nelson, and Elizabeth Tandy Shermer. *The Right and Labor in America: Politics, Ideology, and Imagination*. Philadelphia: University of Pennsylvania Press, 2012.

London, Jack. "A Piece of Steak." *Saturday Evening Post,* November 1909.

Lloyd, Henry Demarest. *The Safety of the Future Lies in Organized Labor*. Washington, DC: AFL, 1893.

Lopata, Helena Znaniecka. *Occupation: Housewife*. New York: Oxford University Press, 1971.

Mansbridge, Jane J. *Why We Lost the Era*. Chicago: University of Chicago Press, 1986.

Mantler, Gordon K. *Power to the Poor: Black-Brown Coalition and the Fight for Economic Justice, 1960–1974*. Chapel Hill: University of North Carolina Press, 2013.

Mark-Lawson, Jane, and Anne Witz. "From 'Family Labour' to 'Family Wage'? The Case of Women's Labour in Nineteenth-Century Coalmining." *Social History* 13, no. 2 (1988): 151–174.

Marchand, Roland. *Advertising the American Dream: Making Way for Modernity, 1920–1940*. Berkeley: University of California Press, 1985.

Marchand, Roland. *Creating the Corporate Soul: The Rise of Public Relations and Corporate Imagery in American Big Business*. Berkeley: University of California Press, 1998.

Marshall, T. H. *Class, Citizenship, and Social Development*. Garden City, NY: Doubleday, 1964.

Mathews, Donald G., and Jane Sherron De Hart. *Sex, Gender, and the Politics of Era: A State and the Nation*. New York: Oxford University Press, 1990.

Matthews, Glenna. *"Just a Housewife": The Rise and Fall of Domesticity in America*. New York: Oxford University Press, 1987.

May, Elaine Tyler. *Homeward Bound: American Families in the Cold War Era*. Rev. and updated ed. New York: Basic Books, 1999.

May, Martha. "The 'Good Managers': Married Working Class Women and Family Budget Studies. 1895–1915." *Labor History* 25, no. 3 (1984): 351–372.

McArthur, Judith N., and Harold L. Smith. *Minnie Fisher Cunningham: A Suffragist's Life in Politics*. New York: Oxford University Press, 2003.

McCartin, Joseph A. *Collision Course: Ronald Reagan, the Air Traffic Controllers, and the Strike that Changed America*. New York: Oxford University Press, 2011.

McDuffie, Erik S. *Sojourning for Freedom: Black Women, American Communism, and the Making of Black Left Feminism*. Durham, NC: Duke University Press, 2011.

McGaw, Judith A. *Early American Technology: Making and Doing Things from the Colonial Era to 1850*. Chapel Hill: University of North Carolina Press, 1994.

McGirr, Lisa. *Suburban Warriors: The Origins of the New American Right*. Princeton, NJ: Princeton University Press.

McGovern, Charles. *Sold American: Consumption and Citizenship, 1890–1945*. Chapel Hill: University of North Carolina Press, 2006.

Meier, August, and Elliott M. Rudwick. *Black Detroit and the Rise of the UAW*. Ann Arbor: University of Michigan Press, 2007.

Merithew, Caroline Waldron. "'We Were Not Ladies': Gender, Class, and a Women's Auxiliary's Battle for Mining Unionism." *Journal of Women's History* 18, no. 2 (2006): 63–94.

Meyer, Stephen. *The Five Dollar Day: Labor Management and Social Control in the Ford Motor Company, 1908*. Albany: State University of New York Press, 1981.

Meyerowitz, Joanne J. *Not June Cleaver: Women and Gender in Postwar America, 1945–1960*. Philadelphia: Temple University Press, 1994.

Mieczkowski, Yanek. *Gerald Ford and the Challenges of the 1970s*. Lexington: University of Kentucky Press, 2005.

Millett, Kate. *Sexual Politics*. Garden City, NY: Doubleday, 1970.

Milkman, Ruth, ed. *Women, Work, and Protest: A Century of US Women's Labor History*. Boston: Routledge and Kegan Paul, 1985.

Milkman, Ruth. *Gender at Work: The Dynamics of Job Segregation by Sex during World War II*. Urbana: University of Illinois Press, 1987.

Mink, Gwendolyn. *The Wages of Motherhood: Inequality in the Welfare State, 1917–1942*. Ithaca, NY: Cornell University Press, 1995.

Mokyr, Joel. "Why 'More Work for Mother?': Knowledge and Household Behavior, 1870–1945." *Journal of Economic History* 60, no. 1 (March 2000): 1–41.

Montgomery, David. *Workers' Control in America: Studies in the History of Work, Technology, and Labor Struggles*. New York: Cambridge University Press, 1979.

Montgomery, David. "To Study the People: The American Working Class." *Labor History* 21 (1980): 485–512.

Montgomery, David. *The Fall of the House of Labor: The Workplace, the State, and American Labor Activism, 1865–1925*. New York: Cambridge University Press, 1987.

Montgomery, David. *Citizen Worker: The Experience of Workers in the United States with Democracy and the Free Market during the Nineteenth Century*. Cambridge: Cambridge University Press, 1993.

Morgan, Robin. "What Robin Morgan Said at Denver." *Journal of Home Economics* 65, January 1973.

Morgan, Ted. *A Covert Life: Jay Lovestone, Communist, Anti-Communist, and Spymaster*. New York: Random House, 1999.

Morganosky, Michelle A., and Brenda J. Cude. "Consumer Response to Online Gorcery Shopping." *International Journal of Retail and Distribution Management* 28, no. 1 (2000): 17–26.

Morris, Charles J. "How the National Labor Relations Act Was Stolen and How It Can Be Recovered: Taft-Hartley Revisionism and the National Labor Relations Board's Appointment Process." *Berkeley Journal of Employment and Labor Law*. 33:1 (2012): 1–71.

Muncy, Robyn. *Creating a Female Dominion in American Reform, 1890–1935*. New York: Oxford University Press, 1991.

Muncy, Robyn. "Cooperative Motherhood and Democratic Civic Culture in Postwar Suburbia, 1940–1965." *Journal of Social History* 38, no. 2 (2004): 285–310.

Murray, Sylvie. *The Progressive Housewife: Community Activism in Suburban Queens, 1945–1965*. Philadelphia: University of Pennsylvania Press, 2003.

Nadasen, Premilla. "Expanding the Boundaries of the Women's Movement: Black Feminism and the Struggle for Welfare Rights." *Feminist Studies* 28, no. 2 (2002): 271–301.

Nader, Ralph. *Unsafe at Any Speed; the Designed-in Dangers of the American Automobile*. Expanded ed. New York: Grossman, 1972.

Navasky, Victor S. *Naming Names*. New York: Hill and Wang, 2003.

Naison, Mark. *Communists in Harlem during the Depression*. Urbana: University of Illinois Press, 2005.

Neuhaus, Jessamyn. "The Way to a Man's Heart: Gender Roles, Domestic Ideology, and Cookbooks in the 1950s." *Journal of Social History* 32, no. 3 (1999): 529–555.

Neuhaus, Jessamyn. *Manly Meals and Mom's Home Cooking: Cookbooks and Gender in Modern America*. Baltimore, MD: Johns Hopkins University Press, 2003.

Nickerson, Michelle M. *Mothers of Conservatism: Women and the Postwar Right*. Princeton, NJ: Princeton University Press, 2012.

Nickles, Shelley. "'Preserving Women': Refrigerator Design as Social Process in the 1930s." *Technology and Culture* 43 (October 2002): 693–727.

Nickles, Shelley. "More Is Better: Mass Consumption, Gender, and Class Identity in Postwar America." *American Quarterly* 54, no. 4 (2002): 581–621.

Nowak, Margaret Collingwood. *Two Who Were There: A Biography of Stanley Nowak*. Detroit, MI: Wayne State University Press, 1989.

O'Connell, Lucille. "The Lawrence Textile Strike of 1912: The Testimony of Two Polish Women." *Polish American Studies* 36, no. 2 (1979): 44–62.

Oberdeck, Kathryn J. "'Not Pink Teas': The Seattle Working-Class Women's Movement, 1905–1918." *Labor History* 32 (Spring 1991): 193–230.

Oestreicher, Richard. "Review Essay: Separate Tribes? Working-Class and Women's History." *Reviews in American History* 19, no. 2 (1991): 228–231.

Offen, Karen. "Defining Feminism: A Comparative Historical Approach." *Signs* 14, no. 1 (1988): 119–157.

Orleck, Annelise. "'We Are That Mythical Thing Called the Public': Militant Housewives during the Great Depression." *Feminist Studies* 19, no. 1 (Spring 1993): 147–172.

Orleck, Annelise. *Common Sense & a Little Fire: Women and Working-Class Politics in the United States, 1900–1965* Chapel Hill: University of North Carolina Press, 1995.

Orleck, Annelise. *Storming Caesars Palace: How Black Mothers Fought Their Own War on Poverty.* Boston: Beacon Press, 2005.

Orloff, Ann Shola. "Gender and the Social Rights of Citizenship: The Comparative Analysis of Gender Relations and Welfare States." *American Sociological Review* 58, no. 3 (1993): 303–328.

Ottanelli, Fraser M. *The Communist Party of the United States: From the Depression to World War II.* New Brunswick, NJ: Rutgers University Press, 1991.

Parr, Joy. *The Gender of Breadwinners: Women, Men, and Change in Two Industrial Towns, 1880–1950.* Toronto: University of Toronto Press, 1990.

Parr, Joy. "Industrializing the Household: Ruth Schwartz Cowan's *More Work for Mother.*" *Technology and Culture* 46 (July 2005): 604–612.

Patel, Raj. *Stuffed and Starved: The Hidden Battle for the World Food System.* Brooklyn, NY: Melville House, 2012.

Perlstein, Rick. *Before the Storm: Barry Goldwater and the Unmaking of the American Consensus.* New York: Hill and Wang, 2001.

Perlstein, Rick. *Nixonland: The Rise of a President and the Fracturing of America.* New York: Scribner, 2008.

Pfeffer, Paula F. "The Women behind the Union: Halena Wilson, Rosina Tucker, and the Ladies' Auxiliary to the Brotherhood of Sleeping Car Porters." *Labor History* 36, no. 4 (1995): 557–578.

Phillips, Kimberley L. *Alabamanorth: African-American Migrants, Community, and Working-Class Activism in Cleveland, 1915–1945.* Urbana: University of Illinois Press, 1999.

Pierce, Jospeh A. *Negro Business and Business Education: Their Present and Prospective Development.* New York: Plenum Press, 1994.

Pitzulo, Carrie. *Bachelors and Bunnies: The Sexual Politics of Playboy.* Chicago: University of Chicago Press, 2011.

Plant, Rebecca Jo. *Mom: The Transformation of Motherhood in Modern America.* Chicago: University of Chicago Press.

Poppendieck, Janet. *Free for All: Fixing School Food in America.* Berkeley: University of California Press, 2010.

Radzilowski, John. "A Social History of Polish-American Catholicism." *U.S. Catholic Historian* 27, no. 3 (2009): 21–43.

Radzialowski, Thaddeus. "View from the Polish Ghetto: Reflections on the First 100 Years in Detroit." *Ethnicity* 1 (1974): 125–150.

Radzialowski, Thaddeus, and Donald Binkowski. "Polish Americans in Detroit Politics." In Angela T. Pienkos, ed., *Ethnic Politics in Urban America: The Polish Experience in Urban America*. Chicago, IL: Polish American Historical Association, 1978.

Ransby, Barbara. *Ella Baker and the Black Freedom Movement: A Radical Democratic Vision*. Chapel Hill: University of North Carolina Press, 2003.

Reitano, Joanne R. *The Restless City: A Short History of New York from Colonial Times to the Present*. 2nd ed. New York: Routledge, 2010.

Rich, Adrienne. *Of Woman Born: Motherhood as Experience and Institution*. 10th anniversary ed. New York: W. W. Norton, 1986.

Rose, Margaret. "'From the Fields to the Picket Line: Huelga Women and the Boycott,' 1965–1975." *Labor History* 31, no. 3 (Summer 1990): 271–293.

Rose, Sonya O. "'Gender at Work': Sex, Class and Industrial Capitalism." *History Workshop* 21 (1986): 113–131.

Rose, Sonya O. "Class Formation and the Quntessential Worker." In John R. Hall, ed., *Reworking Class*. Ithaca, NY: Cornell University Press, 1997.

Rosen, Ruth. *The World Split Open: How the Modern Women's Movement Changed America*. New York: Viking, 2000.

Rosswurm, Steven. *The CIO's Left-Led Unions*. New Brunswick, NJ: Rutgers University Press, 1992.

Rowe-Finkbeiner, Kristin. *The F-Word: Feminism in Jeopardy: Women, Politics, and the Future*. Emeryville, CA: Seal Press, 2004.

Royko, Mike. *Boss: Richard J. Daley of Chicago*. New York: Dutton, 1971.

Rudd, Elizabeth, and Lara Descartes. *The Changing Landscape of Work and Family in the American Middle Class: Reports from the Field*. Lanham, MD: Lexington Books, 2008.

Ruíz, Vicki. *Cannery Women, Cannery Lives: Mexican Women, Unionization, and the California Food Processing Industry, 1930–1950*. Albuquerque: University of New Mexico Press, 1987.

Rupp, Leila J., and Verta Taylor. *Survival in the Doldrums: The American Women's Rights Movement, 1945 to the 1960s*. Columbus: Ohio State University Press, 1990.

Rutherford, Janice Williams. *Selling Mrs. Consumer: Christine Frederick and the Rise of Household Efficiency*. Athens: University of Georgia Press, 2003.

Sarvasy, Wendy. "Beyond Difference versus Equality Policy Debate: Postsuffrage Feminism, Citizenship, and the Quest for a Feminist Welfare State." *Signs: Journal of Women in Culture and Society* 17, no. 2 (Winter 1992): 329–362.

Scanlon, Jennifer. *Inarticulate Longings: The Ladies' Home Journal, Gender, and the Promises of Consumer Culture*. New York: Routledge, 1995.

Schiller, Ben. "Food Riots Are Coming: Here's Why." *Fast Company*, March 2, 2015.

Schlafly, Phyllis. *A Choice Not an Echo*. Washington, DC: Regnery, 2014.

Schulman, Bruce J. *The Seventies: The Great Shift in American Culture, Society, and Politics.* Cambridge, MA: Da Capo Press, 2001.

Schott, Linda K. *Reconstructing Women's Thoughts: The Women's International League for Peace and Freedom before World War II.* Stanford, CA: Stanford University Press, 1997.

Schreiber, Ronnee. *Righting Feminism: Conservative Women and American Politics.* New York: Oxford University Press, 2008.

Schrode, Georg. "Mary Zuk and the Detroit Meat Strike of 1935." *Polish American Studies* 43, no. 2 (1986): 5–39.

Schudson, Michael. *The Rise of the Right to Know: Politics and Culture of Transparency, 1945–1976.* Cambridge, MA: Belknap Press of Harvard University Press, 2015.

Scott, Anne Firor. *Natural Allies: Women's Associations in American History.* Urbana: University of Illinois Press, 1992.

Scott, Anne Firor. *Pauli Murray & Caroline Ware: Forty Years of Letters in Black And White.* Chapel Hill: University of North Carolina Press, 2006.

Scott, Joan W. "Gender: A Useful Category of Historical Analysis." *American Historical Review* 91, no. 5 (1986): 1053–1075.

Scott, Joan Wallach. *Feminism and History.* New York: Oxford University Press, 1996.

Scranton, Phillip. "None-Too-Porous Boundaries: Labor History and the History of Technology." *Technology and Culture* 29, no. 4 (1988): 722–743.

Sealander, Judith. *As Minority Becomes Majority: Federal Reaction to the Phenomenon of Women in the Work Force, 1920–1963.* Westport, CT: Greenwood Press, 1983.

Seccombe, Wally. "Patriarchy Stabilized: The Construction of the Maile Breadwinner Wage Norm in Nineteenth-Century Britain." *Social History* 2, no. 1 (1986): 53–76.

Shearer, Derek. "How the Progressive Won in Santa Monica." *Social Policy* 12, no. 3 (Winter 1982): 7–14.

Shklar, Judith N. *American Citizenship: The Quest for Inclusion.* Cambridge, MA: Harvard University Press, 1991.

Sklar, Kathryn Kish. "Hull House in the 1890s: A Community of Women Reformers." *Signs: Journal of Women in Culture and Society* 10, no. 4 (1985): 658–677.

Sklar, Kathryn Kish. *Florence Kelley and the Nation's Work: The Rise of Women's Political Culture, 1830–1900.* New Haven, CT: Yale University Press, 1995.

Skocpol, Theda. *Protecting Soldiers and Mothers: The Political Origins of Social Policy in the United States.* Cambridge, MA: Belknap Press of Harvard University Press, 1992.

Sombart, Werner. *Why Is There No Socialism in the United States.* White Plains, NY: International Arts and Sciences Press, 1976.

Smith, Rogers M. *Civic Ideals: Conflicting Visions of Citizenship in U.S. History.* New Haven, CT: Yale University Press, 1997.

Stapleford, Thomas A. "'Housewife vs. Economist': Gender, Class, and Domestic Economic Knowledge in Twentieth-Century America." *Labor: Studies in Working-Class History of the Americas* 1, no. 2 (2004): 89–112.

Stapleford, Thomas A. *The Cost of Living in America: A Political History of Economic Statistics, 1880–2000*. Cambridge: Cambridge University Press, 2009.

Stein, Anne. "Post-War Consumer Boycotts." *Radical America* 9 (July 1975): 156–161.

Stein, Judith. *Running Steel, Running America: Race, Economic Policy and the Decline of Liberalism*. Chapel Hill: University of North Carolina Press, 1998.

Stein, Judith. *Pivotal Decade: How the United States Traded Factories for Finance in the Seventies*. New Haven, CT: Yale University Press, 2010.

Stoltzfus, Emilie. *Citizen, Mother, Worker: Debating Public Responsibility for Child Care after the Second World War*. Chapel Hill: University of North Carolina Press, 2003.

Storch, Randi. *Red Chicago: American Communism at Its Grassroots, 1928–35*. Urbana: University of Illinois Press, 2007.

Storrs, Landon R. Y. *Civilizing Capitalism: The National Consumers' League, Women's Activism, and Labor Standards in the New Deal Era*. Chapel Hill: University of North Carolina Press, 2000.

Storrs, Landon R. Y. "Left-Feminism, the Consumer Movement, and Red Scare Politics in the United States, 1935–1960." *Journal of Women's History* 18, no. 3 (2006): 40–67.

Storrs, Landon R. Y. *The Second Red Scare and the Making of the New Deal Left*. Princeton, NJ: Princeton University Press, 2015.

Strasser, Susan. *Never Done: A History of American Housework*. New York: Pantheon Books, 1982.

Strasser, Susan. *Satisfaction Guaranteed: The Making of the American Mass Market*. Washington, DC: Smithsonian Institution Press, 1995.

Strasser, Susan. *Commodifying Everything: Relationships of the Market*. New York: Routledge, 2003.

Strasser, Susan. *Waste and Want: A Social History of Trash*. New York: Holt, 2014.

Strasser, Susan, Charles McGovern, and Matthias Judt. *Getting and Spending: European and American Consumer Societies in the Twentieth Century*. New York: Cambridge University Press, 1998.

Strom, Sharon Hart. "Challenging 'Woman's Place': Feminism, the Left, and Industrial Unionism in the 1930s." *Feminist Studies* 9 (Summer 1983): 359–386.

Stromquist, Shelton "Claiming Political Space: Workers, Municipal Socialism, and the Reconstruction of Local Democracy in Transnational Perspective." In Leon Fink, ed., *Workers across the Americas: The Transnational Turn in Labor History*. Oxford: Oxford University Press, 2011.

Sugrue, Thomas J. "Crabgrass-Roots Politics: Race, Rights, and the Reaction against Liberalism in the Urban North, 1940–1964." *Journal of American History* 82, no. 2 (1995): 551–578.

Swedberg, Sarah. "Teaching Women's History: I Offered Social History, They Took Away Heroes." *History Compass* 2 (2004): 1–7.

Swerdlow, Amy. *Women Strike for Peace: Traditional Motherhood and Radical Politics in the 1960s*. Chicago: University of Chicago Press, 1993.

Taranto, Stacie. *Kitchen Table Politics: Conservative Women and Family Values in New York.* Philadelphia: University of Pennsylvania Press, 2017.

Tax, Meredith. *The Rising of the Women: Feminist Solidarity and Class Conflict, 1880–1917.* Urbana: University of Illinois Press, 2001.

Tax, Meredith. *Rivington Street: A Novel.* Urbana: University of Illinois Press, 2001.

Taylor, Lynne. "Food Riots Revisited." *Journal of Social History* 30, no. 2 (Winter 1996): 483–496.

Thistle, Susan. *From Marriage to the Market: The Transformation of Women's Lives and Work.* Berkeley: University of California Press, 2006.

Thompson, E. P. *The Making of the English Working Class.* New York: Pantheon Books, 1964.

Thompson, E. P. "The Moral Economy of the English Crowd in the Eighteenth Century." *Past and Present* 50 (February 1971): 76–136.

Tilly, Louise, and Joan Wallach Scott. *Women, Work, and Family.* New York: Methuen, 1987.

Traister, Rebecca. "Feminists Killed Home Ec.: Now They Should Bring It Back—for Boys and Girls." *New Republic* (May 28, 2014).

Triece, Mary Eleanor. *On the Picket Line: Strategies of Working-Class Women during the Depression.* Urbana: University of Illinois Press, 2007.

Trotter, Joe William. *The Great Migration in Historical Perspective: New Dimensions of Race, Class, and Gender.* Bloomington: Indiana University Press, 1991.

Turk, Katherine. *Equality on Trial: Gender and Rights in the Modern American Workplace.* Philadelphia: University of Pennsylvania Press, 2016.

Turner, Katherine Leonard. *How the Other Half Ate: A History of Working-Class Meals in the Twentieth Century.* Berkeley: University of California Press, 2014.

US Department of Labor. *Hours and Earnings in the United States, 1932–1940.* Washington, DC: US Government Printing Office, 1942.

Vanderburg, Timothy W. *Cannon Mills and Kannapolis: Persistent Paternalism in a Textile Town.* Knoxville: University of Tennessee Press, 2013.

Vandenberg-Daves, Jodi. *Modern Motherhood: An American History.* New Brunswick: Rutgers University Press, 2014.

Vorse, Mary Heaton. *Labor's New Millions.* New York: Modern Age Books, 1938.

Vorse, Mary Heaton. "And the Workers Say." *Public Opinion Quarterly* 7, no. 3 (1943): 443–456.

Ward, Barbara McLean, and Strawbery Banke Inc. *Produce and Conserve, Share and Play Square: The Grocer and the Consumer on the Home-Front Battlefield during World War II.* Portsmouth, NH: Strawbery Banke, 1994.

Ware, Caroline, and Gardiner C. Means. *The Modern Economy in Action.* New York: Harcourt, Brace, 1936.

Warner, Judith. *Perfect Madness: Motherhood in the Age of Anxiety.* New York: Riverhead Books, 2005.

Weems, Robert E. Jr. *Desegregating the Dollar: African American Consumerism in the Twentieth Century*. New York: New York University Press, 1998.

Weigand, Kate. *Red Feminism: American Communism and the Making of Women's Liberation*. Baltimore, MD: Johns Hopkins University Press, 2001.

Weiner, Lynn Y. *From Working Girl to Working Mother: The Female Labor Force in the United States, 1820–1980*. Chapel Hill: University of North Carolina Press, 1985.

Weiner, Lynn Y. "Maternalism as a Paradigm: Defining the Issues." *Journal of Women's History* 5, no. 2 (1993): 96–113.

Weiss, Jessica. *To Have and to Hold: Marriage, the Baby Boom, and Social Change*. Chicago: University of Chicago Press, 2000.

Weiss, Jessica. "'Fraud of Femininity': Domesticity, Selflessness, and Individualism in Response to Betty Friedan." In Kathleen G. Donohue, ed., *Liberty and Justice for All? Rethinking Politics in Cold War America*. Amherst: University of Massachusetts Press, 2012.

Welter, Barbara. "The Cult of True Womanhood: 1820–1860." *American Quarterly* 18, no. 2 (1966): 151–174.

White, Anne Folino. *Plowed Under: Food Policy Protests and Performance in New Deal America*. Bloomington: Indiana University Press, 2014.

Wiese, Andrew. *Places of Their Own: African American Suburbanization in the Twentieth Century*. Chicago: University of Chicago Press, 2004.

Wilentz, Sean. *The Age of Reagan: A History, 1974–2008*. New York: HarperCollins, 2008.

Wilkinson, Patrick. "The Selfless and the Helpless: Maternalist Origins of the US Welfare State." *Feminist Studies* 25, no. 3 (1999): 571–597.

Williams, Fiona. "Race/Ethnicity, Gender, and Class in Welfare States: A Framework for Comparative Analysis." *Social Politics* 2 (1995): 127–159.

Wilson, Jan Doolittle. *The Women's Joint Congressional Committee and the Politics of Maternalism, 1920–1930*. Urbana: University of Illinois Press, 2007.

Wolcott, Victoria W. *Remaking Respectability: African American Women in Interwar Detroit*. Chapel Hill: University of North Carolina Press, 2001.

Wolf, Naomi. *Misconceptions: Truth, Lies, and the Unexpected on the Journey to Motherhood*. New York: Doubleday, 2001.

Wolfinger, James. *Philadelphia Divided: Race & Politics in the City of Brotherly Love*. Chapel Hill: University of North Carolina Press, 2007.

Zaeske, Susan. *Signatures of Citizenship: Petitioning, Antislavery, and Women's Political Identity*. Chapel Hill: University of North Carolina Press, 2003.

Zaretsky, Natasha. *No Direction Home: The American Family and the Fear of National Decline, 1968-1980*. Chapel Hill: University of North Carolina Press, 2007.

Zieger, Robert H. *The CIO, 1935-1955*. Chapel Hill: University of North Carolina Press, 1995.

Zieger, Robert H., and Gilbert J. Gall. *American Workers, American Unions: The Twentieth Century*. Baltimore, MD: Johns Hopkins University Press, 2002.

Zinn, Howard, Dana Frank, and Robin D. G. Kelley. *Three Strikes: Miners, Musicians, Salesgirls, and the Fighting Spirit of Labor's Last Century.* Boston: Beacon Press, 2001.

Zweiniger-Bergielowska, Ina. *Austerity in Britain: Rationing, Controls, and Consumption, 1939–1955.* New York: Oxford University Press, 2002.

Index